52 WEEK

DAILY DEVOTIONALS

AND ALOPECIA AFFIRMATIONS

Cultivate Empowerment And Self-Love
Every Day Of The Year

Stephanie Anderson, DPC, MPC, BSM

IT Girl Apps Publishing

First published by IT Girl Apps Publishing 2025

FIRST EDITION

Dedication

To my beloved family and dear friends, whose unwavering support lights my path,

To my cherished clients, who inspire me with your resilience and strength,

And to everyone navigating the journey of alopecia and appearance-related challenges,

This book is dedicated to you. May you find hope in the affirmations, wisdom in the scriptures, and encouragement in the words within these pages.

Remember, each day is a new opportunity to embrace your unique path. Take it one day at a time, and know that you are not alone. May you be blessed abundantly on your journey toward acceptance and love for yourself.

With heartfelt gratitude and love,

Stephanie

TABLE OF CONTENTS

Dedication iv

Week 1 Embracing My Unique Beauty 1

Week 2 Confidence In My Journey 10

Week 3 Overcoming Fear And Doubt 19

Week 4 Loving Myself Completely 28

Week 5 Strength In My Identity 37

Week 6 Walking In Purpose 46

Week 7 Cultivating Inner Peace 55

Week 8 Building Unshakable Faith 64

Week 9 Embracing Joy In The Journey 73

Week 10 Letting Go Of Comparison 82

Week 11 Strength Through Community 90

Week 12 Living Boldy And Unapologetically 99

Week 13 The Power Of Gratitude 108

Week 14 Trusting In God's Timing 117

Week 15 Finding Beauty In The Process 126

Week 16 Healing From Within 135

Week 17 Thriving Beyond Alopecia 144

Week 18 Speaking Life Over Myself 153

Week 19 Releasing The Past 161

Week 20 Courage To Be Seen 170

Week 21 My Journey Is My Testimony....179
Week 22 Renewing My Mind Daily....188
Week 23 Accepting My Reflection....196
Week 24 Faith Over Fear....205
Week 25 Owning My Power....214
Week 26 Choosing Happiness....223
Week 27 Walking In Freedom....231
Week 28 Embracing My Uniqueness....240
Week 29 My Voice Matters....248
Week 30 Loving Every Part Of Me....257
Week 31 Trusting The Process....266
Week 32 Finding Strength In Vulnerability....275
Week 33 Resting In God's Promises....284
Week 34 The Beauty Of Surrender....293
Week 35 Claiming My Joy....302
Week 36 Stepping Into My Best Self....311
Week 37 Speaking Truth Over Lies....319
Week 38 I Am Whole as I Am....327
Week 39 No More Apologies....335
Week 40 Embracing the Journey....343
Week 41 Resilience is My Superpower....351
Week 42 Choosing to Shine....359
Week 43 Fully and Completely Me....367

Week 44 Transforming Pain into Purpose 375

Week 45 The Strength Within Me 383

Week 46 I am More Than Enough.. 391

Week 47 Flourishing In Faith 399

Week 48 Living My Truth 407

Week 49 Walking In Abundance.. 415

Week 50 The Gift Of Self-Love 423

Week 51 Reflecting On My Growth.. 431

Week 52 A Year Of Transformation 439

From My Desk.. 449

Week 1

Embracing My Unique Beauty

JANUARY 1

DAY 1

I AM FEARFULLY AND WONDERFULLY MADE

Affirmation: I am beautifully and wonderfully made. My worth is not defined by my hair but by the essence of who I am.

Scripture: "I praise you because I am fearfully and wonderfully made; your works are wonderful, I know that full well." – Psalm 139:14 (NIV)

Encouragement: Today, I choose to embrace my beauty just as I am. My reflection in the mirror is not defined by society's standards, fleeting trends, or superficial ideals. Instead, it is a testament to the divine craftsmanship of my Creator, who intricately designed every part of me. The uniqueness of my features, the depth of my spirit, and my innate qualities all demonstrate that I am a masterpiece, made with intention and purpose. Whether I have a full head of hair or none at all, I am still me—strong, radiant, and enough in every way. It's essential to understand that our worth isn't measured by external appearances but by the richness of our hearts and minds.

As I step forward into the day, I choose to walk boldly in the light of my identity. I am determined to celebrate the uniqueness that I bring to the table and acknowledge the powerful affirmation of my worth. With every stride, I will carry the understanding that my beauty and worth are unshakable and rooted in something far deeper than appearances. By nurturing a heart of gratitude for my creation, I open myself to experience life in its fullness—a life where I am free to shine, uplift others, and create space for joy, all while being unapologetically myself.

JANUARY 2

DAY 2

I AM MORE THAN MY APPEARANCE

Affirmation: I am more than my appearance; I am a reflection of my values, kindness, and strength.

Scripture: "For we are God's masterpiece. He has created us anew in Christ Jesus, so we can do the good things he planned for us long ago." – Ephesians 2:10 (NLT)

Encouragement: Today, I remind myself that my beauty radiates from within, and I choose to celebrate the attributes that truly define me. It is my character, compassion, and creativity that shape my identity and how I relate to the world around me. By embracing the unique qualities that make me special, I not only cultivate a sense of self-worth but also empower myself to lift others up with my spirit. I recognize that each act of kindness and every moment of understanding contributes to a more profound reflection of who I am, reminding me that my influence can extend far beyond the surface.

As I navigate through the day, I reject any negative thoughts regarding my appearance and replace them with affirmations of my intrinsic value. I understand that true beauty shines through my actions and the intentions behind them. With gratitude for the masterpiece that I am, as highlighted in Ephesians 2:10, I commit to living out the good things that God has planned for me. In doing so, I create a legacy of love and strength that impacts not only my life but also the lives of others, showcasing the light that comes from a heart aligned with grace and purpose.

JANUARY 3

DAY 3

I AM A WARRIOR

Affirmation: I am a warrior, courageous in the face of challenges, including my alopecia.

Scripture: "But those who hope in the Lord will renew their strength. They will soar on wings like eagles; they will run and not grow weary; they will walk and not be faint." – Isaiah 40:31 (NIV)

Encouragement: Today, I wholeheartedly embrace the strength that resides deep within me. Just as an eagle rises majestically above the storm, I choose to elevate myself above the clouds of negativity and self-doubt that may attempt to cloud my vision. I recognize that while my journey may present challenges, each step I take forward is a powerful testament to my unwavering resilience. In this moment, I affirm that my struggles do not define me; rather, they refine me, shaping me into a warrior who embodies courage and tenacity. Each day presents an opportunity for growth, and I am committed to stepping into my power fully.

With every rising sun, I am empowered by my experiences and the lessons they bring. I draw inspiration from my unique beauty and the strength that comes from embracing who I truly am. I remind myself that the path may not always be smooth, but as I align my hope with the Lord, I find renewed strength to carry on, just as Isaiah 40:31 promises. I will soar on wings like eagles, run without growing weary, and walk without becoming faint. Today, I am not only a warrior; I am a beacon of light, resilience, and inspiration for myself and others navigating similar challenges.

JANUARY 4

DAY 4

I CELEBRATE MY JOURNEY

Affirmation: I celebrate my journey and view every experience as a step toward self-love.

Scripture: "And we know that in all things God works for the good of those who love him, who have been called according to his purpose." – Romans 8:28 (NIV)

Encouragement: On this day, I take a moment to deeply honor my past, acknowledging both my struggles and my victories. Each experience has played a pivotal role in shaping the person I am today, serving as stepping stones on my path to self-love. I recognize that every challenge has not only tested my resilience but also strengthened my character. Embracing every part of this journey fills my heart with love and gratitude, reminding me that even in difficulty, there are invaluable lessons to be learned. I release feelings of regret and instead choose to celebrate the growth that arises from my experiences, allowing me to move forward with a renewed sense of purpose and positivity.

As I reflect on Romans 8:28, I find great comfort in the assurance that God is working for my good in all circumstances. This divine truth encourages me to trust in the process and to appreciate the intricate design of my life, woven through every moment and memory. Today, I commit to embracing the entirety of my journey—every joyful moment and every trial—as a vital part of my unique story. Recognizing that I am not defined solely by my hardships or successes, but by the way I navigate and learn from them, empowers me to celebrate my life with authenticity and grace. I am grateful for the path I am on and excited for the future that lies ahead.

JANUARY 5

DAY 5

I AM WHOLE AND COMPLETE

Affirmation: I am whole and complete, lacking nothing, and I accept myself entirely.

Scripture: "For in Christ you have been brought to fullness. He is the head over every power and authority." – Colossians 2:10 (NIV)

Encouragement: As I take a moment to reflect today, I am reminded of the profound truth that I am complete exactly as I am, standing firmly in my identity without the need for external validation. There is a deep sense of peace that comes from acknowledging that my worthiness and value originate from within rather than from fleeting appearances or societal standards. Embracing the concept of wholeness allows me to celebrate every facet of my being, free from comparisons or self-doubt. Today, I choose to honor this completeness by recognizing the richness of my experiences, emotions, and individuality that contribute to my unique essence.

In this journey of self-acceptance, I commit to prioritizing self-care, nurturing my body and spirit with love and kindness. Each mindful action I take is an affirmation of my inherent value and a testament to the truth that I lack nothing. By cultivating self-acceptance, I pave the way for deeper connections with both myself and others, empowering not only my spirit but also those around me. I embrace this day as an opportunity to grow in love and appreciation for the whole person I am, knowing that I stand complete, embraced by the fullness that comes from being rooted in Christ.

JANUARY 6

DAY 6

I SHATTER SOCIETAL NORMS

Affirmation: I confidently shatter societal norms and embrace my individuality.

Scripture: "Do not conform to the pattern of this world, but be transformed by the renewing of your mind." – Romans 12:2 (NIV)

Encouragement: Today, I boldly affirm that I will not be limited by societal expectations or conform to the narrow definitions of beauty that our culture often imposes. My individuality is not merely something to be accepted; it is a vibrant strength that sets me apart. I embrace the fullness of who I am and celebrate the qualities that make me unique. By honoring my true self, I pave the way for others to recognize and act upon their own distinctive qualities. In expressing my individuality with confidence, I inspire those around me to break the mold and appreciate their unique journeys. Together, we can create a community where authenticity is cherished rather than suppressed.

As I commit to breaking free from the shackles of comparison, I recognize that the only path to true fulfillment is to appreciate my distinct journey. Every experience, every challenge, and every triumph shapes me into who I am, and I see the beauty in that process. I will continuously renew my mind, allowing the truth of Romans 12:2 to transform my thinking and guide my actions. With each step I take in embracing my individuality, I am not just challenging societal norms; I am also fostering a culture of acceptance and empowerment. By boldly living out my unique identity, I encourage others to join me in this journey, celebrating our differences and uplifting one another in the process.

JANUARY 7

DAY 7

I EMBRACE MY FUTURE

Affirmation: I embrace my future with excitement and hope, knowing that my beauty shines through every chapter.

Scripture: "For I know the plans I have for you, declares the Lord, plans to prosper you and not to harm you, plans to give you hope and a future." – Jeremiah 29:11 (NIV)

Encouragement: As this week comes to a close, I feel a sense of anticipation swelling within me as I look toward the future. Each day is a canvas filled with endless possibilities, inviting me to explore new paths and experiences. I trust that every new dawn brings opportunities for growth, allowing me to shine in ways I may not yet fully understand. My journey with alopecia is not a detour but an integral part of my beautiful story—one that adds depth and character to my life narrative. It serves as a reminder that I can cultivate beauty from adversity, embracing both the challenges and triumphs with open arms.

As I step forward into the mystery of tomorrow, I choose to face the unknown with grace and courage, knowing that I am surrounded by the divine promise stated in Jeremiah 29:11. This scripture reassures me that God has a future filled with hope specifically crafted for me. Each moment unfolds with divine purpose, and I hold fast to the belief that my beauty and potential are indeed limitless. With excitement and a heart full of hope, I am ready to embrace the adventures that lie ahead, not only celebrating my unique journey but also the resilience that comes from owning my identity as I step boldly into my future.

Week 2

Confidence In My Journey

JANUARY 8

DAY 8

MY CONFIDENCE SHINES FROM WITHIN

Affirmation: My confidence is rooted in my spirit, not my appearance. I carry myself with grace and boldness.

Scripture: "So do not throw away your confidence; it will be richly rewarded." – Hebrews 10:35 (NIV)

Encouragement: Each day, I remind myself that true confidence is not rooted in external appearances, but rather in the richness of my spirit and character. It is easy to become entangled in the web of societal expectations, which often prioritize superficial traits over genuine strength. However, I refuse to shrink back or allow such pressures to dim my light. I am fully aware that my worth is not defined by how I look but by the unique essence that I bring to the world. With determination, I rise above the noise and embrace the boldness that comes from within. Each step I take is an affirmation of my self-assuredness, a testament to my journey of self-discovery and empowerment.

Today, I walk with my head held high, embracing the truth that my confidence ripples far beyond the surface and influences those around me in profound ways. My story of resilience is a source of inspiration not only for myself but also for others who may be struggling with their own insecurities. As I proudly embody grace and strength, I remain grounded in the belief that my inner light is powerful and transformative. With every challenge I face, I am reminded that my confidence is rich and rewarding, as promised in Hebrews 10:35. I stand firm in my identity, knowing that my spirit shines brightly, illuminating the path for myself and others..

JANUARY 9

DAY 9

I EMBRACE MY UNIQUENESS

Affirmation: I embrace my unique beauty as a source of strength and empowerment.

Scripture: "And why do you worry about clothes? See how the flowers of the field grow. They do not labor or spin. Yet I tell you that not even Solomon in all his splendor was dressed like one of these. " – Matthew 6:28-29 (NIV)

Encouragement: Each day presents a beautiful opportunity to celebrate the qualities that make me uniquely me. My baldness, far from being a flaw, stands as a distinctive feature that sets me apart from the crowd. It represents my journey and resilience, and I choose to view this aspect of myself as a powerful gift. In a world that often encourages conformity, I find strength in my individuality. Just as the flowers of the field bloom effortlessly, adorned in their own breathtaking colors and shapes, I too embrace my uniqueness as something that empowers me to shine brightly.

By acknowledging and honoring my individuality, I can break free from society's pressures and expectations, allowing myself to thrive in authenticity. I recognize that my uniqueness is not only my strength but also an inspiration to others who may be struggling with their own sense of self. I am proud of who I am, and I commit to honoring my journey of self-discovery. Just as each flower is perfect in its own way, so am I, and I will continue to celebrate the beautiful tapestry of life that my uniqueness contributes to.

JANUARY 10

DAY 10

MY VOICE MATTERS

Affirmation: My voice is powerful, and I have the right to express my thoughts and feelings.

Scripture: "Let everything that has breath praise the Lord." – Psalm 150:6 (NIV)

Encouragement: I remind myself that my experiences shape my voice, and my voice deserves to be heard. Every moment we live contributes to our unique narratives, and it is through sharing these stories that we foster connection and understanding. By expressing my thoughts and feelings, I am not only affirming my own identity but also providing a platform for others to feel validated and understood. Speaking up can pave the way for growth, healing, and empowerment, both for myself and those around me. My voice is an essential part of this journey, one that has the power to inspire and uplift those who may be struggling with similar challenges.

Today, I will not shy away from expressing my truth or advocating for myself and others with alopecia. I choose to celebrate my story and harness the strength of my voice as a tool for change. Psalm 150:6

reminds us that every breath we take is an opportunity for praise, and in this praise lies the beauty of sharing our experiences. By embracing our voices and using them purposefully, we not only glorify our own journey but also encourage others to join in and share theirs. Together, let us create a chorus of voices that uplifts, empowers, and advocates for all those who seek to be heard.

JANUARY 11

DAY 11

I AM MORE THAN MY HAIR

Affirmation: I define my worth beyond my appearance; I am whole and complete as I am.

Scripture: "Are not two sparrows sold for a penny? Yet not one of them will fall to the ground outside your Father's care. And even the very hairs of your head are all numbered. So don't be afraid; you are worth more than many sparrows." – Matthew 10:29-31 (NLT)

Encouragement: I know that true beauty radiates from my character, kindness, and actions. It's essential to remember that my value is not determined by external appearances but is rooted deeply in my authenticity, compassion, and the love I choose to share with the world around me. Our society often places undue emphasis on superficial qualities, but I refuse to let that define my self-worth. Every day, I choose to embrace the unique tapestry of who I am, recognizing that my character and the way I uplift others are the true measures of beauty. I am deserving of love and appreciation, not just for what is seen on the surface but for the depth of the heart and soul within me.

Moreover, in light of the profound truth found in Matthew 10:29-31, I find comfort in knowing that I am uniquely cared for and valued by my Creator. Just as each sparrow is accounted for, I am reminded that every detail of my existence matters to Him; every hair on my head is numbered, illustrating a deep and personal relationship. This assurance empowers me to cultivate self-love and acceptance, reinforcing that I am indeed more than my outer appearance. I am a masterpiece, intricately designed with purpose and worth. Each day, I will continue to affirm my identity, recognizing that my heart, spirit, and intentions define me far more than anything visible to the eye.

JANUARY 12

DAY 12

I CHOOSE LOVE OVER FEAR

Affirmation: I choose love over fear as I navigate my journey.

Scripture: "Perfect love drives out fear." – 1 John 4:18 (NIV)

Encouragement: Today marks a powerful turning point as I consciously release any fears that have held me back and choose to embrace love as my guiding principle. This decision to prioritize love over fear transforms the way I perceive my journey, allowing me to navigate it with grace and resilience. Love for myself empowers me to acknowledge my strengths and imperfections with equal kindness, fostering a deep sense of self-acceptance. As I extend that love to the community around me, I become part of a supportive network that nurtures growth and connection. By actively choosing love, I create an environment where positivity thrives, enabling me to rise above negativity and comparison, and instead inviting joy, acceptance, and compassion into my life and relationships.

In this journey toward love, I recognize that I am cultivating a mindset that aligns with the truth found in Scripture: "Perfect love drives out fear." This profound realization reminds me that love is not merely an emotion but a powerful force capable of dispelling the shadows of doubt and insecurity. Each moment I choose love, I am rejecting the barriers that fear creates, allowing my heart to open wider to possibilities. By embracing love wholeheartedly, I not only transform my own perspective but also inspire those around me to do the same. Together, we can foster a culture of encouragement and understanding, where love becomes the central theme of our lives, illuminating our paths and guiding our interactions.

JANUARY 13

DAY 13

I CELEBRATE MY JOURNEY

Affirmation: I honor my personal journey and the lessons it has taught me.

Scripture: "I delight greatly in the Lord; my soul rejoices in my God. For he has clothed me with garments of salvation and arrayed me in a robe of his righteousness, as a bridegroom adorns his head like a priest, and as a bride adorns herself with her jewels."– Isaiah 61:10 (NIV)

Encouragement: Each twist and turn in my journey has uniquely contributed to the person I am today. Every experience, whether it brought challenges or victories, has shaped my character and deepened my understanding of life. I embrace the profound lessons learned along the way, recognizing that they have woven a rich tapestry of resilience and wisdom within me. As I reflect on the struggles that once felt insurmountable and the successes that sparked joy, I understand that both have been essential in crafting my narrative. I celebrate my capacity to grow through adversity and remain steadfast in my hope for the future.

Moreover, as I continue on this journey, I am reminded that every step I take serves as a testament to my inner strength and determination. With faith as my foundation and the assurance provided by my belief in God, I can transform challenges into opportunities for growth. Each moment I choose to honor my path reinforces the beauty of my unique story. I adorn myself not just with lessons learned but with an infused sense of purpose, reflecting the righteousness and grace that the Lord bestows upon me. In celebrating my journey, I am empowered to create a future filled with possibilities and to shine brightly in all that lies ahead.

JANUARY 14

DAY 14

I AM A SOURCE OF INSPIRATION

Affirmation: My existence inspires others to embrace their own uniqueness.

Scripture: "You are the light of the world. A town built on a hill cannot be hidden." – Matthew 5:14 (NIV)

Encouragement: As I walk confidently in my journey, I am gradually recognizing the profound impact my presence can have on those around me. My authenticity and the way I embrace my individuality can spark a sense of inspiration in others, prompting them to reflect on their unique qualities and potential. I understand that when I fully accept who I am, I create a ripple effect that encourages friends, family, and even strangers to embrace their own uniqueness. This realization is not just empowering for me; it is a reminder of the innate beauty and potential that resides in each person's journey. Today, I make a conscious choice to let my light shine brightly, illuminating the paths of others as they navigate their own.

With this commitment, I aspire to be more than just an observer in the lives of those around me; I aim to be a true beacon of hope and empowerment. By celebrating my own uniqueness and the distinct journeys of others, I foster an environment where individuals feel valued and inspired to flourish. Every story is significant, and every person has something special to offer. As I embrace and uplift my own spirit, I encourage others to do the same, creating a community where we collectively acknowledge and celebrate our varied experiences. Together, we can inspire each other, reminding one another that no one is truly hidden, and that our diverse lights contribute beautifully to the vibrant tapestry of life.

Week 3

Overcoming Fear And Doubt

JANUARY 15

DAY 15

I RELEASE FEAR AND STEP INTO BOLDNESS

Affirmation: I release fear and doubt. I step forward with courage, knowing I am never alone.

Scripture: "For God has not given us a spirit of fear, but of power and of love and of a sound mind." – 2 Timothy 1:7 (NKJV)

Encouragement: Fear often tries to infiltrate our minds with insidious lies, convincing us that we are inadequate or unworthy of love and success. However, today I choose to confront these misleading thoughts with unwavering truth. I am not defined by my insecurities; rather, I am empowered by the deep understanding that I am indeed powerful, deeply loved, and inherently whole. This realization inspires me to take bold steps forward, refusing to allow fear to dim the vibrant light within me. Each day presents an opportunity to rise above my doubts, embracing my journey with confidence and clarity.

Living with alopecia has taught me that my identity is not dictated by external appearances, but by the strength of my spirit and the depth of my character. I stand resolutely against fear, stepping boldly into my purpose with a renewed sense of autonomy and authenticity. God promises us that we are equipped with a spirit of power, love, and a sound mind, and it is through this divine assurance that I find the courage to live life to the fullest. Today, I will celebrate the fearless person God has created me to be, reminding myself that I am equipped to face any challenge that comes my way—never alone and always empowered.

JANUARY 16

DAY 16

I AM A WARRIOR

Affirmation: I am a warrior, courageous, and resilient in the face of challenges.

Scripture: "The Lord is my strength and my shield; my heart trusts in Him, and I am helped." – Psalm 28:7 (NKJV)

Encouragement: Each challenge I face serves as a powerful opportunity to showcase my inner strength and resilience. I recognize that I am not defined by alopecia or any obstacles that may arise in my path. Instead, these challenges provide a unique chance to rise above and cultivate a deeper sense of courage within myself. Armed with unwavering faith and a heart full of strength, I step into each day ready to embrace whatever comes my way. Each trial transforms into a stepping stone on my journey, guiding me further along the path of self-love and acceptance.

In this journey, I hold onto the truth found in Psalm 28:7, which reminds me that the Lord is my strength and my shield. With a heart that trusts in Him, I find the encouragement I need to confront life's uncertainties. I am empowered to approach every challenge with a warrior's spirit—courageous, tenacious, and resolute. As I continue to harness my faith, I secure victories, not just in overcoming obstacles but in embracing the beautiful person I am becoming. Each day is a testament to my resilience, allowing me to forge ahead with confidence and joy as I cultivate a deeper love for myself.

JANUARY 17

DAY 17

I ACCEPT MYSELF UNCONDITIONALLY

Affirmation: I accept and love myself unconditionally, embracing who I am in this moment.

Scripture: "and have put on the new self, which is being renewed in knowledge in the image of its Creator." – Colossians 3:10 (NIV)

Encouragement: My uniqueness is a beautiful reflection of God's creativity and profound love. Each characteristic that makes me who I am is intentionally crafted, highlighting the intricacies of His divine design. Today, I commit to celebrating myself just as I am, with all my strengths and imperfections. I will actively nurture my self-esteem, choosing to appreciate myself in each moment rather than waiting for a future version of me to embrace fully. This journey of self-acceptance is essential; by recognizing and valuing my inherent worth, I reinforce the understanding that true beauty emanates from within, radiating outwardly in all aspects of my life.

As I continuously strive for growth and improvement, I acknowledge that I am a work in progress. Every step I take toward self-love and acceptance is a testament to my resilience and faith. I am deserving of love and acceptance, not just from others but from myself. With each positive thought and affirmation, I cultivate a deeper sense of inner peace and confidence. I embrace the fact that the path to self-acceptance is ongoing, allowing me the grace to learn and evolve through every experience. In doing so, I draw closer to the image of my Creator, embodying the renewed self that Colossians 3:10 speaks of, and I cherish each moment of this beautiful journey.

JANUARY 18

DAY 18

I CHOOSE JOY OVER FEAR

Affirmation: I choose joy over fear, welcoming positivity into my life.

Scripture: "The joy of the Lord is my strength." – Nehemiah 8:10 (NKJV)

Encouragement: Joy serves as a powerful weapon against the insidious grip of fear, and I resolve to wield it boldly and generously in all circumstances. In those moments when fear threatens to encroach upon my peace, I will choose to respond not with hesitation but with an overwhelming sense of laughter, praise, and gratitude. By cultivating a joyful spirit, I create an atmosphere where fear cannot thrive. Today, I joyfully invite happiness to take root in every corner of my heart, purposefully allowing it to overshadow any doubts that may attempt to seep in. Each joyful thought I embrace acts as a shield, reinforcing my spirit and encouraging those around me.

As I consciously select joy over fear, I remind myself of the profound truth found in Nehemiah 8:10: "The joy of the Lord is my strength." This pivotal scripture empowers me to rise above challenges and confront my fears with a heart full of hope and positivity. By continuously fostering joy, I not only transform my own life but also become a beacon of light for others who may be wrestling with their own fears. I will cultivate an attitude of gratitude that echoes throughout my day, ensuring that joy becomes my default response to life's uncertainties. In choosing joy, I am aligning myself with divine strength, embracing each moment with love and trust in a brighter tomorrow.

JANUARY 19

DAY 19

I TRUST IN MY JOURNEY

Affirmation: I trust in my journey and accept that each step is purposeful.

Scripture: "You were bought at a price. Therefore honor God with your bodies." – 1 Corinthians 6:20 (NIV)

Encouragement: Although the road may be unclear at times, I will trust that God is guiding my steps with love and intention. Each moment, whether filled with joy or challenge, is a vital part of my unique journey. I recognize that every twist and turn serves a purpose, shaping me into the person I am destined to become. By surrendering my need for control, I am allowing space for growth and discovery, which enriches my experience and understanding. Embracing the adventure of life, I remain confident that I am on the right path, supported by a divine plan that exceeds my comprehension.

As I reflect on the journey I am on, I feel a profound sense of peace in knowing that I am not walking this path alone. God has crafted my life with care, and even when the way forward seems daunting or obscured, I trust that His wisdom is greater than my fears. Each step I take holds the potential for transformation, and I am reminded to honor my body and spirit as creations entrusted to me. With every choice I make, I can align myself with God's purpose for my life, celebrating each milestone and learning from every challenge. Thus, I reaffirm my commitment to trust the journey, embracing the lessons it brings and looking forward to the beautiful unfolding of my story.

JANUARY 20

DAY 20

I EMBRACE VULNERABILITY

Affirmation: I embrace vulnerability as a source of strength and connection.

Scripture: "My grace is sufficient for you, for my power is made perfect in weakness." – 2 Corinthians 12:9 (NIV)

Encouragement: In moments of vulnerability, I discover that my greatest strength often arises from the very places where I feel most exposed. By daring to be authentic and open with others, I create a space for love and connection to flourish in my life. Embracing vulnerability means sharing not only my story but also my fears and triumphs, which can serve as a bridge to deeper relationships. When I allow others to see my true self, even my struggles, I foster empathy and understanding—the very foundations that make community and connection thrive. I am learning that in sharing my journey, I find support and solace, reinforcing the truth that I am never alone.

Moreover, the affirmation of embracing vulnerability is a powerful reminder that acknowledging our weaknesses can lead to profound strength. The wisdom in 2 Corinthians 12:9 reminds us that God's grace fills the gaps of our shortcomings, allowing His power to be made perfect precisely where we feel inadequate. Each time I open up about my experiences, I not only liberate myself but also inspire those around me to find the courage to be vulnerable in their own lives. This shared authenticity can lead to healing and growth, illuminating the beauty that can arise from embracing our true selves. I am stronger within my truth, and as I walk this path of vulnerability, I am more connected to others and to the deeper purpose of my life.

JANUARY 21

DAY 21

I AM ENOUGH

Affirmation: I am enough, just as I am; I celebrate my worth every day.

Scripture: "You are my God, and I will give thanks to you; you are my God, I will extol you." – Psalm 118:28 (ESV)

Encouragement: Today, I fully embrace and acknowledge my inherent worth, recognizing that it is not dictated by external achievements or opinions. I understand that I do not need to change who I am or prove myself to anyone in order to be deserving of love, respect, and kindness. I can stand confidently in my identity, grounded in the truth that I am enough for God and for myself just as I am. My self-worth is a gift that I cherish, and I will honor it by celebrating the beautiful individual I am today.

As I reflect on my journey, I choose to celebrate my accomplishments—both big and small—as valuable contributions that shape my life. Each step I take, each experience I have, brings me closer to the fullness of who I am meant to be. I will remind myself of Psalm 118:28, embracing the truth that I am loved and valued by God. In this sacred understanding, I find the strength to nurture my self-worth daily and live authentically, radiant in the knowledge that I am wholly deserving of joy and purpose.

Week 4

Loving Myself Completely

JANUARY 22

DAY 22

I LOVE MYSELF UNCONDITIONALLY

Affirmation: I embrace myself with love and compassion, knowing I am worthy of every good thing.

Scripture: "Love your neighbor as yourself." – Mark 12:31 (NIV)

Encouragement: Loving myself starts with grace—embracing the days when I struggle and finding the strength to navigate moments of insecurity. It's a gentle reminder to celebrate every step of my journey, acknowledging the progress I've made along the way. Each day brings its own challenges, but I choose to extend compassion to myself, recognizing that I am deserving of love and kindness. By speaking kindly to myself and honoring my unique path, I empower my spirit and nurture my resilience. This self-love cultivates a deeper appreciation for who I am, both in my moments of triumph and my moments of difficulty.

Today, I consciously choose to love myself deeply, understanding that this love serves as the foundation for how I interact with others. The more I nurture and embrace my own worth, the more I can radiate positivity and encouragement to those around me. My beauty is not merely a matter of external appearance; it is reflected in my spirit, my kindness, and the way I uplift and support others. Just as the scripture encourages me to love my neighbor as myself, I recognize that this self-love enriches my ability to connect with and uplift those I encounter.

Each day, let my love for myself shine brightly, impacting not only my life but also inspiring and affecting the lives of others in meaningful ways.

JANUARY 23

DAY 23

I AM ENOUGH

Affirmation: I am enough just as I am, and I honor my unique journey.

Scripture: "Therefore, if anyone is in Christ, the new creation has come: The old has gone, the new is here!" – 30

Encouragement: Embracing the profound truth that I am enough just as I am empowers me to release the burdens of comparison and self-doubt that often cloud my perspective. It is through my scars and moments of vulnerability that I have cultivated resilience and strength, forging a unique path that only I can walk. Every experience has shaped me into who I am today, contributing to the rich tapestry of my life. I celebrate my individuality, recognizing that the story I carry is invaluable and worthy of honor. Today, I take a moment to reflect on my journey, acknowledging that it is not defined by societal standards but by the authenticity of my experiences.

In this beautiful journey of life, I am reminded that my worth is not contingent upon my appearance or the opinions of others. I am a masterpiece in progress, intricately crafted with purpose and intention. Just as scripture reminds us that in Christ, we are new creations, I realize that I am continuously evolving, shedding the old and embracing the new. Each day presents an opportunity for growth and transformation, reinforcing the idea that I am inherently valuable and cherished. As I move forward, I do so with confidence, knowing that I am enough and that my unique journey adds depth and richness not only to my life but to the lives of those around me.

JANUARY 24

DAY 24

I CHOOSE JOY

Affirmation: I choose joy daily, allowing it to fill my heart and uplift my spirit.

Scripture: " Let the beloved of the Lord rest secure in him, for he shields him all day long, and the one the Lord loves rests between his shoulders." – Deuteronomy 33:12 (NIV)

Encouragement: Joy is indeed a conscious choice, and I hold the remarkable ability to nurture it within my heart and soul. Regardless of the trials I may face, there are always countless reasons to uplift my spirit and appreciate the world around me. Each day presents new opportunities to discover joy, whether through shared laughter with loved ones, the serene beauty of nature, or the heartfelt connections I forge with others. By intentionally seeking out these moments, I can transform not only my own experience but also the energy I bring to every interaction.

As I embrace the decision to choose joy, I find that it equips me with the resilience needed to transcend life's challenges. This uplifting mindset not only enhances my personal well-being but also radiates positivity to those who cross my path. I recognize that my choice to be joyful can inspire and encourage others to pursue their own happiness. In this shared journey of joy, I am reminded that I am cherished and protected, as reiterated in Scripture. The knowledge that I rest secure in the Lord's love amplifies my ability to spread joy, making it a beacon of hope for others who may be struggling. Today, let me be a vessel of joy, illuminating my surroundings and uplifting the spirits of those I encounter.

JANUARY 25

DAY 25

I AM RESILIENT

Affirmation: I am resilient, capable of overcoming any challenge that comes my way.

Scripture: "I can do all things through Christ who strengthens me." – Philippians 4:13 (NKJV)

Encouragement: Resilience is not just a response to adversity; it is a cultivated trait that grows stronger with each trial we face. Each challenge presents us with an opportunity to learn and develop, reminding us that setbacks are not the end but rather a vital part of our journey. Embracing the difficulties along the way equips us with the tools we need to forge ahead, transforming obstacles into stepping stones on our path to strength. As we navigate through tough times, we should remember to celebrate our past victories and acknowledge the inner power we possess. By fostering this perspective, we can approach each day with renewed hope and the assurance that we have the capacity to rise above any situation.

As I reflect on my resilience, I draw strength from the unwavering promise found in Philippians 4:13: "I can do all things through Christ who strengthens me." This powerful affirmation reminds me that I am never alone in my struggles; divine support is always at hand. With this knowledge, I approach my challenges with a mindset that views them as opportunities for growth and transformation. Today, let us all affirm our resilience, lean into our faith, and stand firm in the belief that every obstacle we encounter serves to illuminate our path forward. Our resilience is indeed a remarkable gift, guiding us as we move toward a brighter and more empowered future.

JANUARY 26

DAY 26

I AM BEAUTIFUL INSIDE AND OUT

Affirmation: My beauty shines from within, illuminating my outer self.

Scripture: "Charm is deceptive, and beauty is fleeting; but a woman who fears the Lord is to be praised." – Proverbs 31:30 (NIV)

Encouragement: True beauty emanates from a loving heart and a kind spirit, transcending the fleeting nature of physical appearance. In a world that often prioritizes external allure, it is vital to remember that our true essence resides within. I celebrate my uniqueness and the qualities that distinguish me, recognizing that each attribute contributes to the beautiful tapestry of my identity. Today, I will dedicate time to nurturing my soul, engaging in meaningful practices of kindness, and expressing heartfelt gratitude for the myriad blessings in my life. By acknowledging these aspects, I fortify my inner strength and spirit, setting the foundation for genuine beauty that resonates with those around me.

As I nurture my inner beauty, I become increasingly aware that it naturally radiates outward, touching the lives of others and illuminating my presence in the world. This divine connection reminds me that true beauty cannot be contained or defined by societal standards; instead, it flourishes from authenticity and love. The wisdom captured in Proverbs 31:30 invites us to cultivate a reverent relationship with the Lord, reinforcing that respect and reverence for our Creator enriches our character and amplifies our inner light. In celebrating my inner beauty, I open myself up to the joy of being authentically me, shining brightly for all to see. Today, I choose to embrace this journey, thriving in the knowledge that my beauty is a reflection of my heart and my faith.

JANUARY 27

DAY 27

I AM WORTHY OF SELF-CARE

Affirmation: I honor myself by prioritizing self-care in my daily life.

Scripture: I will walk among you and be your God, and you will be my people." – Leviticus 26:12 (NIV)

Encouragement: When I prioritize self-care, I am affirming my inherent worth and sending a powerful message to myself that I am deserving of love and attention. Engaging in self-care is far from selfish; rather, it is a critical foundation for rejuvenation and personal growth. It empowers me to better serve others and fulfill my purpose in life. Today, I will intentionally carve out sacred moments just for myself, whether that means indulging in relaxation, immersing myself in hobbies, or practicing mindfulness through meditation. I am taking a stand for my well-being, recognizing that I deserve to nourish my body, mind, and spirit with activities that bring me joy and peace.

As I reflect on the profound truth found in Leviticus 26:12, I am reminded that I am not alone; I walk in the company of a loving God who desires a close relationship with me. This divine connection reassures me that self-care is not only a personal journey, but also a sacred acknowledgment of my unique value in the tapestry of life. By embracing self-care, I align myself with God's intentions for holistic health and well-being. Today, I commit to honoring myself and nurturing my spirit, embracing the grace that comes from allowing myself the time and space to recharge. I honor my unique journey, confident that by practicing self-care, I am fulfilling my role as one of His beloved people.

JANUARY 28

DAY 28

I CELEBRATE MY UNIQUENESS

Affirmation: I celebrate my uniqueness, embracing the qualities that set me apart.

Scripture: "Therefore we do not lose heart. Though outwardly we are wasting away, yet inwardly we are being renewed day by day."– 2 Corinthians 4:16 (NIV)

Encouragement: There is no one else like me in the world, and that is my intrinsic power. Every quirk, interest, and unique perspective contributes to the rich tapestry of life that we all share. These distinctive traits not only shape my identity but also enrich the experiences of those around me. Today, I commit to honoring my individuality, taking the time to acknowledge and celebrate the unique qualities that make me who I am. Instead of succumbing to societal pressures or the desire to fit in, I will embrace my authenticity wholeheartedly. I understand that true fulfillment comes from being unapologetically myself, and in doing so, I create the opportunity for authentic connections with others.

By letting go of the need for conformity, I allow my true self to shine through. This journey of self-acceptance and celebration is essential in recognizing that my differences are not just acceptable; they are vital to the diversity that enhances our shared human experience. As I reflect on 2 Corinthians 4:16, I am reminded that while the external world may change or challenge me daily, my inner renewal and growth continue unabated. Each day presents a fresh opportunity to embrace my uniqueness and celebrate the beauty of individuality, fostering resilience that will carry me through life's ups and downs. So today, I choose to celebrate the remarkable person I am, recognizing that my authenticity not only enriches my life but also weaves a vibrant thread into the lives of those I encounter.

Week 5

Strength In My Identity

JANUARY 29

DAY 29

I STAND FIRM IN WHO I AM

Affirmation: I am strong, resilient, and unwavering in my identity.

Scripture: "Be on your guard; stand firm in the faith; be courageous; be strong." – 1 Corinthians 16:13 (NIV)

Encouragement: My identity is a steadfast foundation that remains unshaken by the opinions and judgments of those around me. Each moment serves as a reminder that I am inherently strong, resilient, and unwavering. I take pride in embracing my authentic self without hesitation or the need for validation. My strength is not derived from external sources; rather, it emanates from within, affirming that I am enough just as I am. Today, I stand boldly in the truth of who I am, refusing to minimize my worth or conform to the expectations set by others.

As I navigate through life's challenges and triumphs, I resolve to show up as my full, unapologetic self. I draw inspiration from the scripture, reminding myself to be courageous and strong, for it is in this authenticity that my true value shines through. With each step I take, I choose to celebrate my uniqueness, knowing that my presence contributes to the world in a meaningful way. By standing firm in my identity, I not only honor myself but also encourage others to embrace their true selves without reservation. Today is a day for self-affirmation and resilience, and I will carry this spirit with me in all I do.

JANUARY 30

DAY 30

I CELEBRATE MY UNIQUENESS

Affirmation: My uniqueness is my superpower, and I embrace it fully.

Scripture: "One thing I ask from the Lord, this only do I seek: that I may dwell in the house of the Lord

all the days of my life, to gaze on the beauty of the Lord and to seek him in his temple." – Psalm 27:4 (NIV)

Encouragement: There is no one else like me in this world, and that is my strength. Embracing my uniqueness allows me to discover and appreciate the qualities that make me who I am, recognizing that my differences and individual traits are what truly set me apart. Today, I take the time to reflect on my own personal journey, understanding that every twist and turn has shaped me into the person I am meant to be. Each experience, both joyous and challenging, contributes to a beautiful tapestry that tells my story. I choose to honor my individuality and celebrate the diverse attributes that enrich my life, standing proud in the distinctiveness that is uniquely mine.

In acknowledging my own exceptional qualities, I find strength in the knowledge that I have been beautifully crafted for a purpose. This uniqueness is not something to be shied away from, but rather embraced fully, as it gives me the ability to see the world through my own lens and offer something truly special to those around me. As I dwell in the presence of the Lord, as expressed in Psalm 27:4, I am reminded that seeking Him allows me to find the beauty in my own being. I commit to cultivating a deeper understanding of myself, celebrating every facet of who I am while continually seeking God's guidance on my path. In doing so, I understand that my individuality is, indeed, my superpower, and I am empowered to shine brightly in a world that desperately needs the light that only I can offer.

JANUARY 31

DAY 31

I AM MORE THAN MY APPEARANCE

Affirmation: My worth and value extend far beyond my appearance.

Scripture: "The Lord does not look at the things people look at. People look at the outward appearance, but the Lord looks at the heart." – 1 Samuel 16:7 (NIV)

Encouragement: Each day, it's essential to remind ourselves that our true worth is not defined by our outward appearance but by the richness of our hearts and the love we carry within us. As we navigate through a world that often prioritizes superficial judgments, we must embrace our unique qualities and understand that they are what truly matter. I am a beautiful soul, brimming with love and purpose, and I choose to celebrate the intricacies of my being that go beyond physicality. This inner beauty fosters resilience and strength, allowing me to stand proudly in my individuality and acknowledge the light I bring to the world around me.

Today, I commit to nourishing my spirit and cultivating a perspective that reflects my inner value. By focusing on the qualities that make me uniquely me—kindness, compassion, and authenticity—I can create a sense of fulfillment that transcends societal expectations. As I meditate on the truth found in 1 Samuel 16:7, I remind myself that the Lord looks beyond the surface, seeing the depth of my heart and character. It is this depth that constitutes my true beauty, and by appreciating my inner strength and purpose, I am empowered to shine brightly, encouraging others to do the same. In recognizing that true beauty radiates from within, I will seek to uplift myself and those around me, fostering a community that celebrates we are so much more than our appearances.

FEBRUARY 1

DAY 32

I AM CAPABLE OF GREATNESS

Affirmation: I am capable of achieving greatness in my life.

Scripture: "So you are no longer a slave, but God's child; and since you are his child, God has made you also an heir." – Galatians 4:7 (NIV)

Encouragement: As I reflect on my journey, I recognize the inherent strength and abilities that lie within me, empowering me to pursue the greatness that is my destiny. I am reminded that my dreams, no matter how grand, are not just figments of my imagination; they are calling me to strive for more. Each challenge I encounter is not merely an obstacle but a profound opportunity for personal growth and transformation. Embracing this perspective allows me to see that with every effort I make, every setback I face, I am sculpting the path toward my aspirations. Today, I choose to acknowledge the limitless potential within me and to take deliberate steps that align with the greatness I am capable of achieving.

I celebrate the promise found in Galatians 4:7 that reinforces my identity as a child of God and an heir to His boundless blessings. This scripture serves as a powerful reminder that my journey toward greatness is not a solitary endeavor; I am supported by a divine inheritance that fuels my confidence and determination. Understanding that I am not bound by limitations but rather freed to explore my potential brings me immense encouragement. As I move forward today, I will hold fast to this truth, taking bold steps filled with hope and assurance, knowing that I am destined for greatness and that every step I take is infused with divine purpose.

FEBRUARY 2

DAY 33

I AM LOVED JUST AS I AM

Affirmation: I am deeply loved and accepted just as I am.

Scripture: "We love because he first loved us." – 1 John 4:19 (NIV)

Encouragement: I am inherently worthy of love, not because of my achievements or the person I aspire to be, but simply for the essence of who I am right now. It's essential to recognize and celebrate the abundance of love that envelops me—from the unwavering support of friends and family to the gentle embrace of the universe itself. Each day, as I navigate the complexities of life, I remind myself that I am a beloved creation, deserving of kindness and acceptance.

Today, I choose to immerse myself in this profound love and allow it to nurture my soul. I will take moments to reflect on the relationships that uplift me, the beauty around me, and the deeper connections that remind me of my worth. By acknowledging and appreciating these love-filled elements of my life, I open myself to healing and growth, grounded in the knowledge that I am cherished, just as I am. Through my journey, I will carry this affirmation with me, being rooted in love and extending that same love to others, knowing we are all deserving of such grace.

FEBRUARY 3

DAY 34

I AM A SOURCE OF INSPIRATION

Affirmation: My journey is inspiring, and I am a source of strength for others.

Scripture: "Let your light shine before others, that they may see your good deeds and glorify your Father in heaven." – Matthew 5:16 (NIV)

Encouragement: I recognize that by embracing my own story, I can uplift and encourage those around me. My unique journey is a testament to resilience and determination, and it serves as a guiding light for others who may be struggling to find their path. When I share my experiences, I not only validate my own journey but also create a space where others can see the beauty in their struggles and triumphs. Just as a spark can ignite a fire, my courage empowers those around me to ignite their inner strength and discover the fortitude that lies within their own identity.

Today, I will share my journey, knowing it can inspire and empower others to embrace their true selves. I am reminded that my story is not just mine; it is intertwined with the lives of those I touch. Every kind word, every act of encouragement, and every lesson learned along the way can resonate deeply with someone who needs hope. As I let my light shine, I create a ripple effect of inspiration that encourages others to do the same, all while glorifying the divine purpose in our lives. Together, we can illuminate the world, revealing the potential within us to uplift one another and fulfill our greater calling.

FEBRUARY 4

DAY 35

I CHOOSE SELF-LOVE EVERY DAY

Affirmation: Each day, I choose to love and honor myself.

Scripture: "Do not be afraid, little flock, for your Father has been pleased to give you the kingdom." – Luke 12:32 (NIV)

Encouragement: Self-love is not merely a destination we strive to reach; it is a vital practice woven into the fabric of our daily lives. Each morning offers me the opportunity to embrace this journey, reminding me that nurturing my mind, body, and spirit is essential for growth and fulfillment. By speaking kindly to myself and acknowledging my own worth, I reinforce a positive self-image that propels me forward. It is through this daily commitment that I learn to appreciate my efforts, regardless of how small they may seem, and to celebrate my progress, which further fuels my motivation to continue on this path.

Today, I wholeheartedly embrace self-love, knowing that it serves as a powerful catalyst for my journey toward authenticity and strength. By recognizing that I am deserving of this love, I open myself up to receiving the abundant blessings that life has to offer. I take comfort in the assurance from Luke 12:32 that I am cared for by something greater, which encourages me to prioritize my own well-being. In choosing self-love today and every day, I empower myself to engage with the world in a more authentic way, fostering resilience, joy, and fulfillment in all aspects of my life.

Week 6

Walking In Purpose

FEBRUARY 5

DAY 36

MY PURPOSE IS GREATER THAN MY STRUGGLES

Affirmation: I am created for a purpose greater than my struggles.

Scripture: "And just as we have borne the image of the earthly man, so shall we bear the image of the heavenly man." – 1 Corinthians 15:49 (NIV)

Encouragement: My journey is undeniably significant, each step woven intricately into the fabric of my purpose. Every challenge and hardship I encounter has not only shaped me into the person I am today but has also been a crucial part of the preparation for the greater things that lie ahead. I have come to understand that my experiences, both the triumphs and the trials, serve a higher calling. They are not mere random events, but rather, divine threads that weave into the larger tapestry of my life. I am reminded that my struggles do not define my worth; instead, they become a powerful testimony of resilience and growth. As I navigate this path, I commit to using my experiences not just for personal empowerment, but to inspire and uplift others who may be experiencing similar trials.

Today, I step boldly into my calling, anchored by the truth that my purpose surpasses any obstacles I face. Like the transition from the earthly image to the heavenly one described in 1 Corinthians 15:49, I embrace the transformation that comes from enduring challenges. Each struggle I overcome enhances my ability to reflect the light of hope and encouragement to those around me. I recognize that part of my purpose is to lift others up, to share my story as a beacon of strength, and to foster community through shared experiences. With unwavering faith, I move forward, knowing that I am not alone on this journey; my purpose is alive, dynamic, and far greater than any temporary setback.

FEBRUARY 6

DAY 37

I AM A BEACON OF HOPE

Affirmation: My light shines brightly in the world.

Scripture: "And the God of all grace, who called you to his eternal glory in Christ, after you have suffered a little while, will himself restore you and make you strong, firm and steadfast."– 1 Peter 5:10 (NIV)

Encouragement: I am not just a survivor; I am a beacon of hope for others in this journey of life. My stories and victories, forged through trials and tribulations, serve as guiding lights for those who may feel lost in their own darkness. It is a profound honor to share my experiences, as they have not only shaped me, but also have the potential to inspire those around me. I embrace my role as an influencer for positive change, fully aware that my purpose involves illuminating the path for others who may be struggling to find their way. Each hardship I've faced has equipped me with the strength to uplift and empower, reminding me of the multitude of paths available even in the bleakest of times.

In acknowledging my role as a beacon, I hold fast to the promise found in 1 Peter 5:10, which assures me that after enduring suffering, God will restore me and make me strong, firm, and steadfast. This divine assurance fuels my commitment to shine brightly, as I trust that my light can penetrate even the darkest corners of despair. As I navigate my journey, I remember that my resilience can serve as a roadmap for others, encouraging them to persevere. By sharing my light, I not only honor my experiences but also invite others to join me on a journey toward healing and hope. Let us emerge from the shadows together, supporting one another, as we become beacons of hope in our communities.

FEBRUARY 7

DAY 38

MY PAIN HAS A PURPOSE

Affirmation: My pain is a part of my journey toward purpose.

Scripture: "The Lord appeared to us in the past, saying: 'I have loved you with an everlasting love; I have drawn you with unfailing kindness.'"– Jeremiah 31:3 (NIV)

Encouragement: Each moment of pain I've endured has contributed to my strength and resilience in profound ways. While the journey through suffering can feel isolating and overwhelming, it has also been a catalyst for tremendous personal growth. Each struggle I've faced has not only tested my limits but has also shaped me into a more compassionate warrior, equipped to understand and empathize with the pain of others. It's through these trials that I've discovered the depths of my own character and the power of perseverance. Today, I find comfort in knowing that my pain is not in vain; it serves a greater purpose in my journey toward fulfillment and healing.

Reflecting on the beauty of the Scripture from Jeremiah 31:3, I am reminded that even in the darkest moments, I am enveloped in God's everlasting love and unfailing kindness. This divine assurance reassures me that my challenges are part of a larger design, one that fosters not only my own healing but also allows me to be a beacon of hope for others who may be struggling. By embracing my pain as part of my journey, I open myself to the possibility of transformation—both personally and within the lives of those around me. As I continue to navigate this path, I hold onto the promise that with each step forward, I am being drawn closer to my true purpose.

FEBRUARY 8

DAY 39

I AM EQUIPPED FOR MY JOURNEY

Affirmation: I have everything I need to fulfill my purpose.

Scripture: "And God is able to bless you abundantly, so that in all things at all times, having all that you need, you will abound in every good work." – 2 Corinthians 9:8 (NIV)

Encouragement: I am wonderfully and fearfully made, equipped with everything I need to navigate my unique journey. Each of us is created with a distinct set of abilities, talents, and gifts, carefully designed for the specific purpose we are meant to fulfill. By acknowledging our strengths and the resources available to us, we can cultivate a deeper trust in ourselves and in the divine guidance that surrounds us. Today, let us embrace the truth that we possess all the necessary tools to move confidently toward our goals, regardless of the challenges we may face.

As I take steps forward, I hold onto the promise that I am fully equipped for the purpose that lies ahead. With faith in God's abundant blessings, I am reminded that at every moment and in every circumstance, I have all that I need to excel in every good work. This assurance empowers me to tackle obstacles and live out my calling with boldness and grace. Each day is an opportunity to step into my purpose wholeheartedly, knowing that I am supported, capable, and ready to shine. Let this day be a testament to the abundant blessings that God provides, affirming that we are indeed equipped for our journey.

FEBRUARY 9

DAY 40

MY VOICE MATTERS

Affirmation: My voice is powerful and deserves to be heard.

Scripture: "Because judgment without mercy will be shown to anyone who has not been merciful. Mercy triumphs over judgment." – James 2:13 (NIV)

Encouragement: I recognize that my thoughts, feelings, and opinions are not only valid but also essential contributions to the tapestry of human experience. Each of us has a unique journey that shapes our perspectives, and it is through sharing these insights that we can foster understanding and connection. By embracing the truth of my experiences, I empower myself and those around me. My voice has the potential to inspire, uplift, and bring encouragement to others who may be struggling to find their own. Therefore, I will step into my power and refuse to shy away from expressing my truth, knowing that it can spark hope and motivation in someone else's life.

Today, I choose to speak boldly and authentically about my experiences, recognizing that this act can create a ripple effect of empowerment. My voice carries weight; it has the ability to reach hearts, encourage minds, and change lives. In doing so, I align myself with the profound wisdom found in James 2:13, which reminds us of the importance of mercy and compassion. By sharing my journey, I not only honor my own voice but also create a space where others may feel safe to do the same. In this communal sharing, we triumph over judgment and cultivate a culture rooted in empathy and understanding, reinforcing that mercy truly does triumph over judgment.

FEBRUARY 10

DAY 41

I AM UNIQUELY GIFTED

Affirmation: My gifts and talents are uniquely mine and serve a purpose.

Scripture: "As each has received a gift, use it to serve one another, as good stewards of God's varied grace." – 1 Peter 4:10 (ESV)

Encouragement: I celebrate my unique gifts and talents, taking time to acknowledge that they are integral to my divine design and purpose in this world. Each of us is crafted with distinct abilities, and recognizing this truth empowers me to embrace who I am. I commit to using my gifts not only for my personal growth but also to uplift those around me. With every act of kindness and every moment of service, I deepen my connection with others and honor the grace bestowed upon me.

Today, I will wholeheartedly embrace my individuality and dedicate myself to sharing my talents in service of a greater purpose. In doing so, I become a vessel of support and inspiration for those in need. It's vital to understand that when we utilize our unique gifts, we contribute to a beautiful tapestry of communal strength and compassion. I am reminded that my contributions, no matter how small they may seem, play a significant role in illustrating God's varied grace in action. Together, through our shared gifts, we can create a powerful impact that echoes far beyond ourselves.

FEBRUARY 11

DAY 42

I CHOOSE TO TRUST THE JOURNEY

Affirmation: I trust the journey and the process of becoming.

Scripture: "Trust in the Lord with all your heart, and do not lean on your own understanding." – Proverbs 3:5 (ESV)

Encouragement: Life is not merely about reaching a destination but is profoundly defined by the journey we undertake. Each moment we experience, with all its ups and downs, contributes to our personal growth and development. By choosing to trust the process, I recognize that every step I take—whether it's filled with joy, challenge, or uncertainty—is essential in shaping who I am meant to become. I find peace in surrendering the urge to rush towards an imagined finish line, understanding that each day presents opportunities for learning and transformation. Today, I commit to appreciating the present and living with intention, aware that this journey is a vital part of fulfilling my divine purpose.

As I navigate this journey, I remind myself of the wisdom found in Proverbs 3:5, which encourages us to place our trust in the Lord wholeheartedly rather than relying solely on our own understanding. This scripture reinforces my faith that there is a greater plan unfolding in my life, even when circumstances feel unclear. By leaning on this divine assurance, I can let go of doubts and fears, allowing myself to move forward with confidence. Today, I will focus on walking in faith, trusting that every twist and turn on this path is leading me precisely where I am meant to be, enriching my spirit and aligning me closer to my true calling.

Week 7

Cultivating Inner Peace

FEBRUARY 12

DAY 43

PEACE BEGINS WITHIN ME

Affirmation: I choose peace over worry, calm over chaos, and trust over fear.

Scripture: "You will keep in perfect peace those whose minds are steadfast, because they trust in you." – Isaiah 26:3 (NIV)

Encouragement: True peace is not found in the absence of challenges, but instead flourishes in the presence of unwavering faith. Today, I consciously release every anxious thought, casting aside the worries that threaten to cloud my heart and mind. Instead of succumbing to fear, I choose to rest confidently in God's perfect peace. My heart will not be troubled by circumstances beyond my control; rather, I redirect my focus to the steadfast nature of God's love and support. In doing so, I acknowledge that my strength lies not in my own understanding, but in a higher purpose that guides me. Each moment of stillness serves as a reminder that I am enveloped in divine grace, a comforting shield against the chaos of the world.

As I breathe deeply, I reaffirm my commitment to choose calm over chaos, trusting in the divine wisdom that brings clarity amid uncertainty. With each inhale, I welcome tranquility, and with each exhale, I release the burden of worry. I understand that peace is not merely an absence of noise, but a profound assurance that stems from trusting in God's promises. I allow myself to be anchored in this peace, allowing it to permeate my thoughts, actions, and interactions with others. No matter the external storms I may face, I will remain steadfast, knowing that my faith will guide me through and that I am continually supported by God's unwavering presence.

FEBRUARY 13

DAY 44

I AM GROUNDED IN SERENITY

Affirmation: My heart is steady, my mind is calm, and my soul is at rest.

Scripture: "The Lord gives strength to his people; the Lord blesses his people with peace." – Psalm 29:11 (NIV)

Encouragement: As I navigate the challenges that today may bring, I affirm my commitment to remain grounded. The world can often feel chaotic, filled with pressures and demands that seek to pull me away from my center. However, I choose not to allow those external forces to dictate my inner state. Instead, I embrace each moment with a steady heart and a calm mind. With every deep inhalation, I invite gratitude into my spirit, acknowledging the blessings in my life. As I exhale, I release all negativity and burdens, letting go of what no longer serves my highest good. In this practice, I reaffirm my belief that God's peace is not just a fleeting emotion but a profound and ever-present reality that guides and sustains me through life's storms.

Today, I consciously choose to walk in serenity, recognizing that I am continually supported by divine love. With each step, I cultivate an inner sanctuary of calm, where nothing can disturb my peace. As Psalm 29:11 reminds me, the Lord blesses His people with strength and peace, empowering me to face any challenge with grace. I stand firm in this truth, anchoring my thoughts in the serenity that comes from faith. The divine presence envelops me, assuring me that I am never alone. As I carry this tranquility into my interactions, I spread the gift of peace to those around me, creating a ripple effect of serenity in a world that often needs it most.

FEBRUARY 14

DAY 45

I LET GO AND LET GOD

Affirmation: I surrender my worries to God, knowing He has everything under control.

Scripture: "Cast all your anxiety on him because he cares for you." – 1 Peter 5:7 (NIV)

Encouragement: Holding onto worries does not serve me, and it's essential to recognize that by clinging to my anxieties, I only hinder my own peace and well-being. Today, I consciously open my hands, releasing my burdens and entrusting my concerns to God. I remind myself that I do not have to shoulder every challenge alone; in fact, there's profound strength in surrendering my worries to a higher power. His relentless love and unwavering guidance provide me with the support I need, allowing me to experience a sense of calm and reassurance.

As I embrace this truth, I feel lighter, unencumbered by the weight of fear that once held me back. Knowing that I am eternally cared for, I find freedom in letting go. This act of surrender opens the door to a deeper relationship with God, one grounded in trust and faith. I am reminded that His plans for me are greater than my worries, and in every uncertain moment, I can find solace in His presence. Today, I choose to rest in this comforting truth, acknowledging that by letting go, I can fully embrace the life He has in store for me.

FEBRUARY 15

DAY 46

MY SPIRIT IS CALM AND STILL

Affirmation: I welcome stillness and allow my spirit to be refreshed.

Scripture: "Be still, and know that I am God." – Psalm 46:10 (NIV)

Encouragement: In the fast-paced world we live, it is essential to carve out intentional moments of stillness amidst the chaos. When I take the time to pause, I create space for reflection and rejuvenation. By quieting my mind and gently softening my heart, I allow myself to fully engage with God's presence. This is not merely a fleeting moment but a sacred opportunity to recharge my spirit. Within this stillness, I often discover profound clarity that guides my thoughts and actions. It becomes easier to recognize that true strength does not come from the turmoil around me but from the peace I nurture within.

Choosing to prioritize a calm and unwavering heart is a powerful act of faith. It's a reminder that regardless of my circumstances or the noise that surrounds me, I have the ability to anchor myself in the serenity of God's love. When I embrace the stillness, I am reminded of Psalm 46:10, which encourages me to be still and recognize God's sovereignty in my life. By welcoming this peace, I not only replenish my spirit but also cultivate resilience to navigate through life's challenges with grace. In moments of uncertainty, may I continually return to this stillness, finding comfort and strength in the knowledge that I am held in the embrace of the Divine.

FEBRUARY 16

DAY 47

I RADIATE PEACE AND POSITIVITY

Affirmation: My inner peace shines outward, bringing light and calm to those around me.

Scripture: "Peacemakers who sow in peace reap a harvest of righteousness." – James 3:18 (NIV)

Encouragement: My peace is not just for me—it is a profound gift meant to be shared with everyone I encounter on my journey. When I cultivate and nurture a sense of tranquility within myself, it allows me to extend that serenity outward, creating an environment where others can likewise find solace. Today, I consciously choose to be a source of calm, joy, and reassurance, knowing that my very presence can uplift those around me. As I embody peace, I become a living testament to the divine love that permeates my life, inspiring others to seek that same tranquility.

Moreover, the light that radiates from my inner peace has the power to touch lives in ways I may not even realize. Each word I speak can serve as a comforting balm for someone in need, and every action I take can reflect the unconditional love of God. By embracing my role as a peacemaker, I participate in the beautiful cycle of sowing and reaping that James 3:18 describes. As I sow seeds of peace in my interactions, I trust that I will reap a harvest of righteousness, fostering a deeper connection with others and contributing to a more harmonious world. Let my life be a beacon of positivity, leading others to experience the profound gift of peace as well.

FEBRUARY 17

DAY 48

I TRUST IN GOD'S PERFECT TIMING

Affirmation: I release the need to control and trust that all things unfold in divine timing.

Scripture: "There is a time for everything, and a season for every activity under the heavens." – Ecclesiastes 3:1 (NIV)

Encouragement: Rushing, worrying, and forcing outcomes can often rob us of the peace that God desires for us. When we become tangled in the frustration of wanting things to happen on our timeline, we can easily overlook the beauty in the journey itself. Today, I consciously choose to prioritize trust over control, recognizing that God's timing is always perfect, even when it may not align with my own expectations. By surrendering my ambitions and desires to Him, I can embrace a sense of calm and assurance, knowing that everything is unfolding according to a divine plan.

As I cultivate this mindset of trust, I find my heart growing lighter and my thoughts clearer. The worries that once consumed my mind begin to fade, replaced by a profound sense of gratitude for the present moment. It is in this sacred space that I can fully appreciate the little blessings that surround me, understanding that they are all part of a greater design. My spirit is uplifted as I reflect on Ecclesiastes 3:1, which reminds me that there is indeed a time for everything under the heavens. I release the need to rush and instead allow myself to rest in the perfect timing of God, embracing each day with an open heart and a willing spirit.

FEBRUARY 18

DAY 49

I AM AT PEACE WITH MY JOURNEY

Affirmation: My journey is unfolding exactly as it should, and I embrace it with peace.

Scripture: "And the peace of God, which transcends all understanding, will guard your hearts and your minds in Christ Jesus." – Philippians 4:7 (NIV)

Encouragement: My path is uniquely mine, and I embrace it with gratitude, fully aware that every twist and turn has contributed to my growth. In acknowledging that I no longer compare my journey to others, I liberate myself from the burden of unrealistic expectations. Each experience, whether joyful or challenging, has shaped who I am today, and I recognize that this journey is a part of my divine story. I am precisely where I need to be in this moment, and I trust wholeheartedly in the divine plan that has been laid out for me. This understanding allows me to let go of regrets and misgivings, making space for acceptance and peace in my heart.

Today, I walk forward with confidence, knowing that peace is my constant companion. Philippians 4:7 reassures me that the peace of God, which transcends all understanding, will guard my heart and mind as I navigate life's complexities. It reminds me that even amid uncertainty, I can find solace in my faith. This divine peace gives me the strength to face each day with courage and clarity, embracing my journey as it unfolds. With every step I take, I am surrounded by love and guidance, affirming that I am perfectly positioned in life, trusting the process and discovering joy in each moment. In doing so, I cultivate an environment within me that resonates with tranquility and purpose.

Week 8

Building Unshakable Faith

FEBRUARY 19

DAY 50

MY FAITH IS STRONG AND UNWAVERING

**ffirmation:** My faith is my foundation, unshakable and steadfast.

Scripture: "Now faith is confidence in what we hope for and assurance about what we do not see." – Hebrews 11:1 (NIV)

Encouragement: Life may present challenges that seek to undermine our spirit, but it is during these moments of trial that my faith truly keeps me anchored. The storms of doubt and uncertainty may surround me, yet my faith stands as a robust foundation, immovable and steadfast. In moments when I cannot perceive the complete picture or understand the path laid before me, I choose to trust in God's divine plan. This trust empowers me to face each challenge head-on, allowing my faith to flourish even amidst adversity.

Moreover, I recognize that my faith is not merely a passive belief but an active and dynamic force that grows stronger with each trial I encounter. Each obstacle becomes an opportunity to deepen my understanding and reliance on God's promises. Today, I remind myself that I am never alone, as He walks beside me every step of the way. With renewed conviction, I move forward with unwavering trust, knowing that my faith assures me of hope in the unseen and strengthens my resolve to persevere in life's journey. I embrace the power of this faith, which transcends circumstances and illuminates my way, empowering me to face whatever comes my way with grace and resilience.

FEBRUARY 20

DAY 51

I EMBRACE GOD'S PROMISES

Affirmation: I trust in God's promises; they are my guiding light.

Scripture: "Not that we are competent in ourselves to claim anything for ourselves, but our competence comes from God." – 2 Corinthians 3:5 (NIV)

Encouragement: Today, I choose to fully embrace the promises that God has made to me, recognizing that they serve as both a source of strength and a beacon of hope in my life. His plans are intricately woven with love and purpose, designed to inspire and uplift me, especially during moments of uncertainty. In the face of challenges, I refuse to allow fear to overshadow my faith. Instead, I opt to walk boldly in the light of His guidance, continuously reminding myself that I am on a journey directed by divine intention. Each step forward is not just a movement through life; it is a reflection of my unwavering trust in God's provision and direction.

With every breath I take, I reaffirm my belief that I am not only a cherished creation but one that is destined for greatness. I am reminded that my competence and strength come not from my own abilities, but from the limitless power of God. As I lean into His promises, I find a sense of security that transforms my perspective, encouraging me to embrace the fullness of His grace. I will hold fast to the truth that God equips me for every challenge I face, infusing me with the confidence and resilience I need to thrive. Today, I rest in the assurance that I am never alone; His promises illuminate my path and empower me to live with purpose and joy.

FEBRUARY 21

DAY 52

I TRUST THE JOURNEY

Affirmation: I trust the journey that God has laid before me.

Scripture: "When I am afraid, I put my trust in you. In God, whose word I praise—in God I trust and am not afraid." – Psalm 56:3-4 (NIV)

Encouragement: While the path may twist and turn, I have faith that God is leading me exactly where I need to be. In acknowledging that I cannot foresee every bump or detour, I find solace in the truth that His plan for me is perfect. I release the need to control every aspect of my life and lean into the wisdom of His guidance. Each moment is a step in my journey, contributing to my growth and strength. I recognize that even the challenges I face serve a purpose and that they are part of a greater story being woven together by His loving hand. I trust that even in uncertainty, I am being perpetually uplifted by a divine force that knows my name and intimately understands my heart.

As I navigate this journey, I am reminded that my fears can be transformed into trust when I surrender them to God. Psalm 56:3-4 reassures me that I can find peace even in moments of anxiety, for when I am afraid, I can confidently choose to put my trust in Him. This act of trust does not imply a lack of struggle; rather, it allows me to embrace the process while resting in the assurance of His promises. I hold on to the belief that I am not alone on this path, and that each step, no matter how daunting, draws me closer to the fullness of His purpose for my life. Indeed, in God, whose word I praise, I find not only a refuge but also the courage to face whatever comes my way, rooted in His unwavering support.

FEBRUARY 22

DAY 53

I AM A VESSEL OF HOPE

Affirmation: I am a vessel of hope, spreading light wherever I go.

Scripture: "Submit to God and be at peace with him; in this way, prosperity will come to you." – Job 22:21 (NIV)

Encouragement: My faith is not just a personal journey; it serves as a radiant beacon that has the power to touch and transform the lives of those around me. This truth reminds me that I have the ability to be a vessel of hope, spreading light and positivity to others even in the midst of my own vulnerabilities. When I lift my eyes towards God and submit to His will, I find a peace that enriches my life and empowers me to encourage those who may be facing their own struggles. Each act of kindness and every word of affirmation I share can spark a glimmer of hope in someone else's heart.

Today, I choose to shine brightly, serving as a reflection of the unwavering love and grace I receive from God. I understand that my journey, with all its ups and downs, is not solely for my growth; it's also a testament to the strength and resilience that comes from faith. So, as

I navigate this path, I trust that my experiences may inspire others to seek peace and prosperity in their own lives. By holding onto my belief and sharing it openly, I create an environment where hope can flourish, not just for me, but for everyone who crosses my path.

FEBRUARY 23

DAY 54

I LET GO OF DOUBT

Affirmation: I release all doubt and embrace the certainty of God's love.

Scripture: "So do not fear, for I am with you; do not be dismayed, for I am your God." – Isaiah 41:10 (NIV)

Encouragement: Doubt has no place in my heart, for I am embraced by God's unwavering love. In acknowledging this divine assurance, I find the strength to surrender my worries and anxieties. As I let go of uncertainty, I cultivate an atmosphere where faith can take root and flourish. Each time that doubt attempts to invade my thoughts, I choose to reflect on the countless ways God has consistently proven His faithfulness in my life. This journey is not merely a battle against doubt but also a profound understanding of the depth of God's unwavering support.

Today, I step forward free from doubt, anchored by the assurance that I am loved unconditionally and supported in every endeavor. With each step I take, I embrace the knowledge that God walks beside me, guiding my path and reminding me of His presence. The scripture reminds me not to fear or be dismayed, for I am never alone. As I choose faith over doubt, I am empowered to face challenges with courage, knowing that my heart is fortified by the certainty of divine love surrounding me. In this truth, I find peace and strength, emboldening me to live a life of purpose and confidence.

FEBRUARY 24

DAY 55

I RENEW MY MIND DAILY

Affirmation: I renew my mind daily with thoughts of faith and positivity.

Scripture: "For in him we live and move and have our being." – Acts 17:28 (NIV)

Encouragement: Each day is a new opportunity to refresh my perspective and ground my thoughts in faith. I am intentional about nurturing a mindset that aligns with God's truth and love. By consciously choosing to focus on the positive aspects of my life, I create an environment where hope can thrive. When challenges arise, I remind myself that I have the strength to rise above them. My faith flourishes when I fill my mind with hope, gratitude, and determination, and in doing so, I engage in a powerful transformation that begins in my heart and radiates outward into my actions and interactions with others.

As I renew my mind daily, I align myself with the divine presence that sustains me, echoing the truth of Acts 17:28—"For in him we live and move and have our being." This profound truth assures me that my existence is rooted in a higher purpose. Each moment spent in faith not only elevates my spirit but also equips me to face life's uncertainties with unwavering confidence. By cultivating a heart filled with positivity and an unwavering trust in God, I open myself to experience the fullness of life as intended. This ongoing renewal is not merely an exercise of the mind but a transformative journey that deepens my relationship with God and enriches my daily experiences.

FEBRUARY 25

DAY 56

I STAND FIRM IN MY FAITH

Affirmation: I stand firm in my faith amidst every storm.

Scripture: "He brought me out into a spacious place; he rescued me because he delighted in me." – 2 Samuel 22:20 (NIV)

Encouragement: Just as a sturdy tree withstands the fiercest winds, I too can stand firm in my faith during life's storms. Each trial is not merely a challenge but rather an opportunity to deepen my reliance on God, allowing me to acknowledge and celebrate His unwavering power in my life. In moments of adversity, I will not be swayed; instead, I will rise with courage and strength, confidently trusting in the promises given to me. With each struggle, I have the chance to refine my character and develop resilience, resting assured that I am anchored in my faith. Today, I stand resolute in my belief as I affirm that divine strength will guide me through any turbulence I face.

Moreover, it is essential to remember that I am not alone in these trials. The Almighty Creator has already gone before me, preparing a pathway through the storm. Just as the scripture reminds us, He brings us into spacious places, offering hope and refuge when the winds of uncertainty blow fiercely. I can lean into His promises, knowing He delights in me and actively works for my good. As I navigate the challenges ahead, I will embrace the assurance that my faith is a fortress, allowing me to weather any storm with grace and perseverance. By embracing this perspective, I am empowered to move forward, confident that my foundation is built on a rock that will never falter.

Week 9

Embracing Joy In The Journey

FEBRUARY 26

DAY 57

I CHOOSE JOY IN EVERY SEASON

ffirmation: No matter what comes my way, I choose to embrace joy.

Scripture: " He raises the poor from the dust and lifts the needy from the ash heap; he seats them with princes and has them inherit a throne of honor." – 1 Samuel 2:8 (NIV)

Encouragement: Joy is not just a fleeting emotion; it is a purposeful choice I make each day, a commitment to embrace a positive outlook regardless of life's inevitable challenges. Even when faced with difficulties, I hold onto joy because I have faith in the unwavering truth that God's presence surrounds me, providing comfort and strength. In choosing joy, I actively resist allowing external circumstances to rob me of my peace. Instead, I cultivate a heart of gratitude, recognizing that each moment, big or small, holds an opportunity for joy and growth. Today, I intentionally celebrate the little moments that bring warmth to my spirit, reinforcing my resilience in the midst of trials.

In the light of 1 Samuel 2:8, which reminds us that God raises the poor from the dust and lifts the needy from the ash heap, I find profound encouragement to embrace a life filled with joy. This powerful imagery illustrates God's desire to elevate us, offering us honor and dignity despite our circumstances. As I walk in the fullness of joy that is mine to claim, I remember that my story is woven with purpose, where joy can flourish even in uncertain seasons. I am deeply grateful for the assurance that I am not alone; instead, I am seated among those who are blessed, inheriting a throne of honor in His kingdom. This truth fuels my spirit, motivating me to reflect joy in every season of my life.

FEBRUARY 27

DAY 58

I AM A JOYFUL BEING

Affirmation: I radiate joy wherever I go.

Scripture: "Rejoice in the Lord always. I will say it again: Rejoice!" – Philippians 4:4 (NIV)

Encouragement: Every day presents us with a unique opportunity to share joy and inspiration with everyone we encounter. When we consciously choose to embrace a joyful mindset, we not only nourish our own spirit but also create an uplifting environment for those around us. This ripple effect of positivity can transform our interactions, helping others to discover happiness in their own journeys. Therefore, let us remember that joy is not just a fleeting emotion but a powerful choice we can make each day. By deliberately radiating joy, we contribute to a culture of encouragement and support.

Today, I commit to being a beacon of joy, allowing my light to shine brightly in the world. As I walk through my day, I will actively seek moments to celebrate, to connect, and to uplift the spirits of others. Joy is contagious, and through my simple acts of kindness and positivity, I can inspire someone else to embrace their own joy. With each smile shared, each encouraging word spoken, and each moment of genuine laughter experienced, I become part of a larger tapestry of happiness that weaves through the lives of everyone I encounter. Let us rejoice in the beauty of this day and spread our joy far and wide, fulfilling the calling to "rejoice in the Lord always" and reflect that joy back into our communities.

FEBRUARY 28

DAY 59

JOY IS MY STRENGTH

Affirmation: I find my strength in joy, which uplifts my spirit.

Scripture: "You make known to me the path of life; in your presence, there is fullness of joy." – Psalm 16:11 (ESV)

Encouragement: Joy is a profound and vital source of strength that fuels my perseverance through life's challenges. In times of difficulty, it is the joy that springs from a deep connection with God that uplifts my spirit. This joy not only enhances my ability to cope with obstacles but also empowers me to embrace each day with renewed resilience and courage. When I actively lean into the joy offered by God, I find that it infuses my heart with peace and optimism, guiding me along the path of life. I choose to focus on the blessings around me and remind myself that even in tough times, I can cultivate a joyful heart.

Today, I will intentionally seek out moments that bring me joy, whether it's through appreciating the beauty of nature, cherishing time with loved ones, or simply reflecting on the blessings in my life. It's important to remember that joy is not merely the absence of troubles but the presence of God in my life. As Psalm 16:11 reminds me, I am never alone on this journey; God's presence is the wellspring of joy that sustains me. Embracing this truth helps me to stay grounded and hopeful, knowing that I can navigate every twist and turn with faith as my guide. I will hold on to joy, for it strengthens my spirit and lights the way ahead.

FEBRUARY 29

DAY 60

I CELEBRATE MY JOURNEY

Affirmation: I celebrate every step of my journey, finding joy in the process.

Scripture: "This is the day that the Lord has made; let us rejoice and be glad in it." – Psalm 118:24 (ESV)

Encouragement: Life is composed of moments, and each moment deserves to be cherished. Each step of my journey is a building block that contributes to the canvas of my life, woven together with experiences that shape who I am. As I navigate this journey, I will embrace the importance of celebrating not just the milestones, but also the small victories along the way. Every lesson learned and every challenge overcome is an opportunity for growth and reflection. With each day that unfolds, I recognize the beauty in every twist and turn, allowing gratitude to fill my heart.

Today, I will dedicate time to joyfully reflect on the richness of my unique story, reminding myself that every experience holds value. This journey is not simply about the destination; it is about the incredible growth and transformation that occurs in the process. By honoring each moment and cultivating a spirit of thankfulness, I can fully appreciate the journey I am on. As Psalm 118:24 invites us to rejoice in the day that the Lord has made, I will embrace each day with open arms, celebrating the very essence of my journey and the joys that come with it

MARCH 1

DAY 61

MY JOY IS UNSHAKEABLE

Affirmation: My joy is unshakeable, regardless of my circumstances.

Scripture: "Though the fig tree should not blossom, nor fruit be on the vines, the produce of the olive fail and the fields yield no food, yet I will rejoice in the Lord; I will take joy in the God of my salvation." – Habakkuk 3:17-18 (ESV)

Encouragement: There may be days filled with uncertainty and challenges that threaten to overshadow my spirit, but I choose to stand firm in my joy as a conscious act of faith. This joy is not a fleeting emotion; it is the anchor that keeps me steady amid life's storms and turbulent seas. Even when I face trials, I recognize that true joy stems from a deep-seated trust in God, the source of my strength. Today, I will remind myself that my joy is firmly rooted in my faith and the unchanging nature of God who promises to be with me through every season of life. In doing so, I cultivate a perspective that allows me to see beyond my present circumstances and grasp the bigger picture of God's goodness and grace.

Even when the fig tree does not bloom and there seems to be a lack of abundance around me, I can still declare, as Habakkuk did, that my heart will rejoice in the Lord. This rejoicing is an act of defiance against despair; it is a commitment to seek joy in the God of my salvation. I will choose to be steadfast in my joy, drawing on the wellspring of hope found in God's promises rather than allowing my circumstances to dictate my emotional state. In this way, I acknowledge that joy is a decision I make, not just a reaction to what happens in my life. By holding on to joy with both hands, I open myself to the transformative power of God, enabling me to be a beacon of light and encouragement for others who may be navigating their own storms.

MARCH 2

DAY 62

I CHOOSE JOY OVER WORRY

Affirmation: I release worry and embrace the joy of today.

Scripture: "Do not be anxious about anything, but in every situation, by prayer and petition, with thanksgiving, present your requests to God." – Philippians 4:6 (NIV)

Encouragement: Worry can often cloud my joy and diminish my ability to fully engage with the beauty of the present moment. It can create a heaviness in our hearts, distracting us from the blessings that surround us. However, I have the profound power to choose an alternate path—one that leads to joy and gratitude. By turning to prayer, I can actively surrender my anxieties to God, acknowledging that He invites me to lay down my burdens at His feet. Through this process of releasing what troubles me, I open my heart to the transformative joy that flows from His presence.

As I shift my focus from worry to a joyful anticipation of what each day holds, I remind myself of the promise found in Philippians 4:6. In every situation, no matter how small or significant, I can present my concerns to God with thanksgiving. This act of faith not only lightens my emotional load but also allows me to trust in the goodness that is woven into each aspect of my life. Today, I will consciously choose to fill my thoughts with hope and delight in the Lord, embracing the fact that joy is a choice I can make amidst the uncertainties of life.

MARCH 3

DAY 63

I AM GRATEFUL FOR JOY

Affirmation: I am grateful for the joy that floods my heart.

Scripture: "Let us come before His presence with thanksgiving; let us make a joyful noise to Him with songs of praise!" – Psalm 95:2 (ESV)

Encouragement: Gratitude is truly the gateway to joy, opening our hearts to the beauty that surrounds us. When we take a moment to express gratitude for the myriad of gifts—big and small—that we encounter each day, we not only elevate our own spirits but also create a nurturing environment where joy can flourish abundantly. Whether it's the warmth of the sun on our skin, the laughter of loved ones, or the simple pleasures of daily life, acknowledging these blessings allows us to shift our focus from what we lack to the abundance we already possess. Today, I consciously choose to recognize these wonderful gifts and to articulate my appreciation for them, as doing so transforms even the mundane into moments of unexpected beauty.

As the Scripture reminds us, entering His presence with thanksgiving inspires a sense of community and shared joy. When we lift our voices in songs of praise, we not only celebrate our individual gratitude but also invite others to join us in this uplifting experience. Sharing our joy and gratitude can be contagious, encouraging those around us to also reflect on their own blessings. As we sing, shout, or share our appreciation, we weave a tapestry of positivity that can uplift and inspire others. In this way, gratitude becomes a powerful instrument, turning our hearts toward joy and inviting those nearby to partake in the vibrancy that gratitude brings into our lives. Let us carry this spirit of thanksgiving into our daily routines, enriching our souls and those of others along the way.

Week 10

Letting Go Of Comparison

MARCH 4

DAY 64

MY JOURNEY IS UNIQUELY MINE

Affirmation: I release the need to compare myself to others. My journey is uniquely mine and divinely guided.

Scripture: "Each one should test their own actions. Then they can take pride in themselves alone, without comparing themselves to someone else." – Galatians 6:4 (NIV)

Encouragement: Comparison is a thief of joy, and when I allow it to creep into my thoughts, I risk undermining the significance of my own journey. Each time I measure myself against someone else's achievements or challenges, I overlook the unique beauty and lessons that my experiences bring. Today, I consciously release the urge to compare, understanding that my path is divinely orchestrated and tailored specifically for me. No one else can walk my journey or share my precise struggles, victories, and insights; this individuality is what empowers my story.

As I embrace my uniqueness, I recognize that my journey holds its own distinct beauty and purpose. I am reminded of the wisdom in Galatians 6:4, which encourages self-reflection and pride in our individual progress. Today, I choose to celebrate each step along my path, knowing that every experience adds depth to my story. I trust that I am exactly where I need to be in this moment, and I look forward to the growth that lies ahead, secure in the knowledge that my life is unfolding according to a divine plan that only I can fulfill.

MARCH 5

DAY 65

EMBRACING MY OWN STORY

Affirmation: I embrace the unique chapters of my life and the lessons they bring.

Scripture: "I have been crucified with Christ and I no longer live, but Christ lives in me."

– Galatians 2:20 (NIV)

Encouragement: My story is filled with growth and transformation, serving as a testament to the unique journey that God has laid out for me. Each twist and turn illuminates invaluable lessons that contribute to my personal development and spiritual maturity. Instead of succumbing to the temptation to envy others' experiences, I choose to cherish the richness of my own narrative and the profound strength that emerges from it. Embracing the trials and victories that have shaped me allows me to recognize the beauty of my individuality.

Life is a beautiful tapestry, woven together by diverse threads that represent moments of joy, sorrow, and resilience. Each part of my story tells a piece of who I am, revealing the intricate design of God's purpose in my life. I am reminded that I have been crucified with Christ, and it is through Him that I find my identity and strength. In embracing my unique chapters, I can trust that they all serve a greater purpose—one that ultimately leads me closer to Him and fully into the life that He intended for me. With faith and gratitude, I will continue to honor my journey, knowing that it is a reflection of His work within me.

MARCH 6

DAY 66

ABUNDANT SELF-LOVE

Affirmation: I cultivate love and compassion for myself, knowing I am enough just as I am.

Scripture: "You are altogether beautiful, my darling; there is no flaw in you." – Song of Solomon 4:7 (NIV)

Encouragement: Self-love is not just a concept; it is a vital foundation for my personal journey and growth. I recognize that I am a unique masterpiece, deliberately crafted by the Creator, reflecting divine beauty and purpose. By embracing and nurturing the love I have for myself, I create a pathway toward a more fulfilled and meaningful existence. Rather than focusing on perceived imperfections, I choose to appreciate my individuality and acknowledge my inherent worth. Today, I commit to filling my heart with kindness and compassion towards myself, celebrating my unique qualities and the beauty of my being.

As I immerse myself in self-love, I discover the profound truth that I am enough just as I am. When I treat myself with respect and grace, I not only enhance my own well-being but also cultivate a deeper capacity to love and support others. This journey requires intentionality and practice, but I am determined to practice self-affirmation daily. I will reflect on the beauty within me, inspired by the words of Scripture that remind me of my flawlessness in the eyes of the Creator. With each act of self-compassion, I am not just lifting myself up; I am empowering my spirit to thrive and flourish. Today, I choose to honor my existence and cultivate a heart that is overflowing with love, starting from within.

MARCH 7

DAY 67

LETTING GO OF THE FEAR OF JUDGMENT

Affirmation: I release the fear of judgment from others; I am free to be my authentic self.

Scripture: "Do not judge, or you too will be judged." – Matthew 7:1 (NIV)

Encouragement: The fear of judgment can often act as a heavy weight, stifling our true expression and keeping us from embracing who we genuinely are. This fear may lead us to adopt facades or behaviors that don't align with our true selves, causing us to miss out on the joy of authenticity. Letting go of the fear of what others may think liberates us to be the unique individuals we were created to be. By boldly stepping into our authenticity, we not only honor ourselves but also invite relationships and experiences that resonate with our true essence.

As we navigate the journey of self-discovery, it becomes increasingly clear that authenticity attracts positivity and meaningful connections. When we shed the inhibitions imposed by the fear of judgment, we find empowerment in our vulnerability. Today, I make the conscious choice to embrace my worthiness, celebrating every aspect of who I am. I remind myself that I am deserving of love and acceptance, just as I am. Focusing on my authentic self opens doors to genuine relationships and experiences that uplift my spirit and nourish my soul, allowing me to walk freely in my truth..

MARCH 8

DAY 68

CELEBRATING MY UNIQUE ABILITIES

Affirmation: My abilities are my strength, and I celebrate them wholeheartedly.

Scripture: "We have different gifts, according to the grace given to each of us." – Romans 12:6 (NIV)

Encouragement: I am uniquely gifted in ways that are completely my own, and this individuality is something to be celebrated. Instead of falling into the trap of comparing my talents to those of others, I choose to embrace my strengths with joy and confidence. The abilities I possess are not just mere skills; they are valuable gifts bestowed upon me. By recognizing and cherishing what I bring to the world, I am empowered to share my talents freely and openly. In doing so, I contribute to a vibrant tapestry of diverse gifts that enrich our community.

Every time I take a moment to celebrate my unique abilities, I not only acknowledge my own worth but also create a ripple effect of inspiration around me. My joyful expression of gratitude for my gifts encourages others to recognize and appreciate their own talents as well. As we each honor our distinct contributions, we foster an environment of mutual respect and admiration. Together, we can cultivate a culture where everyone feels empowered to shine in their own right, understanding that our individual strengths collectively enhance the beauty of our shared experiences.

MARCH 9

DAY 69

RECOGNIZING MY WORTH

Affirmation: My worth is inherent, not measured by others' opinions or achievements.

Scripture: "You are precious and honored in my sight, and I love you." – Isaiah 43:4 (NIV)

Encouragement: I am worthy just as I am, and it's essential to embrace this truth every day. In a world that often places a premium on external validation, it is all too easy to fall into the trap of measuring my worth against the successes and achievements of others. However, today, I consciously reject this misleading belief. I remind myself that my life has its own intrinsic value, one that is not contingent upon societal standards or the opinions of those around me. Each step of my unique journey contributes to my personal growth and fulfillment, affirming that I am enough simply because I exist.

As I reflect on the power of my inherent worth, I honor every moment that has shaped me into the individual I am today. I recognize that my experiences—both the triumphs and the challenges—serve to enrich my understanding of myself and my place in the world. I choose to celebrate my individuality, knowing that it is a reflection of my inner strength and resilience. Isaiah 43:4 reminds me that I am precious and honored, cherished for who I am rather than what I do. This divine affirmation empowers me to fully embrace my identity without the need for external validation, allowing me to thrive in confidence and self-love.

MARCH 10

DAY 70

THE GIFT OF GRATITUDE

Affirmation: I live in gratitude, appreciating my journey and the lessons it brings.

Scripture: "Give thanks in all circumstances; for this is God's will for you in Christ Jesus." – 1 Thessalonians 5:18 (NIV)

Encouragement: Gratitude has a remarkable power to transform our perspective, shifting our focus from the voids in our lives to the abundance that already surrounds us. When we express gratitude, we acknowledge not only the significant moments but also the small details that contribute to our growth and happiness. Today, I encourage you to take a moment to reflect on your unique journey. Consider the people who have crossed your path, the lessons that have shaped you, and the experiences that have contributed to who you are today. Each step in your journey is a chapter of growth and understanding, deserving of appreciation.

As we embrace gratitude, we create a heart filled with joy and appreciation that allows us to view our lives through a lens of abundance rather than scarcity. Living in gratitude means consciously choosing to release the burdens of comparison and instead fully engaging with our own path, understanding that it is perfectly designed for us. When we thank God in every situation, as encouraged in 1 Thessalonians 5:18, we align ourselves with His will and invite a deeper sense of peace and fulfillment. Let this practice of gratitude be a daily commitment—the more we recognize what we have, the more we open ourselves to joy and contentment in our lives.

Week 11

Strength Through Community

MARCH 11

DAY 71

I AM UPLIFTED BY MY COMMUNITY

Affirmation: I am surrounded by love and support. My community strengthens me.

Scripture: "Therefore encourage one another and build each other up, just as in fact you are doing." – 1 Thessalonians 5:11 (NIV)

Encouragement: I do not have to walk this journey alone, for God has graciously surrounded me with a vibrant community of individuals who uplift and encourage me. This network of love and support is a vital part of my life, reminding me that I am never isolated in my struggles. In moments of doubt or difficulty, I can lean on these genuine connections, drawing strength from the friendships and relationships that enrich my days. Embracing this support allows me to feel grounded, encouraging me to face challenges with renewed hope and resilience. I recognize that these relationships are not merely coincidence; they are divine placements meant to remind me of God's unwavering presence through others.

In return, I am committed to being a source of encouragement for those around me, fostering a culture of kindness and support. Each small act of upliftment can create ripples of positivity, reinforcing the belief that together, we are indeed stronger. I look to remind my community members of their worth and the unique roles they play in our collective journeys. We are called to uplift one another, as 1

Thessalonians 5:11 reminds us. As I share words of encouragement, I hope to bolster their spirits and help them recognize the power of unity in overcoming life's hardships. Together, we can create a supportive atmosphere where every individual feels valued and empowered, reinforcing our bonds and inspiring one another to thrive.

MARCH 12

DAY 72

I FIND HEALING IN CONNECTION

Affirmation: I embrace the power of connection, knowing that healing happens in community.

Scripture: "Carry each other's burdens, and in this way, you will fulfill the law of Christ." – Galatians 6:2 (NIV)

Encouragement: There is profound power in unity, and it is through connection that we discover the true essence of healing. When I choose to share my journey with others, I not only invite them into my story, but I also tap into a reservoir of strength that transcends my individual experience. The weight of my struggles is significantly lightened when I realize that I am not alone in this journey. By opening my heart to others, I cultivate an environment rich with love, encouragement, and the potential for shared victories. Each conversation, every moment of vulnerability, creates a tapestry of support that weaves our paths together, reminding me of the strength found in collective resilience.

Today, I wholeheartedly embrace the gift of community and the transformative healing it brings. In our shared experiences, we are reminded that we are all interconnected, and each interaction serves as a stepping stone toward wholeness. When we carry each other's burdens, we fulfill the law of Christ, creating a sacred bond that fosters not just individual healing, but a collective restoration. So, let us lean into this community, intertwining our lives in a way that uplifts and empowers. Through this support, we can face life's trials not just as isolated individuals, but as a united front, ready to conquer challenges and celebrate triumphs together.

MARCH 13

DAY 73

I CELEBRATE OUR SHARED JOURNEYS

Affirmation: I celebrate the unique stories and journeys of those around me. Our experiences unite us.

Scripture: "For we are each other's, and we are part of one another." – Ephesians 4:25 (NIV)

Encouragement: Every person I meet enriches the tapestry of my life, contributing unique threads that enhance its complexity and beauty. Our varied experiences, struggles, and triumphs come together to create a vibrant and inspiring narrative of resilience and strength. Each story is significant, reflecting the intricate details of our shared humanity. As I navigate my own path, I am reminded that my journey is intertwined with the journeys of others. This interconnectedness not only deepens my appreciation for the individual stories around me, but also emphasizes how we all contribute to the collective experience of life.

Today, I choose to honor and celebrate the diverse journeys of those within my community. I recognize that each person's path carries wisdom, lessons, and insights that can uplift and inspire. In acknowledging our unique stories, we can find comfort and solidarity in the truth that we are indeed stronger together. As the scripture in Ephesians reminds us, we are part of one another, and it is through this unity that we can support and uplift each other. Let us celebrate our shared journeys and find joy in the beautiful connections that make our lives richer and more meaningful.

MARCH 14

DAY 74

I AM A SOURCE OF LIGHT

Affirmation: I shine brightly within my community, sharing positivity and hope.

Scripture: "But grow in the grace and knowledge of our Lord and Savior Jesus Christ. To him be glory both now and forever! Amen." – 2 Peter 3:18 (NIV)

Encouragement: My attitude and outlook hold incredible power, capable of uplifting those around me in profound ways. Just as a single light can pierce through the thickest darkness, my positive spirit can become a beacon of hope for those who may feel lost or discouraged. By embracing this role, I have the opportunity to not only enhance my own life but also to touch the hearts of others. Today, I will be intentional in my interactions, seeking ways to spread joy and light. Whether through a warm smile, a thoughtful word, or an act of kindness, I will encourage those in my community to recognize their own worth and potential, inspiring them to let their light shine brightly alongside mine.

As I grow in the grace and knowledge of our Lord and Savior Jesus Christ, I am reminded that living a life filled with positivity is not just a personal choice; it is a calling. Each moment presents a new opportunity to reflect His love and goodness, ultimately transforming my surroundings. By choosing to embody this light, I can create an atmosphere of hope and encouragement that resonates deeply with others. Let us remember that even the smallest gestures can create ripples of positivity. Together, we can illuminate the world with our collective brightness, lifting each other up and creating a community anchored in faith and love.

MARCH 15

DAY 75

I EMBRACE VULNERABILITY

Affirmation: I am brave enough to be vulnerable, allowing authenticity to strengthen my community.

Scripture: "Confess your sins to each other and pray for each other so that you may be healed." – James 5:16 (NIV)

Encouragement: Vulnerability is often misinterpreted as a form of weakness, yet it is, in reality, one of the greatest strengths we can possess. When we allow ourselves to share our authentic selves with others, we cultivate an atmosphere that invites deeper connections and fosters trust. Each time we decide to open up, we create ripples of courage that encourage others to step out of their comfort zones and embrace their own imperfections. This collective authenticity not only strengthens our communities but also unites us in our shared experiences and struggles. It reminds us that we are not alone in our journeys, and through our openness, we can lift each other up.

As I reflect on the wisdom found in James 5:16, I am reminded of the healing power of genuine connections. Confessing our struggles and praying for one another serves as a vital process of restoration that goes beyond mere acknowledgment of pain; it lays the groundwork for profound healing. Today, I will embrace my vulnerability with full awareness of its potential to nurture profound relationships. By creating a safe space for openness, we empower one another to share our burdens and celebrate our victories. In this sacred exchange, we discover that vulnerability is indeed a bridge that connects our hearts and enriches our communities.

MARCH 16

DAY 76

I AM GRATEFUL FOR MY SUPPORT NETWORK

Affirmation: I am thankful for the support and love my community provides.

Scripture: "Every good and perfect gift is from above, coming down from the Father." – James 1:17 (NIV)

Encouragement: Gratitude opens the door to joy and serves as a profound reminder of the blessings that surround us. Recognizing and appreciating the unwavering love and support of my community fills my heart with warmth and gratitude. Each gesture, no matter how small, weaves a thread of connection that strengthens our relationships. In moments when life feels overwhelming, it's often the steadfast presence of friends and loved ones that provides the comfort we need. Today, I commit to not only acknowledging these gifts but to actively expressing my gratitude. I will take time to share with those around me how much their kindness and encouragement mean to me.

By vocalizing my appreciation, I reinforce the bonds that tie us together, creating an atmosphere of encouragement and love. As I reflect on the words of James 1:17, I am reminded that every good and perfect gift comes from above, illuminating the grace that flows through my support network. My gratitude becomes a catalyst for joy, inspiring others to recognize the abundance in their own lives as well. Together, we can cultivate a spirit of appreciation that elevates our shared experiences and deepens our connections, reminding us all of the power of community and the importance of leaning on one another in this beautiful journey of life.

MARCH 17

DAY 77

I CREATE SPACE FOR OTHERS

Affirmation: I create an open and welcoming space for others in my community.

Scripture: "Let mutual love continue. Do not neglect to show hospitality to strangers." – Hebrews 13:1-2 (ESV)

Encouragement: My community thrives when I intentionally cultivate a space where everyone feels valued and accepted. Each person who enters this space adds a unique thread to the fabric of our collective experience, and it is my responsibility to ensure that these threads are woven together with care and love. By fostering an environment of understanding and compassion, I become a beacon of hope for those who may feel lonely or marginalized. I recognize that each unique story brings richness to our shared journey, and today I commit to extending warmth and kindness to all, embracing both the familiar faces and newcomers that cross my path.

As I seek to welcome new connections, I understand that hospitality is not just about physical space but also about an open heart. The scripture reminds us to sustain mutual love and actively offer hospitality, reflecting the kindness that fills our own lives. Today, I will take deliberate steps to engage with others, whether through simple conversations or acts of kindness, creating opportunities for connection. Together, we can ensure that our community continues to grow stronger, united by compassion and shared experiences. By creating an atmosphere that encourages openness, I not only uplift others but also enrich my own life, as we thrive together in this journey of fellowship.

Week 12

Living Boldy And Unapologetically

MARCH 18

DAY 78

I AM FEARLESSLY AUTHENTIC

Affirmation: I embrace my true self without apology. I am confident in who I am.

Scripture: "For you are a people holy to the Lord your God. The Lord your God has chosen you out of all the peoples on the face of the earth to be his people, his treasured possession." – Deuteronomy 7:6 (NIV)

Encouragement: Today, I choose to show up as my most authentic self, fully embracing the vibrant individuality that God has instilled within me. It is essential to recognize that I have been lovingly crafted to reflect the divine image in a way that is uniquely mine. I will not shrink, hide, or apologize for the person God created me to be. Instead, I will stand firm in my identity, celebrating the gifts and quirks that make me who I am. My uniqueness is not just a characteristic; it is a divine calling, a reflection of God's creativity and purpose in my life. By walking in this boldness, I free myself from the chains of comparison and self-doubt, understanding that I am enough just as I am.

As I acknowledge my authenticity, I am reminded of Deuteronomy 7:6, which beautifully affirms my status as a cherished and chosen individual in God's eyes. I am part of a special people, intentionally selected to be treasured by the Creator of the universe. Embracing my true self aligns me with this sacred identity, empowering me to shine brightly in a world that often encourages conformity. Today, I will not only acknowledge my worth but also encourage others to embrace theirs. I will foster an atmosphere of acceptance and love, reminding myself and those around me that we are all precious in God's sight, called to express our true selves without reservation. Together, we can celebrate the beauty of our differences, creating a community that thrives on authenticity and connection.

MARCH 19

DAY 79

I AM MORE THAN ENOUGH

Affirmation: I am enough, just as I am, and I do not need to seek validation from others.

Scripture: "You will be a crown of splendor in the Lord's hand, a royal diadem in the hand of your God."

– Isaiah 62:3 (NIV)

Encouragement: I refuse to seek approval from the world because I am already approved by God. In a world filled with fleeting trends and ever-changing standards, it is so easy to fall into the trap of seeking validation from others. However, I choose to stand firm in my identity as a beloved child of God, knowing that my worth is unshakeable and anchored in His love. I embrace my unique qualities and attributes that set me apart, realizing that they are a reflection of my divine creation. I recognize that true validation comes from understanding that I am enough just as I am, and no external approval can add to my inherent value.

I celebrate the profound truth that my worth is not determined by the opinions of others but by the unchanging and eternal truth of who I am in Christ. As Isaiah 62:3 reminds us, I am a crown of splendor in the Lord's hand—a royal diadem in the hand of my God. This affirmation empowers me to rise above the noise, reject negativity, and embrace the beauty of my God-given identity. By recognizing my intrinsic value, I find strength and confidence to walk boldly in my purpose, knowing that I am equipped and cherished just as I am. Today, I affirm that I am enough, and I will continue to thrive in the assurance that God sees me as His precious creation.

MARCH 20

DAY 80

I WALK IN BOLDNESS AND POWER

Affirmation: I step forward in confidence, knowing I am powerful and strong.

Scripture: "The wicked flee though no one pursues, but the righteous are as bold as a lion." – Proverbs 28:1 (NIV)

Encouragement: I am called to live boldly and without fear, for I am empowered by a strength that comes from within. Each step I take is a declaration of my confidence, a testament to the power that resides in my spirit. I recognize that my presence carries an undeniable force, shining brightly in the midst of darkness. As I navigate through life, I choose to embrace my journey with unwavering courage. Fear may attempt to whisper doubts, but I refuse to let those voices overshadow the truth of my identity. I am not just a bystander; I am an active participant in my own life, equipped to face challenges and seize opportunities with resilience.

In embracing this truth, I realize that the boldness I possess is a reflection of my faith and conviction. Just as Proverbs 28:1 reminds us, while the wicked may flee in fear, I stand firm like a lion, unshaken and resolute. This strength is a gift that empowers me to overcome obstacles and inspire others along the way. I walk forward, knowing that I am not alone, but supported by divine purpose and guidance. Each day presents a new opportunity to affirm my power, share my light, and live out the courage that defines my journey. As I walk in this boldness, I not only uplift myself but also encourage those around me to embrace their own strength and walk in their truth.

MARCH 21

DAY 81

I SPEAK MY TRUTH WITH COURAGE

Affirmation: My voice matters, and I will use it to uplift, inspire, and empower.

Scripture: "She is clothed with strength and dignity; she can laugh at the days to come." – Proverbs 31:25 (NIV)

Encouragement: My story is indeed a powerful testament to resilience, and my voice is meant to resonate in the hearts of those around me. In a world that often seeks to muffle authentic expression, I refuse to silence myself merely to appease others. Instead, I choose to share my truth with love and unwavering confidence, embracing the unique journey that has shaped me. Each word I speak holds the potential to uplift, inspire, and empower those who may feel silenced or overlooked. I recognize that my experiences have the capacity to serve as a beacon of hope and healing for others, illuminating the path for those navigating their own struggles.

As I rise in courage to share my truths, I embody the strength and dignity spoken of in Proverbs 31:25. My voice matters— it carries not only my story but also the collective strength of countless others who have felt hesitant to speak up. With each act of courage, I help to cultivate an environment where honesty is celebrated, and vulnerability is embraced. Today, I stand firm in the knowledge that I am equipped with the strength to face whatever tomorrow holds, eager to share my journey with authenticity and purpose. My voice has power, and I will use it to create a ripple effect of encouragement and positivity in the world.

MARCH 22

DAY 82

I CELEBRATE EVERY PART OF MYSELF

Affirmation: I love and accept myself fully, embracing every part of my journey.

Scripture: "I will give thanks to you, Lord, with all my heart; I will tell of all your wonderful deeds." – Psalm 9:1 (NIV)

Encouragement: Every part of me is worthy of love, and I wholeheartedly celebrate the journey that has shaped me into who I am today. It's essential to recognize that our experiences, both positive and negative, contribute to our unique story. Instead of dwelling on imperfections or past struggles, I consciously choose to embrace my growth and resilience, acknowledging how they have fortified my character. Each challenge I've encountered has been a stepping stone that has led me to greater self-awareness, reminding me that every chapter of my life is significant and contributes to my overall narrative.

As I reflect on my journey with gratitude and acceptance, I become more attuned to the beauty of who I am today. The affirmation of self-love invites me to celebrate not just the milestones but also the quieter moments of personal triumphs and breakthroughs. I am reminded that my worth is inherent, shaped by my experiences and the lessons learned along the way. With each new day, I commit to nurturing a spirit of appreciation for everything that constitutes my being, acknowledging that I am a work in progress and that my story is unfolding beautifully with every heartbeat.

MARCH 23

DAY 83

I SHINE WITHOUT APOLOGY

Affirmation: I allow my light to shine unapologetically, inspiring those around me.

Scripture: "I keep my eyes always on the Lord. With him at my right hand, I will not be shaken." – Psalm 16:8 (NIV)

Encouragement: I was not created to blend in or hide my brilliance; rather, I was designed to stand out and illuminate the world around me. Today, I choose to shine brightly, unapologetically embracing my unique gifts and talents. By stepping into the fullness of my purpose, I radiate confidence that can inspire and uplift others. When I allow my light to shine, I create a ripple effect that encourages those around me to discover and express their own inner brilliance, fostering a community of empowerment and positivity.

As I keep my focus on the Lord, I am reminded that I am never alone in this journey. His presence at my side ensures that I will not be shaken by doubts or fears that might try to diminish my shine. Instead, I find strength in His unwavering support to live authentically and boldly. Each moment I choose to shine not only enriches my life but also serves as a beacon of hope and encouragement for others to follow. Together, we can create a world illuminated by our collective light, empowering each individual to shine freely and fearlessly.

MARCH 24

DAY 84

I AM WALKING IN MY PURPOSE

Affirmation: I boldly step into my purpose, trusting that I am exactly where I need to be.

Scripture: " The sun will no more be your light by day, nor will the brightness of the moon shine on you, for the Lord will be your everlasting light, and your God will be your glory." – Isaiah 60:19 (NIV)

Encouragement: I was created with intention and purpose, designed to shine brightly in the world. Every step I take is not just a movement but a deliberate action guiding me closer to my divine calling. It is important for me to remember that I am not alone on this journey; the Lord walks beside me, illuminating my path even when the way seems uncertain. I refuse to play small or allow fear to dictate my choices. Instead, I embrace my courage and strength, stepping forward with boldness. I trust that I am precisely where I need to be at this moment, fulfilling the unique purpose that God has intricately woven into the fabric of my life.

As I navigate each day, I hold tightly to the promise found in Isaiah 60:19, which assures me that the Lord will be my everlasting light. Just as the sun brightens the day and the moon shines at night, God's presence in my life brings clarity and direction. I am encouraged to radiate His glory through my actions, knowing that my life is a testament to His love and purpose. Each moment of courage I summon is a celebration of the divine plan unfolding within me, and I am committed to moving forward with faith and assurance. With each bold stride, I reaffirm my commitment to embrace the journey, confident that I am walking in alignment with God's will for my life.

Week 13

The Power Of Gratitude

MARCH 25

DAY 85

I AM GRATEFUL FOR MY JOURNEY

Affirmation: I embrace gratitude for every experience, knowing it shapes my growth.

Scripture: " Have mercy on me, Lord, for I call to you all day long." – Psalm 86:3 (NIV)

Encouragement: Every step of my journey, including the challenges and obstacles I have faced, has played a pivotal role in shaping the person I am today. I consciously choose to embrace gratitude over complaints, understanding that each experience, whether joyous or difficult, serves as a valuable lesson and a hidden blessing. By acknowledging this truth, I shift my focus from what I lack to the richness of my experiences, cultivating a deeper appreciation for life's varied moments. Today, I open my heart to the transformative power of gratitude, allowing it to illuminate the path before me and to reshape my perspective in profound ways.

In moments of trials and tribulations, it's essential to remind ourselves that our struggles can lead to personal growth and resilience. Recognizing that God walks with me through every secret tear and joyful smile, I find strength in the belief that each experience is part of a greater plan. As I reflect on Psalm 86:3, I am reminded to call upon His mercy and guidance, trusting that I am supported in my journey. Today, I choose to view my life through the lens of gratitude, allowing it to fill my heart with peace and to inspire me to recognize the beauty in every chapter of my story.

MARCH 26

DAY 86

I FIND JOY IN THE SMALL THINGS

Affirmation: I am mindful of and grateful for the little blessings in my life.

Scripture: "Give, and it will be given to you. A good measure, pressed down, shaken together and running over, will be poured into your lap. For with the measure you use, it will be measured to you." – Luke 6:38 (NIV)

Encouragement: Life's beauty often resides in the small, everyday moments that we tend to overlook amid our busy routines. A kind word from a friend, the genuine smile of a stranger, or the warm embrace of sunlight breaking through the clouds—these seemingly insignificant blessings hold the power to transform our day and uplift our spirits. Recognizing these little treasures fosters a deeper appreciation for life itself and reminds us that joy is not always found in grand events but often in the simplicity of our surroundings. Today, as I take a intentional pause from my hectic schedule, I choose to be fully present and attentive to the delicate wonders that life offers.

Cultivating a grateful heart allows us to truly embrace the richness of these small moments. When we intentionally express gratitude for the little things, we invite abundance into our lives, as echoed in Luke 6:38. The scripture beautifully illustrates this principle: when we give our attention to the small blessings, we open ourselves to experiencing even greater joy and fulfillment. As I acknowledge the gifts surrounding me—be it the gentle rustle of leaves, laughter shared over a meal, or the comforting presence of loved ones—I commit to nurturing an attitude of gratitude. In doing so, I not only elevate my own spirit but also create a ripple effect of positivity in the lives of others. Let's cherish these little blessings together, allowing them to inspire our hearts and minds to flourish.

MARCH 27

DAY 87

I CULTIVATE AN ATTITUDE OF GRATITUDE

Affirmation: I choose to focus on gratitude in all situations.

Scripture: "Let the peace of Christ rule in your hearts, since as members of one body you were called to peace. And be thankful." – Colossians 3:15

Encouragement: Gratitude is not merely a feeling; it is a powerful choice that has the ability to transform our mindset and cultivate peace in our lives. By deliberately choosing to focus on gratitude in every situation, we create a shift in our perspective that enables us to see the blessings around us, even amidst uncertainty. When challenges arise, it can be easy to dwell on what is lacking or what is difficult. However, when I consciously redirect my thoughts toward acknowledging the good, I open my heart to an abundance of joy. Each moment of thankfulness becomes an invitation for peace to dwell in my heart, reinforcing the idea that we are interconnected as members of one body, called to uplift one another through gratitude.

As I embrace this practice of gratitude, I recognize that it is not always easy, but it is profoundly rewarding. Focusing on what I am thankful for illuminates the path forward, guiding me through trials with a sense of purpose and resilience. The peace of Christ becomes my anchor, allowing me to navigate life's uncertainties with grace. I am reminded that, regardless of external circumstances, my heart can remain a sanctuary of peace and thankfulness, nourishing my spirit and inspiring those around me to do the same. In recognizing the blessings that surround me, I cultivate an inner environment ripe for joy and harmony, reflecting the profound truth of Colossians 3:15.

MARCH 28

DAY 88

I AM THANKFUL FOR MY STRENGTH

Affirmation: I honor the strength that has carried me through tough times.

Scripture: " Therefore he is able to save completely[a] those who come to God through him, because he always lives to intercede for them." – Hebrews 7:25 (NIV)

Encouragement: Every challenge I've faced has contributed to the tapestry of strength that defines who I am today. Each obstacle has forged resilience within me, shaping my character and deepening my courage. I reflect on the moments when I felt overwhelmed, yet somehow managed to rise above, and I recognize that it was not solely my own power but the grace of God working through me. Today, I consciously acknowledge my own strength, giving thanks for the perseverance that has seen me through dark times, allowing me to emerge even more capable and determined.

As I consider the promise found in Hebrews 7:25, I am reminded that I am not alone in this journey. The assurance that Jesus lives to intercede on our behalf brings me comfort and hope. Knowing that He actively supports me reinforces my gratitude for the strength that has carried me through. Therefore, I celebrate not just the victories but the lessons learned along the way. Today, I thank God for His unwavering presence in my life, guiding me through trials and helping me to nurture the strength that lies within me, enabling me to face whatever comes next with courage and grace.

MARCH 29

DAY 89

I SEE BLESSINGS ALL AROUND ME

Affirmation: I am open to recognizing the countless blessings in my life.

Scripture: "Bless the Lord, O my soul, and forget not all his benefits." – Psalm 103:2 (ESV)

Encouragement: Sometimes, blessings are hidden in unexpected places, often disguised in the mundane or the routine of our daily lives. Each moment offers us an opportunity to recognize the goodness that surrounds us, even in the simplest acts of kindness or moments of joy. Today, I choose to open my eyes and my heart to fully embrace these gifts. It's easy to overlook the small blessings that bring light to our days, but when we consciously decide to see them, we invite a profound sense of gratitude into our lives. I will actively seek out these blessings, allowing them to fill me with joy and appreciation, reminding myself that abundance is often present, waiting to be recognized.

I refuse to take my blessings for granted; instead, I will cherish and acknowledge them with a grateful heart. Each day provides us with numerous reasons to rejoice and give thanks, from the love of family and friends to the beauty of nature around us. As I reflect on Psalm 103:2, I am reminded to bless the Lord and not forget all His benefits. In doing so, I cultivate an attitude of gratitude that transforms my perspective, helping me to see that every moment, even the challenging ones, carries within it the potential for growth and blessing. The more I focus on these gifts, the more I open myself to receiving even greater joys and blessings moving forward.

MARCH 30

DAY 90

GRATITUDE TRANSFORMS MY PERSPECTIVE

Affirmation: Gratitude shifts my mindset, helping me see life with joy and appreciation.

Scripture: " A cheerful heart is good medicine, but a crushed spirit dries up the bones.." – Proverbs 17:22 (NIV)

Encouragement: When I consciously choose to embrace gratitude, I am not just acknowledging my blessings; I am actively inviting peace into my life. This simple yet profound shift in perspective enables me to divert my attention away from what I lack and instead celebrate the abundance that surrounds me. Each moment becomes an opportunity to appreciate the beauty in the mundane and find joy in the little things. Gratitude transforms my mindset, allowing me to see the world through a lens of joy and appreciation. I realize that even in challenging times, there is always something to be thankful for, and these moments of gratitude can become my strongest anchor.

As I reflect on the wisdom of Proverbs 17:22, I understand that a cheerful heart truly acts as good medicine. Just as a healthy body thrives on nourishment, my spirit flourishes when I cultivate gratitude. It is with this cheerful disposition that I can turn trials into triumphs and obstacles into opportunities for growth. By allowing gratitude to guide my thoughts, I am illuminating my path with positivity and resilience. Each day presents a fresh canvas on which to paint my experiences, and I choose to fill it with colors of joy and appreciation. Today, let me consciously seek and celebrate the gifts around me and allow my heart to overflow with gratitude.

MARCH 31

DAY 91

I GIVE THANKS FOR THE JOURNEY AHEAD

Affirmation: I trust the path before me and am grateful for what is to come.

Scripture: "For everything God created is good, and nothing is to be rejected if it is received with thanksgiving." – 1 Timothy 4:4 (NIV)

Encouragement: The future is filled with an abundance of promise, and I consciously choose to greet it with a heart overflowing with gratitude. As I step forward on this journey, I trust that the path before me is paved with goodness, crafted by divine hands. Each twist and turn offers new opportunities for growth, learning, and joy, and I embrace them with an open heart. I recognize that every experience, whether big or small, holds a lesson that contributes to my growth and understanding. Today, I give thanks, not only for the blessings I currently possess but also for the countless gifts and opportunities that await me in the future, knowing that they are all part of God's perfect plan.

In acknowledging the promise of tomorrow, I find strength in the assurance that every good thing comes from above. The Scripture reminds me that all of God's creations are inherently good, and it is through a spirit of gratitude that I can truly appreciate the fullness of life. Each moment offers the chance to cultivate a mindset of thankfulness, allowing me to see the beauty in both my present circumstances and the journey ahead. As I look forward, I am filled with hope, knowing that every challenge I face can transform into a stepping stone toward growth. Through this lens of thanksgiving, I not only prepare myself for what is to come but also position myself to recognize and celebrate the abundance of blessings that are already on their way.

Week 14

Trusting In God's Timing

APRIL 1

DAY 92

GOD'S TIMING IS PERFECT

Affirmation: I trust that everything in my life is unfolding exactly as it should.

Scripture: " I will betroth you to me forever; I will betroth you in righteousness and justice,

in love and compassion." – Hosea 2:19 (NIV)

Encouragement: God's plan is always perfect, even when I do not fully understand it. Life often presents us with challenges that can feel overwhelming, and uncertainty can creep in, leading us to question the direction we're headed. However, in these moments of doubt, we must remind ourselves of the truth found in Hosea 2:19—that we are betrothed to God in righteousness and compassion. This intimate promise assures us that God's love and justice are woven into the very fabric of our lives. As we navigate through our daily experiences, let us release our worries, knowing that God's timing is impeccable and that He has a divine purpose for every season we encounter.

Today, I will consciously choose to rest in faith, trusting that everything is unfolding as it should. I will embrace the journey and acknowledge that each step I take is part of a greater plan. Instead of rushing ahead or feeling anxious about the future, I will lean into the assurance that what is meant for me will come at precisely the right moment. This trust allows me to cultivate a spirit of patience and gratitude, celebrating the unfolding of God's perfect will in my life. In this space of surrender, I invite peace to fill my heart, knowing that I am held in God's loving embrace throughout my journey.

APRIL 2

DAY 93

I LET GO AND LET GOD

Affirmation: I surrender my plans to God and trust in His greater purpose.

Scripture: "Commit to the Lord whatever you do, and he will establish your plans." – Proverbs 16:3 (NIV)

Encouragement: At times, the excitement of our hopes and desires can create an overwhelming urge to rush towards our goals. We may find ourselves fixated on immediate outcomes, anxious for everything to fall into place according to our timeline. However, it's essential to pause and remind ourselves that God's plan is not only intricately designed but also perfectly timed. By surrendering our ambitions and allowing Him to guide our steps, we open ourselves up to the extraordinary possibilities that await us. Trusting in God's greater purpose helps alleviate our worries and invites peace into our hearts.

In moments of doubt or impatience, it is vital to return to the promise found in Proverbs 16:3. This scripture encourages us to commit our endeavors to the Lord, assuring us that He will establish our plans. We may not always see the full picture or understand the delays we face, but we can rest in the knowledge that God is at work behind the scenes, orchestrating every detail for our ultimate good. When we let go of our need for control and embrace the journey with faith, we can expect remarkable growth and transformation in our lives. Trusting God isn't just a decision; it's a powerful testament to the hope we hold in Him, allowing us to confidently move forward on the path He has set before us.

APRIL 3

DAY 94

I WAIT WITH PATIENCE AND FAITH

Affirmation: I remain patient and faithful, trusting that God's promises will be fulfilled.

Scripture: "But if we hope for what we do not yet have, we wait for it patiently." – Romans 8:25 (NIV)

Encouragement: Waiting can often feel like a difficult and burdensome task, yet it is a crucial part of our journey. During this season of anticipation, I consciously choose to anchor myself in steadfast faith, understanding that each moment of waiting serves a purpose in God's grand plan. I recognize that, while it is easy to become impatient, I can find solace in the assurance that God is at work behind the scenes, crafting something beautiful that aligns with His perfect will for my life. Each day spent in expectation is a day closer to the fulfillment of His promises, and this gives me hope and encourages my spirit.

As I lean into this waiting period, I remind myself of the importance of patience and the role it plays in my spiritual growth. Waiting is not merely a passive state; it requires active trust and a firm belief in the goodness of God's timing. Romans 8:25 reminds us to hope and wait patiently for what we do not yet see, reinforcing the idea that our faith is strengthened in the process of waiting. Therefore, I choose to fill this time with prayer, gratitude, and an open heart, confident that God's plan for my life is unfolding perfectly. In my waiting, I will remain alert to the blessings already surrounding me and to the lessons God is teaching me.

APRIL 4

DAY 95

I AM EXACTLY WHERE I NEED TO BE

Affirmation: I trust that my current season is a part of God's divine plan.

Scripture: "The Lord makes firm the steps of the one who delights in him." – Psalm 37:23 (NIV)

Encouragement: Even when circumstances feel uncertain or confusing, I hold on to the unwavering belief that I am exactly where I need to be at this moment. The journey I am on, with all its twists and turns, is a vital component of God's divine plan for my life. Each day, I remind myself that every experience—both joyful and challenging—contributes to my growth and prepares me for the blessings that await on the horizon. By cultivating a mindset of gratitude, I become more attuned to the lessons inherent in my current season, allowing me to see beyond the surface and recognize the purpose in each moment.

As I navigate this season, I choose to approach it with a heart full of faith, trusting that God is guiding my steps. Psalm 37:23 reassures me that as I delight in Him, He establishes my path and makes my steps firm. This promise empowers me to embrace the present with confidence, knowing that my trust in Him is not misplaced. By focusing on the nature of God's faithfulness and the assurance that He is working all things together for my good, I can engage fully in the experiences of today, anticipating the beauty and growth that will emerge from this season of my life.

APRIL 5

DAY 96

I TRUST THAT DELAYS ARE NOT DENIALS

Affirmation: I believe that delays are divine redirections leading me to something greater.

Scripture: "For the vision is yet for an appointed time; though it linger, wait for it; it will certainly come and will not delay." – Habakkuk 2:3 (NIV)

Encouragement: When things don't unfold as swiftly as I would like, I take a step back and remind myself that God is never late; His timing is always impeccable. These moments of waiting can feel heavy and frustrating, but they are truly divine redirections designed to guide me toward something greater than I could ever envision on my own. Delays are not personal setbacks or signs of unworthiness; instead, they provide valuable opportunities for growth, preparation, and alignment with His perfect plan. Just as a seed must be nurtured and cared for before it can blossom, so too must my dreams and aspirations go through a season of development before the fullness of their potential is revealed.

As I embrace this perspective, I find comfort in the assurance of Scripture: "For the vision is yet for an appointed time; though it linger, wait for it; it will certainly come and will not delay" (Habakkuk 2:3, NIV). This reminder instills hope in my heart, encouraging me to trust in the timing of God rather than my own. I can draw strength from the belief that every delay is infused with purpose, crafting the right circumstances to lead me to my destiny. So, in the moments of waiting, I choose to lean into faith, cherishing the growth I experience and looking forward to the beautiful outcomes that await me on the other side of patience.

APRIL 6

DAY 97

GOD'S PLANS FOR ME ARE GOOD

Affirmation: I trust that God's plans for me are filled with hope and a future.

Scripture: "For he chose us in him before the creation of the world to be holy and blameless in his sight." – Ephesians 1:4 (NIV)

Encouragement: God has already crafted a beautiful and fulfilling future for me, one that is filled with purpose and promise. Even when the path ahead seems unclear or when obstacles arise, I hold firm to the belief in His divine goodness. I understand that my perspective is limited, but I choose to trust in His omniscience and unwavering love. It is in moments of uncertainty that faith truly shines, allowing me to release my fears and anxieties. With each step I take, I do so with confidence, knowing that God is intimately involved in my journey, guiding me toward His perfect will.

As I reflect on the assurance found in Ephesians 1:4, I am reminded that I was chosen long before I even existed—crafted with intention to be holy and blameless in His sight. This deepens my sense of purpose and fills me with hope for the future He has designed for me. In embracing this truth, I can find the strength to overcome doubt and embrace the adventure ahead. With every heartbeat, I am encouraged to walk boldly in faith, assured that my Creator is at work, weaving all things together for my good and His glory.

APRIL 7

DAY 98

I WALK IN FAITH, NOT FEAR

Affirmation: I choose faith over fear, trusting that God's timing is always best.

Scripture: "We walk by faith, not by sight." – 2 Corinthians 5:7 (NIV)

Encouragement: Fear has a subtle way of creeping into our minds, attempting to disrupt the peace that faith provides. It whispers lies that lead us to doubt our circumstances and question God's plans for our lives. However, it's essential to remember that fear is not our ally; it is merely an illusion that can cloud our judgment. Instead of succumbing to these anxieties, I can hold steadfast to the truth of my faith, which reassures me that God is sovereign and has a perfect plan for every situation I encounter. By choosing to embrace faith over fear, I align my thoughts and actions with the belief that God's timing is perfect and His guidance is unfailing.

As I walk through life, I am reminded through Scripture that "We walk by faith, not by sight," which invites me to take a step forward even when the path before me is unclear. Each day presents new challenges, but I refuse to let uncertainty dictate my decisions. Instead, I will confidently step forward, armed with the assurance that God is actively working in my life. Trusting in Him allows me to look beyond my immediate circumstances and embrace the promise of His presence and guidance. With each step I take in faith, I affirm my choice to walk unburdened by fear, knowing that my trust in God's perfect timing illuminates the way ahead.

Week 15

Finding Beauty In The Process

APRIL 8

DAY 99

I EMBRACE MY JOURNEY

Affirmation: Every step of my journey holds purpose and beauty.

Scripture: "Being confident of this, that he who began a good work in you will carry it on to completion until the day of Christ Jesus." – Philippians 1:6 (NIV)

Encouragement: Life is undeniably a process, filled with a myriad of experiences that contribute to our growth and transformation. Each moment, whether it presents itself as a high or a low, plays a crucial role in shaping our character and spirit. Today, I choose to embrace the beauty embedded within every step of my journey, recognizing that each challenge and triumph serves a purpose. I hold tightly to the promise that God is actively involved in my life, continually refining me and preparing me for His greater purpose. It brings me comfort and strength to know that I am not alone; I am guided by divine hands that ensure my progress.

As I reflect on Philippians 1:6, I am reassured of the commitment God has towards me. The work He has begun in me is not merely incidental; it is a continuation of His divine plan that will be brought to fruition. This unwavering confidence fuels my spirit and encourages me to persevere through trials. I remind myself that every step I take is part of a masterpiece in progress, crafted by a loving God who is devoted to my development. In this journey, I find hope and inspiration, knowing that His presence is with me, nurturing my growth until it blooms into the fullness of His design.

APRIL 9

DAY 100

I FIND JOY IN THE SMALL WINS

Affirmation: I celebrate every step forward, no matter how small.

Scripture: "Do not despise these small beginnings, for the Lord rejoices to see the work begin." – Zechariah 4:10 (NLT)

Encouragement: Progress is still progress, no matter how small. It is essential to recognize that every step we take, no matter how minor it may seem, contributes to our overall journey and growth. Rather than allowing ourselves to become overwhelmed by the distance we still need to cover, we can enrich our lives by acknowledging and celebrating each victory along the way. Embracing these small wins instills a sense of motivation and hope, reminding us that every effort counts. Each little milestone serves as a building block, gradually leading us to greater transformation and fulfillment.

Moreover, small steps can be significant in the grand scheme of life, influencing our perspectives and encouraging us to maintain a positive mindset. When we celebrate our progress, we cultivate a heart filled with gratitude and joy, which further fuels our desire to move forward. In doing so, we align ourselves with the wisdom found in Zechariah 4:10, which encourages us not to despise small beginnings. By honoring these initial steps, we invite divine joy into our lives, acknowledging that each small action is a vital part of a greater journey orchestrated by the Lord. Thus, let's commit to recognizing the beauty in our small victories, cherishing the process of growth, and trusting that each step brings us closer to our goals.

APRIL 10

DAY 101

I TRUST THE PROCESS

Affirmation: I trust that God is guiding me through every step of my journey.

Scripture: "Trust in the Lord with all your heart and lean not on your own understanding; in all your ways submit to him, and he will make your paths straight." – Proverbs 3:5-6 (NIV)

Encouragement: The path may not always be clear, but I trust that God is leading me in the right direction, even in the midst of uncertainty. Life's journey often presents challenges and detours that can make us question our footing. It is in these moments of doubt that we must remember to lean into our faith and the promise that God is intricately involved in our lives. By surrendering our own understanding and trusting in His divine wisdom, we allow ourselves the freedom to navigate through challenges without the heavy burden of having to control every outcome. Even when things seem chaotic around me, I choose to hold fast to the belief that He is orchestrating each step I take, guiding my feet along a path designed for my growth and purpose.

I recognize that walking in faith means embracing the journey, even when it feels uncertain or uncomfortable. As Proverbs 3:5-6 reassures us, by submitting our will to Him, we open ourselves up to the extraordinary possibilities that He has in store for us. Each twist and turn along this journey is not without intention; there are lessons to be learned and blessings to be discovered. With each step taken in trust, my perspective broadens, allowing me to witness the beauty of His plan unfold. It is through this unwavering faith that I cultivate resilience and strength, knowing that the Divine is continually at work to make my paths straight, illuminating the way toward a brighter tomorrow filled with hope and purpose.

APRIL 11

DAY 102

I AM A WORK IN PROGRESS

Affirmation: I give myself grace as I grow and evolve.

Scripture: "And we all, who with unveiled faces contemplate the Lord's glory, are being transformed into his image with ever-increasing glory, which comes from the Lord, who is the Spirit." – 2 Corinthians 3:18 (NIV)

Encouragement: Growth is a beautiful journey that unfolds at its own pace. It's essential to remember that every step you take, no matter how small, is part of a larger tapestry of transformation woven by God's hand. By allowing yourself the grace to grow and evolve, you acknowledge the incredible work that the Holy Spirit is doing within you. Just as the butterfly does not emerge from its chrysalis overnight, your own metamorphosis requires patience and acceptance of where you are right now. Embracing the process means celebrating your progress, learning from challenges, and understanding that each experience shapes you into a more refined reflection of His glory.

As you continue on this journey of growth, remind yourself of the promise found in 2 Corinthians 3:18. You are being transformed into the image of the Lord, with every moment contributing to your increasing glory. This process is ongoing; there is no need to rush or force yourself into a mold of perfection that does not align with God's design for you. Instead, immerse yourself in the knowledge that you are exactly where you need to be in this moment. With each passing day, trust that you are evolving into the person God intended you to be, filled with purpose and strength. Allow each experience to deepen your understanding and appreciation for the unique path that you are on.

APRIL 12

DAY 103

I SEE BEAUTY IN THE UNEXPECTED

Affirmation: I embrace the unexpected and trust that it brings new blessings.

Scripture: "And your fame spread among the nations on account of your beauty, because the splendor I had given you made your beauty perfect, declares the Sovereign Lord."– Ezekiel 16:14 (NIV)

Encouragement: Life doesn't always follow a predictable path, and it is often in these moments of deviation from our plans that the most beautiful experiences emerge. Embracing the unexpected allows us to remain open to new opportunities and blessings that we might not have considered otherwise. Every twist and turn can reveal a facet of God's grace that transforms our challenges into remarkable testimonies of His faithfulness. By shifting our perspective, we can see that these unexpected moments are not just interruptions but divine appointments, meant to enrich our lives and deepen our appreciation for the journey.

As we navigate through life's uncertainties, it is essential to remind ourselves that God is continually at work behind the scenes, orchestrating events for our ultimate good. He has a vision for our lives that often surpasses our own understanding, and in this divine process, we can find assurance and hope. Just as the splendor that God imparts upon us brings forth beauty, so too do our unanticipated experiences shape us into the people He desires us to be. In trusting His plan, we can cultivate a heart that not only anticipates blessings in every situation but also radiates beauty and joy, allowing us to flourish amid life's unpredictable nature.

APRIL 13

DAY 104

I LET GO OF THE NEED FOR PERFECTION

Affirmation: I release unrealistic expectations and allow myself to grow with grace.

Scripture: " You are my refuge and my shield; I have put my hope in your word." – Psalm 119:114 (NIV)

Encouragement: Perfection is an illusion that often keeps us trapped in a cycle of self-doubt and unrealistic expectations. Today, I choose to release that burden and embrace my authentic self, understanding that making mistakes is a vital part of my growth journey. Each misstep provides the opportunity to learn, adapt, and emerge stronger. Instead of striving for an unattainable ideal, I will celebrate the progress I make, knowing that God's grace surrounds me like a comforting embrace. I remind myself that being human means I will encounter challenges, and it is during these moments of struggle that I can truly experience the depth of His love and support.

As I navigate through life's uncertainties, I hold onto the promise found in Psalm 119:114, recognizing that God is both my refuge and my shield. In trusting His word, I find reassurance and strength. I may stumble, but I will not fall into despair; I will walk confidently in the knowledge that God's grace is enough to cover my imperfections. With every step I take, I am committed to allowing myself to grow with grace, cherishing the lessons learned, and responding to life's challenges with a spirit of resilience. In this journey of faith, I am learning to embrace who I am while resting in the assurance that I am always held in God's unwavering love.

APRIL 14

DAY 105

I AM BECOMING WHO I AM MEANT TO BE

Affirmation: I embrace every part of my transformation with gratitude and confidence.

Scripture: ""Then the Lord God formed a man from the dust of the ground and breathed into his nostrils the breath of life, and the man became a living being." – Genesis 2:7 (NIV)

Encouragement: I am on a profound journey of growth, healing, and transformation, a pilgrimage that allows me to continuously evolve into the person I am meant to be. Each day presents new opportunities for self-discovery, and I acknowledge that I am neither defined by my past nor fully realized in my future. I celebrate the progress I've made, honoring the lessons learned from challenges and setbacks. Gratitude fills my heart as I reflect on the significance of each step along this winding path. Embracing the beauty of my transformation encourages me to remain open and receptive to the changes that mold me. I trust that each experience, each moment of personal development is a vital part of God's divine plan in my life.

As I journey onward, I find strength in the knowledge that I am a masterpiece in progress, created by God with purpose and intention. Just as He breathed life into man, He breathes inspiration and hope into my spirit each day, allowing me to grow and flourish in His light. I hold onto my affirmation with confidence, knowing that my transformation is a continuous process that unfolds in perfect timing. With every moment of reflection and self-acceptance, I become more aligned with the vision God has for me. Today, I not only embrace the steps of my journey but also cherish the wisdom and strength they impart, trusting wholeheartedly that I am becoming who I am meant to be.

Week 16

Healing From Within

APRIL 15

DAY 106

I ALLOW MYSELF TO HEAL

Affirmation: I give myself permission to heal emotionally, spiritually, and physically.

Scripture: "He heals the brokenhearted and binds up their wounds." – Psalm 147:3 (NIV)

Encouragement: Healing is a journey, not a destination. It is a process that takes time, and it is essential to recognize that each step forward, no matter how small, is significant. Today, I choose to grant myself the grace and patience I need as I work through my past pain. This journey involves embracing my emotions, acknowledging my struggles, and understanding that healing is not linear. God is actively at work within me, gently guiding me toward restoration and wholeness in my heart, mind, and body. As I open myself up to this healing, I also open the door for God's love and compassion to wash over me, reminding me that I am never alone in my struggles.

Each day I release the layers of hurt, I am reminded of the promise found in Psalm 147:3 that reassures us of God's commitment to heal the brokenhearted and bind up their wounds. This scripture serves as a powerful reminder that I am in the hands of a loving Creator who desires my wholeness. As I navigate this process, I can trust that God is carefully tending to my wounds, working to heal me from the inside out. Just as a beautiful flower takes time to bloom, so too does my emotional and spiritual healing. I will celebrate the progress I make and hold onto the hope that comes from trusting in God's restorative power in my life.

APRIL 16

DAY 107

I RELEASE WHAT NO LONGER SERVES ME

Affirmation: I let go of past hurts, fears, and doubts to make room for peace and joy.

Scripture: "Forget the former things; do not dwell on the past. See, I am doing a new thing!" – Isaiah 43:18-19 (NIV)

Encouragement: Holding on to past pain and negative experiences can create a heavy burden that stifles our ability to move forward and embrace the fullness of life. Each moment spent dwelling on old wounds, fears, and doubts keeps us anchored in a place that no longer serves our highest good. Today, I invite myself to make a conscious and empowering choice to release these burdens. This act of letting go is not a sign of weakness; rather, it is a demonstration of strength and resilience. By consciously releasing what no longer aligns with my emotional and spiritual growth, I open my heart to the endless possibilities that await me.

As I let go, I begin to embrace the new opportunities that God is placing in my path. This isn't merely about creating space; it's about nurturing a fertile ground for growth, peace, and joy to flourish. I hold firm to the promise found in Isaiah 43:18-19, which reminds me that God is always doing a new thing in my life. I trust in His guidance, knowing that the journey of renewal is not only possible but inevitable when I relinquish the past. Today is a day for fresh starts; it's a reminder that each moment is filled with potential and that joy is waiting for me just around the corner.

APRIL 17

DAY 108

I NOURISH MY MIND, BODY, AND SOUL

Affirmation: I care for myself holistically, knowing that true healing starts from within.

Scripture: "Dear friend, I pray that you may enjoy good health and that all may go well with you, even as your soul is getting along well." – 3 John 1:2 (NIV)

Encouragement: Healing is a multifaceted journey that encompasses not just the physical aspect, but also the emotional and spiritual dimensions of our being. It's essential to recognize that when we nurture ourselves, we are engaging in a holistic practice that fosters true well-being. Today, I consciously choose to fill my body with nutritious food that energizes and revitalizes me. I will cultivate positive thoughts in my mind, rejecting negativity that can cloud my perspective. By surrounding myself with uplifting influences, I open the door for positivity to flow into my life. In doing so, I'm building a solid foundation for my emotional health, which supports my overall journey toward healing.

Moreover, as I nourish my soul with the comforting and affirming truths found in God's Word, I am reminded that my spiritual health is intricately linked to my overall well-being. The scripture from 3 John 1:2 emphasizes a deep connection between our physical state and the wellness of our soul, showcasing the importance of caring for each part of our being. Each intentional choice I make today leads me one step closer to achieving holistic wholeness. Embracing this self-care approach is an act of love and gratitude towards myself, recognizing that I am worthy of health in every aspect of my life. As I walk this path, I trust that my efforts will manifest in abundant well-being, resonating not just within myself, but also radiating out to those around me.

APRIL 18

DAY 109

I TRUST THE HEALING PROCESS

Affirmation: I am patient with my healing and trust that God is working in my life.

Scripture: "The Lord will sustain him on his sickbed and restore him from his bed of illness." – Psalm 41:3 (NIV)

Encouragement: Healing is a journey that unfolds at its own pace; it requires patience and understanding. It's essential to recognize that while some days may feel heavy and burdensome, others can bring glimmers of hope and inspiration. I have learned to embrace each moment—whether joyous or challenging—seeing them as valuable parts of my healing process. Every step, no matter how small, contributes to my overall restoration. With each passing day, I am reminded that my faith is not in the absence of difficulty, but in the assurance that God is with me, guiding and supporting me through every physical and emotional trial.

I hold fast to the promise that God sustains and restores me, as beautifully illustrated in Psalm 41:3. This verse reassures me that I am never alone on my sickbed; instead, I am surrounded by divine grace and love. I choose to lean into this support, acknowledging that my healing is in progress, and I willingly accept the time it may take. In doing so, I cultivate patience and resilience, knowing that my trust in God's plan is pivotal. As I continue this journey, I remain confident that God is actively working in my life, preparing me for a stronger, healthier future.

APRIL 19

DAY 110

I CHOOSE PEACE OVER WORRY

Affirmation: I release anxiety and embrace the peace that surpasses all understanding.

Scripture: "Do not be anxious about anything, but in every situation, by prayer and petition, with thanksgiving, present your requests to God. And the peace of God, which transcends all understanding, will guard your hearts and your minds in Christ Jesus." – Philippians 4:6-7 (NIV)

Encouragement: Worry does not serve me, and I recognize that it often distracts me from the grace and love present in my life. In choosing peace, I am redirecting my focus away from anxiety and placing my trust in the divine guidance that God offers. Each time I feel the flutter of worry rise within me, I am reminded that my faith can lift me above those troubled feelings. In embracing peace, I am opening myself to the transformative power of God's presence, inviting His assurance to envelop every aspect of my life. Today, I intentionally choose to replace my worries with unwavering faith and surrender my fears to the comforting embrace of peace.

As I journey through this day, I lean into the promise found in Philippians 4:6-7, remembering that I am called to bring all my concerns to God through prayer and gratitude. I hold on to the assurance that God hears my petitions and responds with a peace that transcends human understanding. This divine peace guards my heart and mind, shielding me from the chaos of worry that seeks to take root. By cultivating a heart of thanksgiving, I open myself to receive this precious gift, anchoring my spirit in a place of calm and reassurance. I trust wholeheartedly that God is taking care of me and my healing, and in this trust, I find the courage to face each moment with grace and tranquility.

APRIL 20

DAY 111

I AM STRONGER THAN MY STRUGGLES

Affirmation: My challenges do not define me—I am defined by my resilience and faith.

Scripture: "But now he has reconciled you by Christ's physical body through death to present you holy in his sight, without blemish and free from accusation." – Colossians 1:22 (NIV)

Encouragement: My struggles are not merely setbacks—they are transformative experiences that serve as setups for strength and personal growth. Each challenge I confront is an opportunity to cultivate resilience and deepen my faith. In the face of adversity, I discover hidden reservoirs of strength within myself that I never knew existed, illuminating the path toward my personal evolution. With every obstacle, I am reminded that I am not alone; God walks beside me, guiding me through the darkness and into the light. I am constantly evolving, and each trial only amplifies my connection to my true self.

I will continue to forge ahead, buoyed by the knowledge that God has equipped me with everything I need to navigate life's complexities. His reconciliation through Christ as stated in Colossians 1:22 reminds me that I have been made whole and blameless in His sight, free from any accusations that may weigh me down. As I embrace my journey, I hold onto my faith and resilience as my defining attributes, understanding that these struggles are integral to my story. With each step forward, I affirm that I am stronger than my struggles, and I will emerge from each trial more empowered and equipped to fulfill my purpose.

APRIL 21

DAY 112

MY HEALING IS A TESTIMONY

Affirmation: My healing journey is a powerful testimony of God's grace and faithfulness.

Scripture: "Come and hear, all you who fear God; let me tell you what he has done for me." – Psalm 66:16 (NIV)

Encouragement: My journey of healing is not just for me; it has a far-reaching impact, serving as a testimony that can inspire and uplift those around me. Every challenge I have faced and overcome reflects the grace and faithfulness of God in my life. I choose to embrace this process wholeheartedly, recognizing that God can turn my struggles into powerful stories of hope and resilience. As I share my experiences, I trust that they will resonate with others who may be walking a similar path, providing them with a glimmer of hope when they need it most. Through my journey, I aim to demonstrate that healing is not just a destination but a transformative process that strengthens my faith and my connection to God.

I am a living example of His love and restoration, and I am reminded of the words of Psalm 66:16, encouraging me to share my testimony with all who fear God. As I recount the miraculous ways He has worked in my life, I become a vessel of encouragement for others. My story is a beacon of light that can lead others to seek and experience God's goodness for themselves. By openly sharing my healing journey, I allow others to see that they, too, can find strength amid their struggles. In my vulnerability lies the power to inspire, and I pray that through my words and experiences, others may find the courage to trust in God's promises and embrace their own healing journeys.

Week 17

Thriving Beyond Alopecia

APRIL 22

DAY 113

I AM MORE THAN MY HAIR

Affirmation: My identity is not tied to my hair; I am a complete and powerful individual.

Scripture: "Before I formed you in the womb I knew you, before you were born I set you apart." – Jeremiah 1:5 (NIV)

Encouragement: My value is not based on my appearance, but rather on the essence of who I am and the impact I have on those around me. The love I share, the kindness I extend, and the wisdom I carry are the true reflections of my identity. When I look in the mirror, I choose to see beyond the surface; I see a unique individual who has purpose and strength. Each day, I celebrate the qualities that make me, me—my resilience, my compassion, and my ability to uplift others, regardless of the challenges I face. It is this inner beauty that shines forth, illuminating the lives of those I encounter.

In embracing my uniqueness, I am empowered to thrive not only in spite of alopecia but also because of it. My journey has shaped me into a complete and powerful individual, set apart and known even before my existence. The words from Jeremiah 1:5 serve as a profound reminder that my worth is deeply rooted in something far greater than physical traits. I am wonderfully made, designed with intention and love. Each day, I reaffirm my identity, drawing strength from the knowledge that I am cherished and valued, not for how I look but for who I truly am.

APRIL 23

DAY 114

I WALK IN CONFIDENCE

Affirmation: I carry myself with confidence and grace, knowing I am beautifully made.

Scripture: "As for God, his way is perfect: The Lord's word is flawless; he shields all who take refuge in him." – 2 Samuel 22:31 (NIV)

Encouragement: Confidence transcends mere appearances; it is deeply rooted in the appreciation and understanding of oneself. Today, I choose to embrace my unique qualities, recognizing that true beauty radiates from within. I stand tall and proud, knowing that my worth is not dictated by societal expectations or the fleeting opinions of others. Rather, I am defined by the love I carry for myself and the grace with which I navigate the world. As I celebrate my individuality, I affirm that I am bold, beautiful, and blessed, living authentically according to my own values and beliefs.

In this journey of self-discovery, let the assurance found in God's word guide me. The verse from 2 Samuel reminds me that God's ways are perfect, and in seeking refuge in Him, I find strength and protection. As I walk with confidence, I become a testament to the flawless love and work of my Creator. Today, I will not only carry myself with poise; I will also share this confident spirit with those around me, uplifting others to recognize their own worth and encouraging them to embrace their divine design. Together, we can cultivate a community rooted in acceptance and love, reflecting the beautiful affirmation that we are marvelously made.

APRIL 24

DAY 115

I DEFINE MY OWN BEAUTY

Affirmation: Beauty radiates from within me; I define what beauty means for myself.

Scripture: "Your beauty should not come from outward adornment... rather, it should be that of your inner self, the unfading beauty of a gentle and quiet spirit, which is of great worth in God's sight." – 1 Peter 3:3-4 (NIV)

Encouragement: The world may have its own definition of beauty, but I choose to create my own. In a society often obsessed with external appearances, it is essential to recognize that true beauty radiates from the heart and soul. I define what beauty means for myself, embracing the understanding that it is not about fitting into narrow standards set by others, but about celebrating the unique qualities that make me who I am. Each aspect of my character—my kindness, compassion, authenticity, and resilience—shapes the essence of my beauty. It flourishes as I love deeply and uplift those around me, illuminating the world with my inner light.

As I reflect on 1 Peter 3:3-4, I am reminded that my worth is not dictated by outward adornments but is rooted in the unfading beauty of my inner self. This gentle and quiet spirit, which holds great value in

God's sight, is a powerful testament to the beauty I possess. By nurturing my inner self, I am empowered to unleash a beauty that transcends physical appearances. I am encouraged to cultivate this inner glow daily, fostering a deep-seated confidence that no external measure can replicate. As I embrace and define my own beauty, I can inspire others to do the same, creating a ripple effect that celebrates the diversity and richness of inner beauty.

APRIL 25

DAY 116

I AM THRIVING, NOT JUST SURVIVING

Affirmation: I am not just getting by—I am thriving in every area of my life.

Scripture: "The thief comes only to steal and kill and destroy; I have come that they may have life, and have it to the full." – John 10:10 (NIV)

Encouragement: Alopecia may be a chapter in my story, but it does not define my entire book. While it has presented its challenges, I see it as just one part of a much larger narrative filled with resilience and growth. I have decided to live fully, embracing joy, success, and love in every area of my life. Each day is an opportunity to reflect on the blessings that surround me, and I consciously choose to celebrate every victory, no matter how small. I know that my worth and identity are not tied to external circumstances but are rooted in the strength and spirit within me. In doing so, I refuse to merely exist; instead, I choose to thrive and cultivate a life rich with purpose and meaning.

Furthermore, I understand that life is a precious gift, and I am determined to make the most of it. I acknowledge that I have the power to shape my experiences and how I respond to them, transforming challenges into stepping stones for personal growth. The promise of John 10:10 reassures me that I am destined for a fulfilling life—not merely in survival but in the abundant joys that God offers. I embrace not only my journey but also the lessons that come with it, knowing that thriving means flourishing in body, mind, and spirit. With this perspective, I am equipped to face any obstacle, knowing that I am capable of achieving greatness and living a life filled to the brim with love and purpose.

APRIL 26

DAY 117

I AM FEARLESS IN PURSUING MY DREAMS

Affirmation: Alopecia does not limit me; I chase my dreams with courage and determination.

Scripture: " Keep this Book of the Law always on your lips; meditate on it day and night, so that you may be careful to do everything written in it. Then you will be prosperous and successful." – Joshua 1:8 (NIV)

Encouragement: No condition, no circumstance, and no doubt can hold me back from pursuing my dreams with fervor. Each new day is an opportunity to rise above any limitations that may seek to confine me. I am capable, strong, and inherently worthy of achieving every goal I set for myself, regardless of the obstacles I might face along the way.

Alopecia is simply a chapter in my unique story; it may shape my experiences, but it does not dictate my destiny. Instead, it fuels my passion and determination to strive for greatness, reminding me that I have the power to write my own narrative filled with courage and triumph.

As I meditate on the teachings of Scripture, I find reassurance in the promise that success awaits those who commit themselves to their path. With every step I take, I draw strength from the knowledge that God is guiding me, and His words instill in me an unwavering confidence. Just as Joshua was encouraged to hold fast to the Book of the Law, I too will hold onto my vision and pursue it relentlessly. My dreams are within reach, and with each courageous step, I declare that I am fearless in the face of adversity and committed to achieving the life I envision for myself.

APRIL 27

DAY 118

I SHINE MY LIGHT FOR OTHERS

Affirmation: My journey inspires others; I am a beacon of hope and strength.

Scripture: "As for you, the anointing you received from him remains in you, and you do not need anyone to teach you. But as his anointing teaches you about all things and as that anointing is real, not counterfeit—just as it has taught you, remain in him." – 1 John 2:27 (NIV)

Encouragement: My experiences, my triumphs, and my resilience serve as encouragement for others on their own unique journeys. Every challenge I have faced has not only shaped me but also positioned me to uplift those around me. I embrace my role as a source of strength, understanding that my light shines bright even on difficult days. When I share my story, I create a connection that can foster hope in those who may feel lost or uncertain. This shared journey serves as a reminder that we are never alone, and that our struggles can lead to profound growth and inspiration for others.

As I navigate my path, I am aware that my journey can illuminate the way for someone else. Just as the anointing mentioned in 1 John 2:27 assures me of my intimate relationship with the divine, I know that the strength I possess within can radiate outward, touching lives in transformative ways. I am committed to remaining rooted in this truth, allowing my light to shine bright in all its facets. By doing so, I not only honor my own journey but also offer encouragement and hope to those who may need it most. Together, we can all draw strength from one another and forge a brighter path forward.

APRIL 28

DAY 119

I LOVE MYSELF UNCONDITIONALLY

Affirmation: I accept and love myself fully, just as I am.

Scripture: "Just as a body, though one, has many parts, but all its many parts form one body, so it is with Christ." – 1 Corinthians 12:12 (NIV)

Encouragement: Self-love is a profound journey that goes beyond the pursuit of perfection; it involves embracing my authentic self at every stage of my life. Today, I choose to honor the unique qualities and experiences that contribute to my individuality. By recognizing that I am a beautiful creation, deserving of love and acceptance, I affirm my inherent worth. Each moment spent nurturing my self-love reinforces my belief that I am not defined by my flaws but by my resilience and growth. Just as the many parts of my body work together in harmony, I too can appreciate the different aspects of who I am and how they collectively contribute to the person I am becoming.

In celebrating self-love, I am reminded that my journey is a reflection of God's handiwork, and that He has uniquely designed me for a purpose. As I move forward, I commit to acknowledging my strengths and practicing kindness toward myself, even in times of struggle. Each challenge I face becomes an opportunity for growth, allowing me to deepen my love for myself. By embracing my journey with courage and compassion, I can fully embody the wonderful promise of 1 Corinthians 12:12, recognizing that, like the body of Christ, I am part of a greater whole, beautifully crafted and infinitely valued in the eyes of the Creator. Today, I affirm my self-love not only as an integral aspect of my personal journey but as a vital part of my spiritual path as well.

Week 18

Speaking Life Over Myself

APRIL 29

DAY 120

MY WORDS HAVE POWER

Affirmation: I speak life, love, and abundance over myself daily.

Scripture: "The tongue has the power of life and death, and those who love it will eat its fruit." – Proverbs 18:21 (NIV)

Encouragement: My words shape my reality in profound ways. The power of our speech is often underestimated, yet it is in the act of speaking that we can ignite hope and positivity within ourselves. Today, I consciously choose to speak words that uplift, encourage, and affirm my worth. Each affirmation I declare sends ripples of positivity into my life, allowing me to reinforce a mindset that fosters growth and abundance. By rejecting negativity and surrounding myself with encouraging phrases, I create a nurturing environment that supports my journey and allows my spirit to flourish.

Furthermore, the wisdom in Proverbs reminds me that the tongue holds the power to shape not only my destiny but also the world around me. When I choose words filled with life and love, I am sowing seeds that will ultimately bear fruit in my relationships and goals. Embracing positivity in all that I say allows me to create a reality where I can thrive. I commit to making my words a source of strength and a reflection of the abundance I wish to cultivate in my life. By continuously affirming my intrinsic worth and the potential that lies within me, I lay the groundwork for a fulfilling and prosperous future.

APRIL 30

DAY 121

I DECLARE VICTORY OVER MY LIFE

Affirmation: I speak victory, healing, and breakthrough into my life.

Scripture: "For the Lord your God is the one who goes with you to fight for you against your enemies to give you victory." – Deuteronomy 20:4 (NIV)

Encouragement: No matter what challenges I face, I declare that I am victorious. The promises of God reassure me that no obstacle is too great and no struggle too daunting for His power. Each day, I choose to speak words of victory, healing, and breakthrough over my life, reminding myself that I am not alone in this journey. God stands beside me, ready to battle my adversities with me. This knowledge fuels my confidence and inspires me to remain steadfast in my faith, even during the toughest of times. I am empowered by His presence, knowing that He is orchestrating every step I take toward a brighter future.

As I meditate on the truth found in Deuteronomy 20:4, I am reminded that my God is a warrior who actively fights on my behalf. This verse serves as a powerful affirmation that His support is unwavering, and His desire is for me to experience victory. I can embrace each day with resilience, trusting that God's favor surrounds me like a shield. In every challenge I encounter, His strength is my foundation, and His promises are my assurance. Therefore, I move forward with boldness, declaring triumph over my circumstances, and eagerly anticipating the breakthroughs that are on the horizon.

MAY 1

DAY 122

I SPEAK LOVE OVER MYSELF

Affirmation: I speak words of love and kindness to myself daily.

Scripture: "Gracious words are a honeycomb, sweet to the soul and healing to the bones." – Proverbs 16:24 (NIV)

Encouragement: I deserve to be spoken to with kindness—especially by myself. It's easy to internalize negative self-talk and allow harsh judgments to overshadow our self-worth. However, recognizing our own value is essential. Today, I consciously choose to surround myself with uplifting affirmations that foster a nurturing environment within. By speaking words of love and kindness to myself, I open the door to healing emotions and cultivate a sense of peace that resonates deep within my soul.

This deliberate act of kindness toward oneself isn't just a fleeting gesture; it is a powerful commitment to self-love and respect. As Scripture reminds us, "Gracious words are a honeycomb, sweet to the soul and healing to the bones" (Proverbs 16:24). By choosing to weave gracious words into my daily narrative, I enhance not only my well-being but also my resilience against the challenges I may face. Each kind affirmation becomes a step toward a more compassionate inner dialogue, allowing me to embrace the divine love that fuels my spirit and nourishes my journey. Today, let us draw from the well of kindness within and speak balms of love over ourselves, transforming our hearts and minds in the process.

MAY 2

DAY 123

MY WORDS CREATE MY FUTURE

Affirmation: I speak into existence the life I desire and deserve.

Scripture: "You will also decree a thing, and it will be established for you; and light will shine on your ways." – Job 22:28 (NIV)

Encouragement: Every word I speak carries immense power and potential. It is vital to recognize the weight that our words hold, as they can shape our realities and influence the trajectory of our lives. Instead of allowing negativity, doubt, or fear to seep into my thoughts and conversations, I choose to speak words that nurture hope, strength, and positivity. By consciously declaring success, joy, and peace over my life, I actively align my spoken affirmations with God's promises. This practice not only empowers me to manifest the life I desire and deserve but also reinforces my faith in the divine plan laid out for me.

As I continue this transformative journey, I am reminded of the profound truth found in Job 22:28, which assures me that when I decree a thing, it will indeed be established for me. My words are a reflection of my beliefs and intentions, and through them, I can invite light to shine upon my path. Each declaration I make serves as a stepping stone toward the abundant life God has envisioned for me. I will embrace this power with gratitude and intention, firmly believing that the future I desire is within my grasp, as I speak it into existence.

MAY 3

DAY 124

I SPEAK PEACE OVER MY MIND AND HEART

Affirmation: I declare peace over my thoughts, emotions, and spirit.

Scripture: "Peace I leave with you; my peace I give you. I do not give to you as the world gives. Do not let your hearts be troubled and do not be afraid." – John 14:27 (NIV)

Encouragement: Today, I choose to release the heavy burdens of stress, worry, and anxiety that often seek to overshadow my daily life. In doing so, I invite tranquility into my heart and mind, fully aware that by speaking peace over my circumstances, I align myself with the divine assurance provided by God. His peace is not just a fleeting emotion but a profound state of being that transcends any chaos I may be facing. This peace has the power to calm restlessness and dispel fears, allowing me to embrace a spirit of serenity that rests in His promises.

As I reflect on the words of John 14:27, I am reminded that the peace God offers is unlike anything the world can give. While the external environment may be filled with turmoil and uncertainty, I have the ability to hold fast to this inner peace that comes from knowing that I am loved and protected. By grounding myself in this truth, I can let go of anxiety and choose faith instead. Today, I reaffirm my commitment to uphold this peace, trusting that my heart will remain untroubled and free from fear as I rest in God's loving embrace.

MAY 4

DAY 125

I SPEAK STRENGTH INTO MY LIFE

Affirmation: I am strong, capable, and resilient. I declare my strength today.

Scripture: " Immediately the boy's father exclaimed, "I do believe; help me overcome my unbelief!" – Mark 9:24 (NIV)

Encouragement: No matter what challenges I encounter on my journey, I must remind myself that I possess an inherent strength that lies within. Life may present numerous obstacles, but I choose to stand firm and resilient, refusing to let difficulties overwhelm me. In acknowledging my capability, I also embrace the truth that I can rise above every trial. By declaring my strength and holding onto the faith that empowers me, I create a powerful foundation for overcoming adversity. I am equipped with the tools necessary to face whatever comes my way, for I am stronger than I often give myself credit for.

As I reflect on the words of the boy's father in Mark 9:24, I recognize the duality of belief and doubt alive within us all. It's a reminder that even in moments of uncertainty, when my faith may waver, I can call upon my inner strength to guide me through. I acknowledge that it's okay to seek assistance in overcoming my unbelief, for it is through these struggles that I grow closer to my true self. Embracing both my vulnerabilities and strengths empowers me to face each day with confidence. Today, I will continue to affirm my resilience and remain grounded in the belief that I am more than capable of meeting the challenges I encounter.

MAY 5

DAY 12

MY WORDS ALIGN WITH GOD'S PLAN

Affirmation: I speak in agreement with God's promises and plans for my life.

Scripture: "In him and through faith in him we may approach God with freedom and confidence."– Ephesians 3:12 (NIV)

Encouragement: As I navigate through each day, I consciously choose to speak words that resonate with God's promises and the potential He has placed within me. I refuse to give power to defeat, fear, or doubt, which only serve to cloud my vision and hinder my progress. Instead, I boldly proclaim that I am embracing the divine purpose He has ordained for my life. By aligning my words with His truth, I actively declare my faith in a future filled with hope and abundance. Each word I speak becomes a stepping stone towards the life God has intricately woven for me, filled with purpose and possibility.

With the assurance that comes from my faith, I lean into the freedom and confidence promised in Ephesians 3:12. This assurance empowers me to approach each situation with an optimistic heart and a resilient spirit. I remain expectant of the great things that lie ahead, knowing that every challenge is an opportunity for growth and every moment is infused with His grace. By committing to speak life and positivity, I am not alone in my journey; instead, I am surrounded by the strength of His promises, paving the way for extraordinary blessings to unfold.

Week 19

Releasing The Past

MAY 6

DAY 127

LETTING GO OF YESTERDAY

Affirmation: I release the weight of the past and embrace the beauty of today.

Scripture: " Eat honey, my son, for it is good; honey from the comb is sweet to your taste.

Know also that wisdom is like honey for you: If you find it, there is a future hope for you,

and your hope will not be cut off." – Proverbs 24:13-14 (NIV)

Encouragement: Today, I make a conscious choice to let go of yesterday's burdens and embrace the gift of the present moment. The weight of the past can often feel overwhelming, but I remind myself that my past experiences do not define who I am or dictate my future. Instead, it is God's purpose that shapes my identity and guides my journey. As I release the chains of regret and disappointment, I open my heart to the possibilities that today holds. Each step I take away from yesterday is a step towards growth, renewal, and the beauty of new beginnings.

In Proverbs 24:13-14, we are reminded of the sweetness of wisdom and the hope that comes with discovering it. Just as honey brings nourishment and joy, embracing the lessons learned from the past can provide a foundation for a brighter tomorrow. I hold fast to the promise that if I seek wisdom, my future will be filled with hope and abundant blessings. Today, I choose to taste the sweetness of this truth and trust in God's plan for my life. With every moment I release old burdens, I create space for new opportunities and experiences, knowing that my hope will not be cut off. Each day is a chance to build a fulfilling future anchored in faith and love.

MAY 7

DAY 128

HEALING FROM PAST WOUNDS

Affirmation: I allow God to heal my heart from past hurts.

Scripture: " Start children off on the way they should go, and even when they are old they will not turn from it." – Proverbs 22:6 (NIV)

Encouragement: The pain of my past no longer has control over me, and I choose to embrace a brighter future filled with hope and healing. By allowing God to work in my heart, I open myself up to the transformative power of His love and grace. Each moment spent in prayer and reflection strengthens my resolve to let go of past hurts and welcomes the restoration that only He can bring. With each step I take, I grow more resilient and equipped to face life's challenges. I understand that healing is a journey, and I am committed to following the path set before me with faith and courage.

As I seek to align my life with God's intentions, I can reflect on the wisdom of Proverbs 22:6, recognizing the profound impact of foundational teachings and values in shaping my life. Just as children are guided on the right path, I too can choose to follow in the ways of love, forgiveness, and strength. This scripture reminds me that the lessons I learn today will remain with me as I navigate my life's journey. I hold fast to the truth that my heart can be renewed, and each day offers a fresh opportunity to cultivate wholeness and embrace the transformative healing process that God has for me.

MAY 8

DAY 129

RELEASING REGRET

Affirmation: I release regret and embrace God's grace.

Scripture: "Therefore, there is now no condemnation for those who are in Christ Jesus." – Romans 8:1 (NIV)

Encouragement: Regret has no place in my heart, for I choose to embrace the abundant grace that God freely offers. It can be all too easy to allow memories of past mistakes to linger, casting shadows over my present and future. However, I am reminded that God's mercy is renewed with each new day, shining a light on the path ahead. I hold on to the truth that I am not defined by my missteps, but rather by the incredible grace of God that invites me to move forward. Each moment is an opportunity for growth and transformation, and I resolve to walk in confidence, shedding the weight of guilt.

In acknowledging that there is no condemnation for those who are in Christ Jesus, I find peace and reassurance. The chains of regret that once held me back are now broken, allowing me to step boldly into the plans God has for my life. I release the burden of guilt and shame, understanding that God sees me through a lens of love and forgiveness. As I continue to let go of my past, I embrace the hope and joy of a future filled with possibility. With gratitude in my heart, I choose to live each day in the fullness of God's grace, looking forward to what He has in store for me.

MAY 9

DAY 130

EMBRACING MY GROWTH

Affirmation: I celebrate the lessons from my past and use them to grow.

Scripture: "The Lord your God is with you, the Mighty Warrior who saves. He will take great delight in you; in his love he will no longer rebuke you, but will rejoice over you with singing." – Zephaniah 3:17 (NIV)

Encouragement: Every experience I have encountered has meticulously shaped me into the person I am today, contributing invaluable lessons that enrich my journey. Looking back, I can clearly see the growth that has stemmed from both joyful moments and challenging obstacles. I celebrate these lessons, acknowledging how they have equipped me with wisdom and resilience. Each step of the journey has taught me about perseverance and has allowed me to refine my character. As I embrace the fullness of my past, I recognize that these experiences serve not only as a foundation but also as a springboard into the next exciting chapter of my life.

The scripture from Zephaniah reminds me of the steadfast presence of the Lord as my Mighty Warrior. I find great comfort in the truth that He delights in me and rejoices over my journey with singing. This affirmation instills a profound sense of hope and encouragement within me. I am not merely a sum of my experiences; rather, I am a being of progress and transformation, loved and celebrated by my Creator. With this realization, I stand ready and empowered to step boldly into the future, carrying the lessons of my past as both a shield and a guiding light towards new opportunities for growth and fulfillment.

MAY 10

DAY 131

FORGIVING MYSELF AND OTHERS

Affirmation: I choose to forgive, releasing myself and others from the past.

Scripture: "Bear with each other and forgive one another if any of you has a grievance against someone. Forgive as the Lord forgave you." – Colossians 3:13 (NIV)

Encouragement: Forgiveness is a profound gift that I offer not only to others but also, and perhaps most importantly, to myself. When I cling to resentment and bitterness, I am essentially carrying a heavy burden that can cloud my mind and weigh down my spirit. Every moment I hold onto past grievances is a moment I deny myself the joy and peace that comes from letting go. By choosing to forgive, I free my heart from the shackles of hurt and disappointment. This intentional act of release allows me to embrace a brighter future, filled with possibilities and genuine connections.

Moreover, I am reminded of the essential truth found in Colossians 3:13, which encourages me to bear with one another and forgive, just as I have been forgiven. This scripture reinforces the notion that forgiveness is not just an act of kindness towards others; it is also a form of self-care and liberation. By embracing forgiveness, I align my spirit with the grace that has been afforded to me, and I create space for healing and restoration in my life. In forgiving, I acknowledge my humanity and the shared experiences of our imperfections, allowing me to step into a new chapter, guided by compassion and understanding.

MAY 11

DAY 132

TRUSTING GOD WITH MY PAST

Affirmation: I trust God to use my past for His purpose.

Scripture: "You intended to harm me, but God intended it for good." – Genesis 50:20 (NIV)

Encouragement: Even the hardest moments of my past have a purpose that transcends my understanding. It's easy to feel weighed down by mistakes, regrets, or painful experiences, but I am reminded that God can weave these challenges into a beautiful tapestry of redemption. I trust that God is using every part of my story for good, aligning my experiences with His greater plan, which is often beyond my current sight. Each setback and hardship serves as a stepping stone that can lead to growth, resilience, and newfound strength, building a foundation upon which I can stand tall in faith.

As I reflect on the truth of Genesis 50:20, I find solace in the knowledge that what was intended for harm can be transformed into something profoundly good by divine hands. This promise reassures me that my past does not define me; rather, it has equipped me with unique insights and empathy that I can share with others. I embrace the belief that God can redirect my past experiences into avenues of hope and healing, not just for myself, but also for those around me. In trusting God with my past, I am not only letting go of burdens but also stepping into a future filled with purpose, courage, and boundless possibility.

MAY 12

DAY 133

STEPPING INTO MY FUTURE

Affirmation: I step boldly into the future God has for me.

Scripture: "Forgetting what is behind and straining toward what is ahead, I press on." – Philippians 3:13-14 (NIV)

Encouragement: As I embark on this journey into my future, I remind myself that my past does not define me; rather, it is a stepping stone to greater things that lie ahead. I turn my back on the weight of regret and disappointment, fully embracing the promise of new beginnings that God has placed before me. Each step I take is grounded in faith, emboldened by the conviction that God's plans for me are good, filled with hope and purpose. I am determined to leave behind any negativity and instead cultivate a mindset that celebrates growth and opportunity.

Today, I choose to celebrate my potential and trust that I am being guided toward a future overflowing with His blessings.

With this unwavering assurance, I press on with confidence, knowing that every challenge I face is merely an opportunity for personal growth. Philippians 3:13-14 reminds us to forget what lies behind and to strain toward what is ahead, encouraging us to envision the beautiful future God desires for us. I hold onto the belief that greater things await me, and I am equipped to pursue them wholeheartedly. With my eyes fixed firmly on the horizon, I embrace the journey ahead, understanding that each moment is part of a divine plan that is unfolding just for me. With God by my side, I will move forward boldly, stepping into a future filled with promise and purpose.

Week 20

Courage To Be Seen

MAY 13

DAY 134

I AM VISIBLE AND VALUABLE

Affirmation: I embrace being seen, knowing that I am worthy of love and acceptance.

Scripture: "For everyone born of God overcomes the world. This is the victory that has overcome the world, even our faith." – 1 John 5:4 (NIV)

Encouragement: I refuse to shrink back in fear or insecurity, for I know that I am designed to shine brightly in this world. It is essential for me to recognize that my very presence is a gift that can inspire and uplift others. I was created with unique gifts and talents that contribute to the beautiful tapestry of life around me. Today, I choose to embrace my visibility, standing tall in the truth of who I am. I am worthy of love and acceptance, not only from others but also from myself. By affirming my value, I cultivate a space where I can express my thoughts, share my heart, and engage with the world authentically.

In a world that often tries to silence our voices, I firmly stand in the knowledge that I can overcome any challenges that come my way. My faith is my strength; it empowers me to break free from the chains of doubt and fear. With every step I take, I will be bold in proclaiming my worthiness and significance. Today, I will be unapologetically visible, knowing that each act of courage contributes to my personal victory over negativity and insecurity. I am not merely a passerby in this life; I am here with purpose and passion, ready to embrace the love and acceptance that I deserve.

MAY 14

DAY 135

I SHOW UP FOR MYSELF

Affirmation: I honor myself by showing up boldly in every area of my life.

Scripture: "Be strong and take heart, all you who hope in the Lord." – Psalm 31:24 (NIV)

Encouragement: Every time I show up for myself, I am taking a powerful stand for my own worth and dignity. This act of self-commitment reflects a deep recognition of my inherent value. When I choose to present myself boldly in every area of my life, I am not only honoring my own needs and desires but also reinforcing the belief that I deserve to be seen and heard. In showing up, I embrace my strength, capabilities, and the unique gifts I bring to the world. There is a profound power in actively participating in my life; it allows me to live authentically and aligns my actions with my true self.

As I navigate through life's challenges, the encouragement from Psalm 31:24 reminds me to be strong and take heart, grounding me in the hope that comes from trusting in the Lord. Each show-up moment becomes a testament to my resilience, reflecting that I am not alone in my journey. With every step I take, I remind myself that my presence matters, and I can face any situation with faith and courage. The more I honor my commitment to myself, the more I cultivate an environment where my aspirations can flourish. In doing so, I not only uplift myself but also inspire others around me to recognize and honor their own journeys.

MAY 15

DAY 136

MY CONFIDENCE INSPIRES OTHERS

Affirmation: My courage to be seen empowers others to do the same.

Scripture: "in purity, understanding, patience and kindness; in the Holy Spirit and in sincere love." – 2 Corinthians 6:6 (NIV)

Encouragement: When I choose confidence over fear, I give others permission to do the same. My story, filled with triumphs and challenges, serves as a beacon of hope for those around me. By openly embracing my own vulnerabilities and demonstrating courage in my actions, I create an environment where authenticity flourishes. It is through my willingness to be seen—flaws and all—that I inspire others to step into their own light, allowing them to shed the weight of insecurity. Just as 2 Corinthians 6:6 reminds us of the importance of embodying qualities like purity and kindness, my journey reflects how these virtues can manifest in our daily lives, encouraging others to rise up and share their unique stories.

In building a foundation of trust and mutual support, I discover that the ripple effect of my confidence can transform not only my own path but also the lives of those around me. Each time I choose to show up authentically and express sincere love, I reinforce the notion that we are all deserving of visibility and acceptance. My courage becomes a source of empowerment, inviting others to recognize their own strength and innate worth. Together, as we apply understanding and patience in our interactions, we create a community where everyone's voice is valued. Ultimately, as I continue to embody confidence, I hold space for others to thrive, igniting a spark that encourages them to boldly embrace their true selves.

MAY 16

DAY 137

I LET GO OF FEAR AND STEP INTO BOLDNESS

Affirmation: Fear does not control me—I walk in courage and faith.

Scripture: "The Spirit of God has made me; the breath of the Almighty gives me life."– Job 33:4 (NIV)

Encouragement: I will not allow fear to hold me back from living fully. Each step I take in boldness brings me closer to the life God has for me. It is essential to remember that fear is often a deceptive force that seeks to hinder our progress and keep us from realizing our true potential. With every decision I make to step forward, I am not merely moving away from fear; I am actively embracing the courage and faith that God has instilled within me. By acknowledging that the Spirit of God breathes life into me, I can draw strength from that divine presence, reminding myself that I am never alone in my journey.

As I continue to step boldly into the unknown, I reaffirm my belief that God has equipped me with everything I need to face challenges head-on. Each moment of courage builds my faith and reinforces my identity as a beloved child of God, created with purpose and passion. The breath of the Almighty fills me with vitality, allowing me to rise above obstacles and trust in His plan for my life. I choose to focus on the promise of a brighter tomorrow, knowing that fear will not dictate my choices or undermine my aspirations. Instead, I will lean into the boldness that God provides, confident that every step forward is a testament to His unwavering love and support.

MAY 17

DAY 138

MY PRESENCE IS A GIFT

Affirmation: I am a gift to this world, and my presence brings value wherever I go.

Scripture: "Now you are the body of Christ, and each one of you is a part of it." – 1 Corinthians 12:27 (NIV)

Encouragement: I have something special to offer this world, and it is essential to recognize the unique value I bring to every situation I encounter. I am not merely an afterthought; my existence holds significance in the grand tapestry of life. Each one of us is uniquely designed and intricately woven into the fabric of the universe, and my gifts, experiences, and perspectives contribute meaningfully to this collective masterpiece. As I navigate through my daily interactions, I can remind myself of the importance of my presence and the positive influences I can have on others. By embracing my identity as a precious gift, I empower myself and those around me to realize their own inherent worth.

Moreover, the scripture in 1 Corinthians 12:27 beautifully emphasizes our role within the larger body of Christ, reinforcing the notion that we are not isolated individuals but vital parts of a greater whole. Each person plays a crucial role, and my contribution is valuable in ways I may not fully understand. Embracing this calling not only cultivates self-worth but also inspires me to uplift others, encouraging them to recognize their own gifts and significance. Together, we can create a vibrant community where everyone feels seen, valued, and appreciated for who they are. My presence, therefore, becomes a source of encouragement and inspiration, reflecting the divine purpose that we all share as interconnected members of this beautiful tapestry.

MAY 18

DAY 139:

I STAND TALL IN MY TRUTH

Affirmation: I stand tall in my truth, embracing my authentic self.

Scripture: "Stand firm, and you will win life." – Luke 21:19 (NIV)

Encouragement: I will not hide who I am any longer. Every chapter of my story, whether it be filled with struggles or triumphs, contributes to the unique tapestry of my life. Embracing my authentic self means honoring all the experiences that have shaped me into the person I am today. Each moment I've faced, every obstacle I've overcome, and all the lessons I've learned have empowered me to stand tall in my truth. I commit to fully expressing my individuality, recognizing that my journey is valuable and worthy of being shared.

As I walk confidently in my purpose, I remember the promise found in Luke 21:19, which encourages me to stand firm. This resilience allows me to navigate life's challenges with grace and strength. I am reminded that embracing my true self and standing firm in my beliefs is not just about individual perseverance; it's also about inspiring others to do the same. By living authentically, I create a ripple effect of courage, inviting those around me to find their own voices and share their stories. Together, we can foster a community built on truth and authenticity, one where everyone is empowered to stand firm and thrive.

MAY 19

DAY 140

I AM READY TO BE SEEN

Affirmation: I no longer hide—I step into the fullness of who I am.

Scripture: "Arise, shine, for your light has come, and the glory of the Lord rises upon you." – Isaiah 60:1 (NIV)

Encouragement: Today, I step forward with boldness and assurance, embracing the truth that I am no longer hidden. I am seen, I am known, and I am deeply loved for who I am. This is a powerful moment of awakening, a calling to shed any self-doubt or insecurity that may have held me captive in the past. I acknowledge that each aspect of my journey has shaped me into the person I am today, and I walk confidently in my purpose, empowered by the knowledge that I am exactly where I am meant to be. The light within me is no longer dimmed; it shines brightly for all to see, reflecting the glory of the Lord that has risen upon me.

As I embrace this truth, I allow my light to touch the lives of those around me, inspiring others to step into their own fullness. The act of being seen is not merely about visibility; it is about authenticity and courage. I am reminded that my presence has value and that my stories, struggles, and triumphs contribute to a greater tapestry of life. With each step I take, I am fulfilling my divine purpose, radiating hope and love to those I encounter. Today, I declare my readiness to shine, to embrace the journey ahead, and to celebrate the beautiful person I have become.

Week 21

My Journey Is My Testimony

MAY 20

DAY 141

MY STORY HAS PURPOSE

Affirmation: Every chapter of my life serves a greater purpose.

Scripture: "On the day when I act," says the Lord Almighty, "they will be my treasured possession. I will spare them, just as a father has compassion and spares his son who serves him." – Malachi 3:17 (NIV)

Encouragement: My journey, with all its ups and downs, is not in vain; rather, it is a vital tapestry woven together by the hands of divine love. Each chapter of my life, filled with triumphs and trials alike, contributes to the greater narrative that God is crafting specifically for me. I find solace in knowing that every experience—both the joyous moments and the challenging times—serves to shape and refine me into the person I am meant to be in His grand design. God's promise, as stated in Malachi 3:17, reassures me that I am cherished and valuable to Him. I can trust that, in His timing, every element of my story is being used for a purpose beyond my understanding.

As I reflect on my life's journey, I am reminded that my trials are not merely obstacles, but rather unique opportunities for growth and transformation. It is within these moments that I lean into my faith, embracing the idea that I am part of something much larger than myself. Understanding that I am a treasured possession of the Lord inspires me to move forward with renewed hope and confidence. God's compassion is evident, as He spares me from despair and guides me with a father's love. Knowing that He is intricately involved in my life encourages me to believe that my story is not just a series of random events, but a purposeful path leading me to greater fulfillment and significance.

MAY 21

DAY 142

I AM NOT DEFINED BY MY STRUGGLES

Affirmation: My struggles do not define me; my faith and perseverance do.

Scripture: "The Lord is close to the brokenhearted and saves those who are crushed in spirit." – Psalm 34:18 (NIV)

Encouragement: I will not allow my past struggles to hold me back. Instead, I embrace them as a vital part of my testimony, a reflection of the journey that has shaped me into who I am today. Each challenge I have faced has been a stepping stone toward greater faith and resilience. I recognize that these experiences, while painful, are not my identity; they are the context within which I have grown. By leaning into my struggles, I am reminded of God's unending faithfulness, His presence in my darkest moments, and the strength He has provided to carry me through. I celebrate every victory, no matter how small, for they are signs of my progress and perseverance.

As I trust in the truth of Scripture, I find comfort in the promise that the Lord is close to the brokenhearted. This assurance fills me with hope, reinforcing my belief that I am not alone in my battles. God's love and support are constant, and they guide me toward healing and renewal. I choose to live from a place of faith rather than fear, grounded in the knowledge that my struggles do not define me; rather, my faith and perseverance do. This journey of resilience is what gives my life meaning and purpose, inspiring me to encourage others who may feel broken or crushed in spirit. Together, we can rise, finding strength in our shared experiences and lifting one another toward a future filled with hope and promise.

MAY 22

DAY 143

I SHARE MY STORY WITH CONFIDENCE

Affirmation: My testimony has the power to encourage and uplift others.

Scripture: "Let the redeemed of the Lord tell their story—those he redeemed from the hand of the foe." – Psalm 107:2 (NIV)

Encouragement: I share my journey not in shame but with confidence, knowing that my story can bring hope and healing to others walking a similar path. Every experience I've faced, whether filled with joy or challenges, plays a crucial role in shaping who I am today. When I openly share these moments, I create a bridge of understanding and connection that reminds others they are not alone in their struggles. My testimony becomes a source of strength, a torch lighting the way for those who may feel lost or uncertain. By bearing witness to my experiences, I can inspire others to embrace their own stories, transforming pain into purpose and despair into resilience.

In sharing my story, I also fulfill the call found in Psalm 107:2, inviting others to witness the transformative work God has done in my life. This isn't just a personal narrative; it's a powerful testament to the faithfulness of God in the midst of adversity. As I recount how I've been redeemed and uplifted, I encourage others to reflect on their own journeys and recognize the strength that lies within their experiences. It's a reminder that we are all woven together through shared struggles and victories, and collectively, our stories affirm the hope we can offer one another. By courageously telling our stories, we participate in a divine narrative of redemption and healing, empowering others to do the same.

MAY 23

DAY 144

MY PAIN HAS TRANSFORMED INTO STRENGTH

Affirmation: What once hurt me has now made me stronger and wiser.

Scripture: " The one who gets wisdom loves life; the one who cherishes understanding will soon prosper."' – Proverbs 19:8 (NIV)

Encouragement: My past pain is no longer a burden; instead, it has become a powerful source of strength in my life. The experiences that once brought me to my knees are now the very experiences that have propelled me forward, giving me the resilience and wisdom to face future challenges with confidence. I have cultivated a deeper understanding of myself and the world around me through my struggles. Each trial has enriched my character, allowing me to rise above adversity and embrace the lessons learned along the way. I stand firm in the belief that what once hurt me has transformed me for the better, and I am filled with gratitude for the growth that has emerged from my hardships.

Embracing this journey of transformation encourages me to cherish my experiences, both good and bad. With every setback, I have discovered new strengths and insights that have shaped my perspective on life. The wisdom I have gained fuels my passion for living fully and authentically. As Proverbs 19:8 reminds us, the one who loves wisdom and cherishes understanding will flourish. I strive to embody this truth, knowing that my past struggles have equipped me with the tools I need to thrive. Each day, I rise with renewed purpose, ready to embrace the possibilities that lie ahead, confident that I can overcome any challenges that come my way.

MAY 24

DAY 145

I WALK IN VICTORY

Affirmation: I am victorious in Christ, and my story reflects His goodness.

Scripture: "But thanks be to God! He gives us the victory through our Lord Jesus Christ." – 1 Corinthians 15:57 (NIV)

Encouragement: I am no longer bound by fear, shame, or doubt. Through my faith in Christ, I embrace the transformative power of His victory over all adversities. Each step I take is a testament to God's unyielding faithfulness, reminding me that my life is not defined by my past struggles but rather by the grace and strength I find in Him. As I walk forward, I am empowered to rise above life's challenges, knowing with confidence that I am grounded in His love and purpose. This journey serves as a powerful reminder that no matter the obstacles I face, I can always lean on the promise of His victory.

Walking in victory means celebrating the goodness that God has poured into my life. I choose to reflect that goodness not only in my triumphs but also in my trials. It is in these moments of challenge that I can truly showcase the resilience He instills within me. I am not merely living for myself; I carry the testimony of His grace, illuminating the way for others who may still be trapped in their own fears and doubts. With each breath, I declare that I am victorious in Christ, for He alone has the power to transform my story into one of hope, redemption, and unwavering faith.

MAY 25

DAY 146

MY JOURNEY INSPIRES OTHERS

Affirmation: My testimony gives others the courage to keep going.

Scripture: " Have you experienced so much in vain—if it really was in vain?" – Galatians 3:4 (NIV)

Encouragement: I never know who might need to hear my story, which is why I share it boldly and authentically. Each moment I've encountered on my journey, whether filled with triumphs or struggles, is a testament to resilience and faith. It's easy to underestimate the impact our experiences can have on others; however, the truth is that our testimonies can light the way for those who are navigating their own valleys. When I recount my journey, I do so with the hope that it will provide solace and strength to someone who might be facing similar challenges, reminding them that they are not alone in their struggles.

When I reflect on the words from Galatians 3:4, I am reminded that there is purpose in every trial I've faced. If I allow my experiences to remain unshared, I risk losing the opportunity to encourage someone else to persevere. The struggles may seem in vain if we keep them to ourselves, but the moment we open up, we allow our stories to transform into beacons of hope. So I continue to embrace vulnerability, trusting that my testimony not only validates my journey but also empowers others to keep moving forward, knowing that their efforts and hardships have meaning too.

MAY 26

DAY 147

I AM LIVING PROOF OF GOD'S GRACE

Affirmation: My life is evidence of God's unending grace and love.

Scripture: "Surely your goodness and love will follow me all the days of my life." – Psalm 23:6 (NIV)

Encouragement: My life is a living testimony of God's grace, a profound reflection of His unyielding love and mercy. Each day, I recognize the countless ways in which His grace manifests in my life, guiding me through challenges and illuminating my path with hope and joy. I embrace this divine grace wholeheartedly, understanding that it is not merely a passive gift but an active force that encourages me to grow and thrive. In every moment of vulnerability and strength, God's love surrounds me, reinforcing the truth that I am never alone on this journey.

As I share my story, I invite others to see the beauty of God's grace at work in their lives as well. I strive to walk in this grace daily, allowing it to shape my interactions and decisions. Each step I take reflects a commitment to living authentically, knowing that God's goodness and love pursue me relentlessly. This assurance lifts my spirit and fuels my determination to extend grace to others, creating a ripple effect of love that echoes God's heart. As Psalm 23:6 reminds us, His goodness follows us throughout our lives, a constant reminder that we are enveloped in His unending grace.

Week 22

Renewing My Mind Daily

MAY 27

DAY 148

MY THOUGHTS SHAPE MY REALITY

**ffirmation:** I align my thoughts with truth, positivity, and faith.

Scripture: "But God demonstrates his own love for us in this: While we were still sinners, Christ died for us." – Romans 5:8 (NIV)

Encouragement: Each day, I have the power to choose what I focus on, and this conscious choice shapes my reality. By releasing negativity and letting go of self-doubt, I create space to embrace thoughts that bring peace, hope, and unwavering confidence. This transformative journey begins with renewing my mind daily, allowing me to align my thoughts with truth and positivity. As I do this, I create a foundation built on faith, trusting that every thought I nurture can lead me toward a life of purpose and joy.

In this divine exchange, I am reminded of the immense love God has for me, as illustrated in Romans 5:8. This truth inspires me to focus on the positive aspects of my life and to celebrate the grace that is always present, even in my imperfections. By grounding myself in this love, I can confidently face each day, knowing that I have the agency to shift my perspective and embrace a mindset that reflects hope and possibility. With every mindful thought, I am not just changing my mindset; I am stepping into a reality that mirrors the truth of God's unwavering love for me.

MAY 28

DAY 149

I CHOOSE PEACE OVER WORRY

Affirmation: My mind is at peace because I trust in God's plan.

Scripture: "He heals the brokenhearted and binds up their wounds."– Psalm 147:3 (NIV)

Encouragement: Worry cannot take root where faith resides. When we place our trust in God and His divine plan, we create an environment where peace flourishes. It's essential to recognize that our anxious thoughts do not define us; instead, they are opportunities to lean deeper into our faith. As we surrender these burdens to Him, we open ourselves to experience the healing power of His love. Each moment we choose faith over fear, we allow God to work within us, guiding our hearts and minds toward serenity. Today, let this understanding empower you to let go of your worries and embrace the peace that comes from knowing He is in control of all things.

Moreover, remember that healing and comfort are integral aspects of God's nature, as beautifully highlighted in Psalm 147:3. He is not only here to mend our physical pains but also to heal the emotional and spiritual wounds we carry. By choosing peace, we align ourselves with His promise to bind up our wounds, restoring us to wholeness. Embrace this divine assurance and realize that in moments of turmoil, there is serenity waiting to be claimed. Let your heart be anchored in the truth that God's plan is unfolding, and as you trust in Him, peace will reign in your life today and always.

MAY 29

DAY 150

I GUARD MY MIND AGAINST NEGATIVITY

Affirmation: I protect my thoughts and focus on what uplifts my spirit.

Scripture: "Above all else, guard your heart, for everything you do flows from it." – Proverbs 4:23 (NIV)

Encouragement: My mind is a powerful tool, shaping my perceptions and influencing my actions. I recognize that I have the authority to choose what I allow to take root in my thoughts. By actively rejecting negativity, I create space for positivity and resilience to flourish. I am committed to surrounding myself with uplifting influences, embracing encouragement that fuels my spirit and wisdom that guides my decisions. It is vital to hold on to the truth, as it serves as a sturdy foundation upon which I can build a life of purpose and joy.

Furthermore, I understand that guarding my heart, as outlined in Proverbs 4:23, is not just a protective measure; it's an intentional practice of nurturing my inner self. The flow of my life is profoundly affected by what I think and believe. When I focus on uplifting thoughts, I create a ripple effect that extends to my emotions and actions, leading to a more fulfilled and meaningful existence. I choose to cultivate a mindset filled with hope, love, and positivity, because I know that every thought I entertain shapes the reality I experience. Every day is an opportunity to reinforce my commitment to a healthy mind and spirit, paving the way for personal growth and a deeper connection with those around me.

MAY 30

DAY 151

MY MIND IS A GARDEN OF POSSIBILITIES

Affirmation: I plant seeds of faith, joy, and success in my mind daily.

Scripture: "Finally, brothers and sisters, whatever is true, whatever is noble, whatever is right, whatever is pure, whatever is lovely, whatever is admirable—if anything is excellent or praiseworthy—think about such things." – Philippians 4:8 (NIV)

Encouragement: My thoughts truly determine my direction in life. Every day presents us with the opportunity to nurture our minds, much like a gardener tending to a garden filled with potential. When I consciously choose to focus on good things—qualities that are true, noble, right, pure, lovely, and admirable—I am actively planting seeds of faith, joy, and success in my mind. These positive thoughts act as the foundation for a thriving life, allowing me to cultivate a mindset that fosters growth, resilience, and abundance in every area. It is important to recognize that what we think shapes our reality; thus, being intentional about our thoughts can lead to transformative change.

As I fill my mind with positivity and excellence, I align myself with the abundant life that is promised to us. Philippians 4:8 reminds us of the power of our thoughts and encourages us to focus on things that inspire us. By doing so, we create a fertile ground for dreams to take root and flourish. Each day, I embrace the opportunity to reflect on what is praiseworthy and uplifting, thus reinforcing a positive mindset that propels me forward on my journey. Let us commit to this uplifting practice, knowing that our thoughts have the power to shape our future and lead us to a life filled with purpose and fulfillment.

MAY 31

DAY 152

I TAKE EVERY THOUGHT CAPTIVE

Affirmation: I am in control of my thoughts, and I choose faith over fear.

Scripture: "We take captive every thought to make it obedient to Christ." – 2 Corinthians 10:5 (NIV)

Encouragement: My mind is not a battlefield for doubt and fear. Instead, it is a sanctuary where hope and faith can flourish. I take authority over every negative thought that attempts to invade my mind, and I recognize that I have the power to choose my responses. By consciously replacing doubt with faith-filled declarations of victory, I enable myself to break free from the chains of anxiety. As I nurture positive thoughts, I cultivate a deeper connection with Christ, allowing His truth to guide my perspective and actions.

I understand that taking every thought captive means actively engaging in this transformative process. It is not merely a passive stance but a bold declaration of my commitment to live in alignment with God's promises. Each time I confront a wave of fear, I remind myself that I am equipped with the strength of faith to overcome. I can consciously replace worry with assurance, knowing that every thought can be redirected to align with the divine purpose for my life. With each victory over fear, I grow stronger in my faith, creating a mindset that reflects hope, courage, and trust in God.

JUNE 1

DAY 153

MY MIND IS BEING RENEWED EVERY DAY

God's truth.

Scripture: "To be made new in the attitude of your minds." – Ephesians 4:23 (NIV)

Encouragement: Renewal is a beautiful journey, one that unfolds gradually and requires both faith and patience. Each day presents an opportunity for growth, as I open my heart and mind to the transformative power of God's truth. I remind myself that the process may not always be immediate or easy, but I choose to embrace this journey with a sense of hope and anticipation. I actively engage with the Scriptures, allowing them to penetrate deep into my soul and reshape my thoughts. By doing so, I cultivate an awareness that my transformation is not only inevitable but also necessary for aligning my life more closely with God's will.

As I reflect on the promise found in Ephesians 4:23, I find assurance that my mindset can be refreshed daily. With each passing moment, I become more attuned to the wisdom and strength that comes from my relationship with God. I recognize that with every challenge I face and every truth I embrace, I am being molded into a stronger version of myself—one filled with confidence and clarity. This journey of renewal is both a gift and a testament to my faith. With trust in God's process, I celebrate the progress I make each day, knowing that He is continually at work within me, guiding my thoughts and actions for His purpose.

JUNE 2

DAY 154

I AM FREE FROM LIMITING BELIEFS

Affirmation: I let go of fear, doubt, and limitations—I am limitless in Christ.

Scripture: "So if the Son sets you free, you will be free indeed." – John 8:36 (NIV)

Encouragement: I refuse to be bound by old beliefs that no longer serve me. The fears and doubts that have held me captive for far too long will not dictate my future any longer. Instead, I choose to step into a renewed mindset, one that is transformed and uplifted by my faith. I embrace the boundless possibilities that God has in store for me. Each day, as I remind myself of this truth, I find the courage to break free from the chains that fear and limiting beliefs have placed around me. I trust in God's promise that I am made new, and through His strength, I can transcend any obstacles that may come my way.

In this journey of freedom, I acknowledge that I am not alone. The assurance in John 8:36 reminds me that if Jesus sets me free, I will indeed be free. This divine liberation grants me the power to explore new horizons and pursue my ambitions without hesitation. As I embrace this freedom, I realize that I am capable of achieving great things—not because of my own abilities, but because of the limitless grace bestowed upon me by Christ. With each step forward, I claim my freedom and invite God's limitless love and possibilities into every aspect of my life, knowing that my potential is unrestrained when anchored in Him.

Week 23

Accepting My Reflection

JUNE 3

DAY 155

MY REFLECTION IS BEAUTIFUL

Affirmation: I see beauty when I look in the mirror.

Scripture: "The Lord himself goes before you and will be with you; he will never leave you nor forsake you. Do not be afraid; do not be discouraged."– Deuteronomy 7:6 (NIV)

Encouragement: My reflection is a masterpiece, beautifully crafted by the hands of God. Each feature, every unique aspect of who I am, is woven together with intention and purpose. Instead of succumbing to self-criticism or societal standards, I choose to embrace the truth that I am fearfully and wonderfully made. I recognize that when I look in the mirror, I am beholding a creation that holds infinite worth, designed to radiate the beauty that reflects God's love. This profound truth empowers me to embrace my authentic self, allowing me to shine brightly in a world that often tries to dim my light.

As I meditate on the profound assurance found in Deuteronomy 31:6, I remind myself that the Lord Himself goes before me, actively guiding my path and instilling strength within me. His unwavering presence promises that I am never alone, and this enveloping love dispels any fear or discouragement I may face. With every glance at my reflection, I affirm not only my beauty but also the divine purpose that resides within me. Each day is a new opportunity to walk in this truth, celebrating my unique journey and sharing the blessings of my authentic self with others. In doing so, I honor the artistry of my Creator, acknowledging the vibrant life He has gifted me.

JUNE 4

DAY 156

I AM MORE THAN MY APPEARANCE

Affirmation: My worth is not tied to how I look but to who I am.

Scripture: "May the Lord our God be with us as he was with our ancestors; may he never leave us nor forsake us." – 1 Kings 8:57 (NIV)

Encouragement: In a world that often prioritizes superficial qualities, it is essential to remind ourselves that our worth transcends mere physical appearance. What truly defines us are the values we hold, our integrity, and the love we share with others. Each act of kindness, every moment of compassion, and the unwavering faith we uphold shape our true identity. As we navigate through life, let us remember that our character is the foundation of who we are, reflecting the light of God's grace in our interactions and relationships. It is within our hearts that we cultivate genuine beauty, one that endures and inspires.

Moreover, as we lean on the truth found in 1 Kings 8:57, we can draw strength from the knowledge that God is always with us, just as He was with our ancestors. We are not alone in our journey; His presence reassures us that we are never forsaken. As we affirm our worth in Him, we can confidently embrace our unique qualities and strengths. In acknowledging that our identity is rooted in our faith, we can foster a deeper sense of self-acceptance and gratitude. Let this serve as a reminder that we are cherished for who we are at our core, and in this self-awareness, we unleash our potential to impact the world around us.

JUNE 5

DAY 157

I SPEAK LOVE OVER MYSELF

Affirmation: I silence negativity and replace it with words of love and affirmation.

Scripture: "The tongue has the power of life and death, and those who love it will eat its fruit." – 2 Corinthians 10:4

Encouragement: What I say about myself truly matters, as the words I speak have the power to shape my reality. The voice within me can be a source of either encouragement or discouragement, and today, I consciously choose to cultivate positivity in my thoughts and spoken words. By silencing negativity and replacing it with affirmations of love, I open the door to a more fulfilling and joyful existence. This commitment to uplifting discourse paves the way for growth, healing, and empowerment as I recognize the incredible potential residing within me. Embracing my reflection with gratitude is not just an act of self-acknowledgment; it is a transformative practice that reinforces my inherent worth.

As I meditate on the scriptural truth that "the tongue has the power of life and death," I find assurance in the idea that my words can bring forth abundance and hope. Each time I affirm love and positivity in my life, I actively choose to foster a nurturing environment for my spirit. This decision ignites a ripple effect, influencing not only my mindset but also the way I interact with others. Ultimately, by speaking life into myself, I invite love, hope, and joy to flourish within my heart and extend this vibrancy to those around me. Today, let us commit together to embrace words of empowerment, consciousness, and gratitude in all that we say about ourselves.

JUNE 6

DAY 158

MY CONFIDENCE COMES FROM WITHIN

Affirmation: I am confident because I am made in God's image.

Scripture: "So God created mankind in his own image, in the image of God he created them; male and female he created them." – Genesis 1:27 (NIV)

Encouragement: My confidence does not come from external sources, achievements, or the validation of others; rather, it is rooted deeply in the profound truth that I am created in the image of a perfect Creator. This foundational realization transcends any fleeting approvals or material gains, setting the stage for a resilient self-assurance that remains steadfast amid life's challenges. When I reflect on the fact that I am crafted with purpose and intent by the Divine, I recognize the inherent worth and dignity that accompanies my creation. This divine craftsmanship instills a sense of pride and strength within me that nothing can diminish.

Moreover, embracing the knowledge that both male and female are uniquely made in God's likeness empowers me to celebrate my individuality and recognize the beauty in diversity. It reassures me that

I possess qualities and abilities designed specifically for my journey in life. As I navigate through my day, I strive to walk confidently, knowing that I reflect the essence of my Creator. This understanding encourages me not only to believe in myself but also to uplift others, reminding them of their own divine design and potential. In a world that often tries to sway our self-worth, let us hold fast to the reality that our identities are anchored in God, giving us the courage to shine our light brightly.

JUNE 7

DAY 159

I CELEBRATE MYSELF DAILY

Affirmation: I find joy in who I am and how I was created.

Scripture: " So Joshua said to the Israelites: "How long will you wait before you begin to take possession of the land that the Lord, the God of your ancestors, has given you?." – Joshua 18:3 (NIV)

Encouragement: I do not wait for others to affirm me; instead, I take the initiative to celebrate myself each and every day. It is empowering to recognize that I am a unique creation, designed with intention and purpose by the Divine. Life presents countless opportunities to appreciate who I am, and I choose to embrace the qualities that make me distinctive. By reflecting on my strengths and values, I embolden myself to pursue my aspirations and dreams. This daily celebration fosters a sense of gratitude within me, allowing me to cultivate joy in each moment and recognize the beauty of my journey.

Moreover, embracing this self-celebration aligns beautifully with the encouragement found in Joshua 18:3, where we are reminded not to delay our possession of what has already been promised to us. I understand that the land God has set before me may require courage and decisive action. By acknowledging and affirming my worth, I empower myself to step boldly into those promises. I refuse to let the opinions or validations of others dictate my sense of self. Instead, I claim my identity, walk confidently in my purpose, and invite others to join me in the joyful journey of self-celebration. Each day is a precious gift, and I choose to honor myself by embracing the fullness of who I am.

JUNE 8

DAY 160

MY SCARS AND STRUGGLES TELL MY STORY

Affirmation: My journey is a testament of strength, resilience, and grace.

Scripture: " She sets about her work vigorously; her arms are strong for her tasks." – Proverbs 31:17 (NIV)

Encouragement: My scars, whether seen or unseen, serve as powerful evidence of my growth and resilience. Each mark tells a story — a testimony of battles fought and won, moments of pain transformed into strength, and challenges faced with unwavering courage. They remind me that it is through my struggles that I have learned to rise again and again, finding deeper layers of faith and hope in the process.

The trials I have endured have only reinforced the incredible power of God's grace in my life, allowing me to emerge not just as a survivor, but as a warrior who carries their story with pride.

As I embrace my journey, I remember the wisdom found in Proverbs 31:17: "She sets about her work vigorously; her arms are strong for her tasks." This scripture encourages me to harness that strength, reminding me that my resilience is rooted in my determination to push through adversity with purpose. Each day, I am called to labor diligently, not just in the face of difficulties but also in celebrating the victories that my scars represent. May I carry my scars with grace, recognizing that they are woven into the beautiful tapestry of my life, showcasing the extraordinary journey of transformation that God has crafted within me.

JUNE 9

DAY 161

I LOVE THE PERSON I SEE IN THE MIRROR

Affirmation: I love and accept myself just as I am.

Scripture: "But who are you, a human being, to talk back to God? Shall what is formed say to the one who formed it, 'Why did you make me like this?'" – Romans 9:20 (NIV)

Encouragement: True self-love begins with a profound sense of acceptance, which serves as the foundation for emotional and spiritual growth. It's essential to recognize that each of us is uniquely designed and intricately formed by a divine Creator. When I embrace who I am—flaws, strengths, and all—I unlock the ability to walk in freedom, freeing myself from the chains of self-criticism and comparison. This acceptance not only enriches my own life but also radiates outward, allowing me to love others more genuinely and deeply. Each day presents a choice: to affirm my worth and appreciate my journey, or to dwell in self-doubt. Today, I wholeheartedly choose to love the person looking back at me in the mirror, celebrating my individuality and existence.

Moreover, the reminder from Romans 9:20 emphasizes our relationship with the Creator, reinforcing that I am beautifully crafted for a specific purpose. Just as a sculpture cannot question the intentions of the artist, I too must understand that my value is inherent, not contingent upon societal standards or comparisons with others. Instead of questioning my design, I will choose to honor the unique qualities I possess. Embracing this truth cultivates an environment of love and acceptance within and around me. As I navigate today, may I carry this affirmation in my heart, proclaiming, "I love and accept myself just as I am," allowing this declaration to transform not only my perspective but also my interactions with others, reflecting the light of self-acceptance in all that I do.

Week 24

Faith Over Fear

JUNE 10

DAY 162

I CHOOSE FAITH OVER FEAR

Affirmation: Fear does not control me—I walk in faith and confidence.

Scripture: "What is mankind that you are mindful of them, human beings that you care for them? You have made them a little lower than the angels and crowned them with glory and honor."– Psalm 8:4-5 (NIV)

Encouragement: Fear may knock at my door, but I refuse to let it in. Instead, I choose faith, fully trusting that God's plan for my life is far more significant than any of my worries or anxieties. Each time I feel the shadows of fear creeping in, I remind myself of the promise in Psalm 8:4-5, which emphasizes that I am not just an insignificant being passing through this world; I am crafted with intention, made a little lower than the angels, and crowned with glory and honor. This glorious truth empowers me to rise above my fears, knowing that I am cherished and valued by my Creator.

In choosing faith over fear, I not only affirm my trust in God's guidance but also embrace the confidence that comes from realizing my worth in His eyes. I hold fast to the belief that I am not alone in my struggles; instead, I am supported by divine strength that nurtures my spirit and fuels my courage. When I focus on God's loving care and His mindful attention to my life, I understand that each challenge I face is an opportunity for growth and deeper connection with Him. With each step of faith I take, I can confidently declare that I am crowned with glory, and fear has no power over me.

JUNE 11

DAY 163

I TRUST GOD'S PLAN FOR ME

Affirmation: I surrender my worries and trust in God's perfect plan.

Scripture: "Trust in the Lord with all your heart and lean not on your own understanding; in all your ways submit to him, and he will make your paths straight." – Proverbs 20:22 (NIV)

Encouragement: In moments of uncertainty and confusion, it's essential to remember that I don't need to have all the answers. Life can often feel overwhelming, and we may find ourselves grappling with doubts and questions about our direction. Yet, in these times, it is vital to embrace the truth that God is actively guiding us through every twist and turn. By surrendering our worries to Him, we open our hearts to the peace that comes from trusting in His perfect plan, which is much greater than our own limited understanding. Even when the path ahead seems unclear, we can rest in the knowledge that God sees the full tapestry of our lives and is weaving it together for our ultimate good.

It is in surrendering our fears and anxieties that we can truly find solace in God's unwavering love and faithfulness. As Proverbs 3:5-6 reminds us, we are called to trust in the Lord with all our hearts and submit to Him in every circumstance. When we choose to lean not on our own understanding, we allow Him to illuminate our paths, making them straight and sure. Each step we take in faith, regardless of how uncertain it may feel, brings us closer to the fulfillment of His glorious plans for us. So let us boldly embrace the journey, secure in the knowledge that God is orchestrating each moment with purpose and intention, guiding us along the way.

JUNE 12

DAY 164

FEAR HAS NO POWER OVER ME

Affirmation: I release fear and embrace God's peace.

Scripture: " Now this is eternal life: that they know you, the only true God, and Jesus Christ, whom you have sent." – John 17:3 (NIV)

Encouragement: I will not allow fear to dictate my actions, for I recognize that it is a thief that robs me of my joy, peace, and purpose. Instead, I choose to stand firm in the remarkable peace that God has promised me. This peace is not merely a fleeting emotion but a steadfast assurance that transcends all understanding. It is rooted in the unwavering truth that God is in control, orchestrating every detail of my life with love and wisdom. I am reminded that fear often arises from the unknown and the uncertainties that surround me, but when I place my faith in God, I can let go of those anxieties.

Moreover, I have been invited into a profound relationship with the only true God and His son, Jesus Christ. This relationship provides me with the ultimate source of strength and comfort. As I deepen my understanding of who God is, I find myself more equipped to navigate life's challenges without the weight of fear holding me back. I embrace the truth that eternal life is not only about what lies ahead but also about the abundant life I can experience now, full of hope, purpose, and divine peace. Each moment I choose faith over fear, I am stepping into a life of empowerment and richness, fully confident in the plan that God has for me.

JUNE 13

DAY 165

MY FAITH IS STRONGER THAN MY DOUBTS

Affirmation: I replace doubt with faith, knowing that God is working on my behalf.

Scripture: " He went on a little farther and bowed with his face to the ground, praying, "My Father! If it is possible, let this cup of suffering be taken away from me. Yet I want your will to be done, not mine." – Matthew 26:39 (NLT)

Encouragement: Even when things seem uncertain and doubts begin to creep in, I consciously choose to cultivate faith over fear in my heart and mind. This decision is not just a fleeting thought but a deep-seated belief that resonates within me. Understanding that God is always working on my behalf provides me with a reassuring sense of peace. Just as Jesus modeled for us in the Garden of Gethsemane, He acknowledged His anguish yet submitted to God's will, demonstrating that even in our most challenging moments, we can lean into faith. I embrace the notion that every trial I face is an opportunity for spiritual growth, strengthening my resilience and deepening my trust in God's perfect plan for my life.

When I face uncertainties and the weight of doubt threatens to overwhelm me, I remind myself of the unwavering truth found in God's word. My faith empowers me to rise above the circumstances that seek to distract or deter me from my divine purpose. I confidently affirm that my faith, fortified by prayer and scripture, becomes a powerful antidote to doubt. By focusing on God's promises and surrendering my fears, I align myself with His greater vision for my life. I am reminded that, like Jesus, I can bring my burdens before God while choosing to trust that His will, which is always good and perfect, will ultimately prevail. This encourages me to remain steadfast and hopeful, knowing that God is in control and has great plans for me.

JUNE 14

DAY 166:

I WALK IN BOLDNESS AND COURAGE

Affirmation: I step forward with courage, knowing that God goes before me.

Scripture: "Be strong and courageous. Do not be afraid; do not be discouraged, for the Lord your God will be with you wherever you go." – Philippians 4:13 (NIV)

Encouragement: As I navigate through life, I am reminded that I am never alone in my journey. Every step I take is accompanied by God's unwavering presence, providing me with the strength and assurance I need to face any challenge that comes my way. The promise that He walks with me instills a deep sense of comfort within my heart, allowing me to embrace each moment with boldness and courage. I am emboldened by the truth that I can step forward into the unknown, knowing that my path is illuminated by His guidance.

Furthermore, as Philippians 4:13 assures me, I am strengthened not by my own abilities but by the divine support that fuels my spirit. When moments of fear and discouragement arise, I can choose to lean into the unshakeable foundation of faith that God provides. I will not allow anxiety or doubt to dictate my actions, for I am anchored in the knowledge that God is with me wherever I go. This divine companionship reassures me that I am equipped to confront obstacles and seize opportunities with confidence, reflecting the courageous spirit He has instilled within me. In every circumstance, I hold fast to this promise: I step forward, unafraid, and embrace the extraordinary plans God has in store for me.

JUNE 15

DAY 167

MY FAITH MAKES ME UNSHAKABLE

Affirmation: My foundation is strong because I trust in God completely.

Scripture: "When you pass through the waters, I will be with you; and when you pass through the rivers, they will not sweep over you. When you walk through the fire, you will not be burned; the flames will not set you ablaze." – Isaiah 43:2 (NIV)

Encouragement: No matter what challenges come my way, I remain steadfast in faith, grounded by my unwavering trust in God. The trials I face, be they emotional, spiritual, or physical, cannot shake the solid foundation that my belief in Him provides. Just as the waters and flames described in Isaiah 43:2 serve as metaphors for life's tribulations, I take comfort in the promise that God is always by my side. In times of difficulty, I find strength in remembering that even when the world feels uncertain, my faith acts as an anchor, keeping me secure and unwavering. With God as my refuge, I can face what lies ahead, confident that His presence will guide and uplift me through every storm.

As I walk through life's fiery challenges, I am reminded that I will not be consumed by them; instead, I will emerge stronger and more resilient. The assurance of God's companionship brings me solace and courage, reinforcing the belief that I am never alone in my struggles. Just as the flame cannot touch the faithful, I know that with each test, my faith only deepens, solidifying the bond I share with my Creator. Each experience becomes an opportunity to witness the powerful truth of His promises being fulfilled in my life. Therefore, I embrace every moment with the confidence that my foundation is strong, and I am unshakable through Him.

JUNE 16

DAY 168

I AM FEARLESS BECAUSE GOD IS WITH ME

Affirmation: I fear nothing because God is always by my side.

Scripture: " People with integrity walk safely, but those who follow crooked paths will be exposed.." – Proverbs 10:9 (NLT)

Encouragement: Fear has no hold over me. I walk in confidence, knowing that God is my protector, my guide, and my strength. The assurance of His unwavering presence empowers me to face each day with courage and joy. In moments of uncertainty or challenge, I remind myself that I am not alone; God walks beside me, illuminating my path and offering me the wisdom to navigate through life's trials. When I embrace this truth, I am filled with a profound sense of peace that allows me to rise above my fears.

As I journey through life, I am equipped with the reassuring knowledge that I can face any situation head-on. God's love envelops me, dispelling the doubts and anxieties that may attempt to creep in. His integrity, as spoken in Proverbs 10:9, serves as a reminder that walking in faith aligns me with His righteousness, ensuring my safety as I follow the paths He has laid out for me. I can confidently move forward, knowing that my heart is anchored in His promises. With each step I take, I declare boldly that I am fearless because God is with me. My faith empowers me to trust in His plan, and as I do, I become a beacon of hope and strength for others in their journeys as well.

Week 25

Owning My Power

JUNE 17

DAY 169

I STAND IN MY POWER

Affirmation: I embrace the strength within me and walk confidently in my power.

Scripture: "God is within her, she will not fall; God will help her at break of day." – Psalm 46:5 (NIV)

Encouragement: I no longer shrink myself to fit into spaces where I am meant to shine. Each of us possesses a unique light, and it is essential to allow that light to shine unfettered. Recognizing that my power is not contingent upon the validation or approval of others liberates me from the constraints that once held me back. Instead of seeking permission to express myself fully, I choose to embrace my innate strength and abilities, allowing them to flow freely in every situation I encounter. By standing confidently in my power, I not only uplift myself but also inspire others to do the same.

In the face of challenges, I remind myself of the divine support that surrounds me. As Psalm 46:5 reassures us, "God is within her, she will not fall; God will help her at break of day." This promise of unwavering support instills a deep sense of faith in my journey. Knowing that the strength I hold within is bolstered by a higher power encourages me to tackle obstacles head-on with courage and resilience. Embracing this truth, I move forward with confidence, fully aware that I am equipped with everything I need to overcome adversity and achieve my dreams.

Today, I step boldly into my greatness, celebrating the beautiful strength that resides within me.

JUNE 18

DAY 170

I AM BOLD AND COURAGEOUS

Affirmation: I move through life with boldness, courage, and purpose.

Scripture: " Better the poor whose walk is blameless than the rich whose ways are perverse." – Proverbs 28:6 (NIV)

Encouragement: Today, I step boldly into the life that God has uniquely crafted for me. I recognize that my voice holds significance and my presence radiates strength. With each step I take, I embrace the courage that comes from knowing that I am walking in alignment with my divine purpose. Every challenge I encounter is an opportunity for growth, and I approach each moment with confidence, knowing that God empowers me to overcome. The affirmation of my boldness serves as a reminder that I am not alone; I am supported by a higher power that fuels my journey.

As I reflect on Proverbs 28:6, I am reminded that true richness lies not in material wealth but in living a life of integrity and authenticity. I choose to embody the values that bring me closer to the heart of God, understanding that my character is far more important than any worldly possession. With each conscious decision I make to move forward with courage and purpose, I am investing in a life that reflects God's love and truth. I encourage you to also embrace your unique journey; let your boldness shine bright as you pursue the path laid out for you.

Together, let us walk with unwavering confidence and demonstrate the power of a purposeful life.

JUNE 19

DAY 171

I RELEASE LIMITATIONS

Affirmation: I refuse to be held back by fear, doubt, or insecurity.

Scripture: "But godliness with contentment is great gain."– 1 Timothy 6:6 (NIV)

Encouragement: I refuse to live in fear of failure, understanding that every challenge I encounter serves as a stepping stone for personal growth. When obstacles arise, I choose to view them as opportunities to deepen my faith and resilience. I remind myself that with each trial, I am being equipped with the tools necessary to rise above my circumstances. It is through these experiences that I develop a stronger character and a clearer understanding of my potential. Embracing this journey allows me to unearth hidden strengths and discover new possibilities I never thought possible.

Equipped with the knowledge that I am not alone in my struggles, I lean into God's strength to face whatever comes my way. I hold fast to the promise that godliness paired with contentment brings great gain, as stated in 1 Timothy 6:6. This scripture encourages me to be at peace with my present situation while striving for growth and improvement. I stand on the truth that my worth is not tied to my accomplishments but rather to my identity as a beloved child of God. As I release limitations imposed by fear, doubt, or insecurity, I open myself to a life of abundance, purpose, and joy. With faith as my foundation, I can overcome anything that stands in my path.

JUNE 20

DAY 172

I AM UNSTOPPABLE

Affirmation: I have the power to create the life I desire.

Scripture: "With man this is impossible, but with God all things are possible." – Matthew 19:26 (NIV)

Encouragement: There is nothing that can stand in my way when I walk in faith. God has equipped me with all the tools and strength I need to overcome obstacles and pursue my dreams. When challenges arise, I am reminded of the divine support that surrounds me, empowering my every step. As I navigate life's journey, I can draw upon the assurance that I am not alone; with God by my side, I have the ability to transform every setback into an opportunity for growth. My faith becomes a shield against doubt and discouragement, allowing me to move forward with unwavering determination and courage.

Moreover, my belief in the possibilities that lie ahead rejuvenates my spirit and fuels my ambition. I am not just a passive participant in my life; I am a dynamic creator of my reality. The promise that "with God all things are possible" ignites a fire within me to dream bigger and aim higher. Each day, I embrace the power that comes from aligning my actions with my faith, reminding myself that I have the capability to manifest my desires. Together with God, I am truly unstoppable, and I will relentlessly pursue the life I envision, trusting that every step I take is guided by divine providence.

JUNE 21

DAY 173

MY POWER COMES FROM GOD

Affirmation: My strength is not my own—God empowers me daily.

Scripture: "But you will receive power when the Holy Spirit comes on you." – Acts 1:8 (NIV)

Encouragement: In moments when I feel overwhelmed or drained, I take a deep breath and remind myself that my strength is not derived from my own efforts or capabilities. Rather, it comes from the boundless well of God's power, which infuses me with resilience and courage. The assurance that His strength is perfected in my weakness is a comforting truth that allows me to embrace vulnerability without fear. I am not alone in my struggles; I have a divine source of strength that empowers me to rise above challenges. This understanding transforms the narrative of my life, shifting it from one of self-reliance to a reliance on the Almighty.

As I reflect on Acts 1:8, I am inspired by the promise that the Holy Spirit empowers us to navigate our daily lives with purpose and boldness. It's a beautiful reminder that I don't have to tackle my burdens in isolation; I can lean into the divine support that surrounds me. Each day, I can wake up with the confidence that God is equipping me with the strength I need to face whatever may come my way. With this truth in my heart, I move forward boldly, trusting that in my moments of weakness, I am truly made strong through Him.

JUNE 22

DAY 174

I AM A LIGHT IN THIS WORLD

Affirmation: I radiate strength, love, and confidence wherever I go.

Scripture: "It is God who arms me with strength and keeps my way secure." – Psalm 18:32 (NIV)

Encouragement: My journey is a profound testimony to the resilience of the human spirit and the transformative power of faith. Every challenge I face and overcome serves as a beacon of hope, illuminating the path for those around me. As I navigate through life, I recognize that my experiences not only shape me but also provide encouragement to others who may feel lost or overwhelmed. By embracing my own strength, love, and confidence, I become a source of inspiration, reminding those in my circle that they, too, possess the incredible ability to shine brightly in their own unique ways.

As I reflect on Psalm 18:32, I am reassured that God equips me with unwavering strength and secures my journey, allowing me to radiate positivity and encouragement wherever I go. I am reminded that my light is not just for myself; it is a gift meant to uplift those who may be struggling. When I share my story and allow my light to shine, I invite others to recognize their own power and potential. Together, we form a tapestry of resilience and hope, illuminating the world with the love and strength that God has bestowed upon us, and encouraging one another to step boldly into our destinies.

JUNE 23

DAY 175

I FULLY OWN WHO I AM

Affirmation: I stand tall in my identity, unapologetically myself.

Scripture: " When I consider your heavens, the work of your fingers, the moon and the stars, which you have set in place, what is mankind that you are mindful of them, human beings that you care for them? You have made them a little lower than the angels and crowned them with glory and honor." – Psalm 8:3-5 (NIV)

Encouragement: I am powerful, worthy, and enough—just as I am. Embracing our true identity is not simply an act of self-acceptance; it is a declaration of our inherent value and purpose. Each one of us is a unique creation, meticulously designed by a higher power, as reflected in Psalm 8:3-5. This scriptural passage serves as a profound reminder that we are not overlooked or insignificant; instead, we have been crowned with glory and honor, which highlights our worthiness. Acknowledging this truth allows us to stand tall in our identity, knowing that we have been intentionally woven into the fabric of creation. We possess the power to shape our lives and impact others positively, tapping into the gifts that God has bestowed upon us.

As we move through life, it is essential to hold on to the affirmation, "I stand tall in my identity, unapologetically myself." This statement is not merely a personal mantra; it reflects the strength that comes from knowing who we are and whose we are. When we declare our identity, we liberate ourselves from the need for validation from external sources, anchoring our self-worth in our relationship with the Creator. In a world that often pressures us to conform, we can draw courage from the understanding that we are made a little lower than the angels and yet so incredibly cherished. Let this truth fill your heart with confidence and empower you to navigate life boldly, fully embracing and celebrating the beautiful, unique individual that you are.

Week 26

Choosing Happiness

JUNE 24

DAY 176

HAPPINESS IS MY CHOICE

Affirmation: I choose joy and happiness in every moment.

Scripture: " It is a sin to despise one's neighbor, but blessed is the one who is kind to the needy." – Proverbs 14:21 (NIV)

Encouragement: In the face of life's many challenges, it's crucial to remember that happiness is a conscious choice we can make every day. Regardless of the obstacles or difficulties that come our way, we hold the power to choose joy and to embrace a positive mindset. It is important to acknowledge that our joy does not hinge upon our external circumstances. Instead, it is rooted in the deep peace and hope that God generously places within us. By focusing on the blessings we have, rather than the hardships we encounter, we can cultivate a spirit of gratitude and resilience that allows us to radiate happiness amidst uncertainty.

Moreover, Proverbs 14:21 reminds us of the profound impact our kindness can have on others. By choosing to be kind to those in need, we not only bless them but also foster an environment where joy can flourish. Acts of kindness often lead to greater fulfillment and happiness, as they create connections and deepen relationships within our communities. When we lift others and share compassion, we enhance our own happiness and affirm our commitment to joyful living. Let us seize each moment as an opportunity to spread joy and kindness, reinforcing the choice of happiness in our hearts and in the lives of those around us.

JUNE 25

DAY 177

MY HAPPINESS IS ROOTED IN GOD

Affirmation: My joy is unwavering because it comes from God.

Scripture: " You gave me life and showed me kindness, and in your providence watched over my spirit." – Job 10:12 (NIV)

Encouragement: True happiness transcends the fleeting pleasures of material possessions and the superficial validation from temporary successes. It is rooted deeply in my relationship with God, who is the wellspring of joy that never runs dry. When I seek fulfillment in the external world, I often find that it leaves me feeling empty and longing for more. However, when I nurture my connection with God, I discover an unwavering joy that withstands life's challenges and uncertainties. His love and kindness affirm my worth and purpose, grounding me in a happiness that is anchored in something far greater than my circumstances.

God's providence continually watches over my spirit, reminding me that I am cherished and valued beyond measure. As Job so poignantly illustrates, acknowledging His active presence in my life allows me to embrace the joy that comes from being known and cared for by the Creator. Even amid trials and tribulations, I can find solace in the fact that my happiness is not contingent upon the highs and lows of life but instead flows from a deep, abiding relationship with Him. In cultivating this connection, I can experience a profound sense of peace and joy that transforms my outlook on life, enriching my spirit and allowing me to share that happiness with others.

JUNE 26

DAY 178

I RELEASE NEGATIVITY

Affirmation: I let go of negativity and focus on the good in my life.

Scripture: "Though you have not seen him, you love him; and even though you do not see him now, you believe in him and are filled with an inexpressible and glorious joy." – 1 Peter 1:8 (NIV)

Encouragement: Today, let us consciously choose to release any negativity that may linger in our thoughts or actions. The world can often present us with challenges and discouraging moments, but it is within our power to redirect our focus toward the positive aspects that enrich our lives. By embracing this decision, we cultivate an atmosphere of gratitude and appreciation for the love, beauty, and blessings surrounding us. As we actively shift our perspective, we engage in a transformative practice that invites joy and fulfillment into our daily existence.

Moreover, remember the profound message found in 1 Peter 1:8, which speaks to the immense joy that comes from believing and trusting in something greater than ourselves. Even when we find ourselves facing unseen trials or circumstances, there lies a remarkable joy rooted in faith that can uplift our spirits and energize our hearts. By allowing this divine joy to permeate our lives, we naturally repel negativity and instead draw in the light and love that sustain us. Let today be a reminder that, despite any negativity that may attempt to encroach upon our minds, we can steadfastly nurture a heart full of hope and joy.

JUNE 27

DAY 179

I AM GRATEFUL FOR EVERY MOMENT

Affirmation: Gratitude fills my heart and brings me joy.

Scripture: " So I strive always to keep my conscience clear before God and man." – Acts 24:16 (NIV)

Encouragement: When I focus on gratitude, I create space for happiness and positivity to flourish in my life. Cultivating an attitude of thankfulness allows me to shift my perspective, enabling me to see the beauty in even the smallest moments. Each morning I wake up with the intention to recognize and appreciate the myriad gifts that surround me, from the warmth of the sun on my skin to the laughter shared with loved ones. By cherishing these moments, I invite a profound sense of joy into my heart. Gratitude doesn't just remind me of what I have; it helps me to understand that life is filled with opportunities for joy, no matter the challenges I may face.

Moreover, embracing gratitude is a conscious choice that transforms my interactions with others and deepens my relationship with God. With a heart full of thankfulness, I strive to keep my conscience clear, aligning my actions with my values and principles, as highlighted in Acts 24:16. This commitment to clarity not only honors my relationships with those around me but also reflects my desire to live a life that is pleasing to God. By acknowledging the blessings in my life, I am empowered to navigate each day with purpose and clarity, reinforcing my ability to be present in every moment. Gratitude serves not only as a reminder of what is good but as a guiding force that propels me toward a fulfilling and joyful existence.

JUNE 28

DAY 180

I ATTRACT JOY

Affirmation: My positive mindset attracts joy and peace.

Scripture: "A cheerful heart is good medicine, but a crushed spirit dries up the bones." – Proverbs 17:22 (NIV)

Encouragement: My joy radiates and uplifts those around me, creating an atmosphere of warmth and connection. When I actively cultivate a positive mindset, I'm not only nurturing my own happiness but also sharing that light with others. Just as a cheerful heart can serve as good medicine, my joyful approach to life encourages others to seek out their own moments of joy. It's incredible how a simple smile or a kind word can brighten someone else's day and foster a sense of community. By choosing joy, I'm making a conscious effort to uplift others, thereby creating a ripple effect of positivity that extends beyond myself.

Moreover, focusing on positivity allows me to construct a life filled with happiness and peace, where challenges appear lighter and more manageable. It's essential to remember, as Proverbs 17:22 reminds us, that a cheerful heart holds tremendous power against negativity. When my spirit is strong and joyous, I cultivate resilience against life's inevitable difficulties. The more I embrace joy, the more I attract it into my life, creating an environment where peace thrives. By aligning my thoughts with positivity, I open myself up to new possibilities, experiences, and deeper connections with those around me. My joy not only enriches my own life but also acts as a beacon of hope for others navigating their own journeys.

JUNE 29

DAY 181

I CHOOSE TO SMILE

Affirmation: My smile is a reflection of my inner joy.

Scripture: "A happy heart makes the face cheerful, but heartache crushes the spirit." – Proverbs 15:13 (NIV)

Encouragement: A simple smile can change not only my day but also the lives of those around me in profound ways. It serves as a universal language that transcends words, effortlessly conveying warmth, understanding, and connection. When I offer a smile, I not only uplift my own spirit but also create an inviting atmosphere for others. This gentle reminder of joy can be contagious, inspiring someone else to reflect that joy back, thereby igniting a ripple effect of positivity. By consciously choosing to smile, I am embracing the radiant joy that resides within, allowing it to shine brightly and touch the hearts of those I encounter.

Moreover, the wisdom found in Proverbs 15:13 reinforces this truth, illustrating that our inner state profoundly influences our outer expression. Aligning my heart with happiness cultivates a cheerful demeanor that reflects my joy to the world. In moments of struggle or heartache, it becomes vital to remember the power of my smile and its ability to lift not just my own spirit but also the spirits of others. I am reminded that a happy heart can rise above challenges and pain, fostering resilience and hope. By choosing to embody joy, I not only strengthen my own heart but also contribute to a more joyful, connected community around me.

JUNE 30

DAY 182

JOY IS MY BIRTHRIGHT

Affirmation: God created me to live in joy and abundance.

Scripture: "You have filled my heart with greater joy." – Psalm 4:7 (NIV)

Encouragement: Joy is not merely a fleeting emotion or a luxury that we may experience occasionally; it is fundamentally my birthright, intricately woven into the very fabric of my existence. Each day is a gift, offering a fresh opportunity to embrace the love, peace, and happiness that God intends for me. By choosing to recognize and cultivate joy in my life, I align myself with the divine purpose that God has so graciously bestowed upon me. This inherent joy serves as a reminder that I am worthy of experiencing abundance and fulfillment in every aspect of my life.

Moreover, as I reflect on the profound truth found in Psalm 4:7, I am comforted by the reminder that God has filled my heart with greater joy. This assurance does not only elevate my spirit but empowers me to share that joy with those around me. It is a powerful and contagious energy, capable of lighting up the darkest corners of life. By acknowledging that joy is an integral part of who I am, I can navigate my circumstances with hope and resilience and inspire others to do the same. Embracing this promise of joy creates a ripple effect, reinforcing my belief that I am truly created to live in joy and abundance, every single day.

Week 27

Walking In Freedom

JULY 1

DAY 183

I AM FREE IN CHRIST

Affirmation: I walk in the freedom that Christ has given me.

Scripture: "Dear children, let us not love with words or speech but with actions and in truth." – 1 John 3:18 (NIV)

Encouragement: Embracing the freedom that Christ has given me means letting go of the chains of fear, doubt, and insecurity that once held me captive. I remind myself daily that I am a beloved child of God, free to experience life to its fullest. The confidence that comes from knowing Christ's love allows me to step into new opportunities and challenges with courage, casting aside any hesitations rooted in past experiences. Each moment presents a chance to act with purpose and intent, living out the truth of who I am in Him. I choose to be a beacon of His love and grace, demonstrating my faith through my actions and the integrity of my heart.

With the wisdom of 1 John 3:18 guiding me, I understand that love must be expressed in ways that transcend mere words. It is in my actions that the essence of Christ's freedom is revealed—not only for me but also to those around me. Today, I commit to living authentically, allowing my faith to inspire others to break free from their own bonds of fear and doubt. By embodying the love and grace I have received, I strive to create an environment where everyone can feel empowered to embrace their own freedom in Christ. Together, let us walk boldly in the light, uplifting one another as we navigate this journey of life, bound only by the promises of God's unending love.

JULY 2

DAY 184

I RELEASE WHAT NO LONGER SERVES ME

Affirmation: I let go of what does not align with my purpose and peace.

Scripture: "For those who find me find life and receive favor from the Lord." – Proverbs 8:35 (NIV)

Encouragement: I refuse to carry burdens that do not belong to me. Each day presents an opportunity to evaluate what we hold onto, and it's essential to distinguish between what uplifts us and what weighs us down. I release past hurts, worries, and expectations that do not serve my highest good, understanding that clinging to these negative influences only distracts me from my purpose and inner peace. By choosing to let go, I make space for healing and growth, allowing God's light to fill the gaps where darkness once lingered. This conscious act of release invigorates my spirit and reconnects me to a deeper sense of clarity and purpose.

As I take this step forward in faith, I trust God to take care of me and to lead me toward the life He envisions for me. The scripture reminds me that in finding God, I discover true life and favor. This serves as a powerful acknowledgment that when I align myself with His will and let go of what does not contribute to my well-being, I am opening myself up to blessings beyond measure. I embrace the freedom that comes from surrendering my burdens, knowing that God's grace allows me to step into a future filled with hope, joy, and abundant possibilities. In this journey, I actively seek the peace that comes from trusting in God's divine guidance, nurturing my soul and fostering resilience in the face of life's challenges.

JULY 3

DAY 185

I AM NOT DEFINED BY MY PAST

Affirmation: My past does not limit my future—I am moving forward in victory.

Scripture: "Forget the former things; do not dwell on the past." – Isaiah 43:18 (NIV)

Encouragement: I am no longer a prisoner of past mistakes, failures, or disappointments. My history does not dictate my identity or define my potential. Instead, I choose to see each day as an opportunity for growth and renewal. God has lovingly extended to me a new beginning, one that invites me to leave behind the burdens of yesteryear. I embrace this fresh start with open arms, confident that each step I take is leading me toward greater purpose and fulfillment. I am committed to seeking the abundant life that lies before me, anchored in faith and trust in God's plan for my journey.

As I reflect on the promise of Isaiah 43:18, I remind myself that my focus should not linger on what once was but rather on the incredible future that awaits me. With each passing moment, I am moving forward in victory, shedding the limitations of my past. I will not allow regret or sorrow to hold me back any longer. Instead, I will harness the lessons learned and channel them into positive action. My future is filled with hope and purpose, and I have the strength to pursue it wholeheartedly. By aligning my thoughts and actions with God's vision for my life, I am empowered to walk boldly into the new chapters that He is writing for me.

JULY 4

DAY 186

I WALK IN CONFIDENCE AND STRENGTH

Affirmation: I am strong, bold, and unshaken by life's challenges.

Scripture: "For the grace of God has appeared that offers salvation to all people." – Titus 2:11 (NIV)

Encouragement: In this journey of life, it is vital to remember that we are not defined by the challenges we face but rather by the strength we find within ourselves and through our faith. I have come to embrace this truth wholeheartedly; I no longer shrink back or hide from the obstacles that cross my path. With a renewed sense of purpose, I walk with my head held high, fully aware that God has equipped me with all the tools I need to not only endure but to thrive in the midst of adversity. My confidence springs from the knowledge that I am never alone—His grace surrounds me, providing courage and resilience in every circumstance.

As I reflect on the powerful message from Titus 2:11, I am reminded that salvation and grace are gifts offered freely to all. This divine assurance fosters my unwavering boldness, allowing me to stand firm against life's uncertainties and pressures. Each day presents an opportunity to embody the strength that God instills within me, transforming fear into courage and doubt into determination. I embrace the reality that my confidence is deeply rooted in Him, and I choose to carry this truth into every aspect of my life, moving forward with the assurance that I am truly strong, bold, and unshaken, ready to confront any challenge with grace and poise.

JULY 5

DAY 187

I EMBRACE MY AUTHENTIC SELF

Affirmation: I love and accept myself just as I am.

Scripture: "May the favor of the Lord our God rest on us; establish the work of our hands for us— yes, establish the work of our hands." – Psalm 90:17 (NIV)

Encouragement: In a world that often encourages comparison and competition, it's essential to remember the profound value of embracing one's authentic self. Each of us is uniquely crafted with gifts and experiences that contribute to the rich tapestry of humanity. When I choose to love and accept myself exactly as I am, I break free from the shackles of societal expectations and external validation. This journey toward self-acceptance is immensely empowering; it allows me to step into my true identity without fear or hesitation. By shedding the need for approval from others, I can fully appreciate my distinct qualities and the purpose I serve in this world.

Moreover, as Psalm 90:17 reminds us, when we embrace our authentic selves, we invite the favor of the Lord into our lives, allowing Him to establish and bless the work of our hands. There is strength in recognizing that our value doesn't diminish in comparison to anyone else. Instead, it shines even brighter as we embrace our individuality. Each step we take toward self-acceptance is a celebration of our divine creation and potential. By focusing on our unique journey, we can confidently contribute our talents and gifts to the world, finding joy and fulfillment in the process. Let us continue to celebrate our authenticity and trust in the path that God has laid before us.

JULY 6

DAY 188

I AM FEARLESS IN PURSUING MY PURPOSE

Affirmation: I pursue my God-given purpose with boldness and determination.

Scripture: " Watch ye and pray, lest ye enter into temptation. The spirit truly is ready, but the flesh is weak." – Mark 14:38 (KJV)

Encouragement: Nothing can stop me from fulfilling the unique and powerful purpose that God has set before me. Despite the challenges and uncertainties that may arise, I am determined to rise above them with unwavering faith. I refuse to let fear dictate my steps or allow distractions to divert my attention from the path He has illuminated for me. Instead, I choose to walk boldly, embracing the courage that comes from knowing that God is my steadfast guide. With each step I take, I am reassured that I am moving forward in alignment with His divine will.

As I pursue my God-given purpose, I hold tightly to the truth that my spirit is ready, even when my flesh may feel weak. I will remain vigilant in prayer and watchfulness, continually seeking strength and wisdom from God to overcome temptations and obstacles. It is in the moments of doubt that I will remind myself of the affirmation I declare daily: I pursue my purpose with boldness and determination. With each challenge I face, I will lean into my faith, trusting that God's powerful presence equips and empowers me to achieve all that He has called me to do.

JULY 7

DAY 189

MY FREEDOM INSPIRES OTHERS

Affirmation: As I walk in freedom, I encourage others to do the same.

Scripture: "You, my brothers and sisters, were called to be free. But do not use your freedom to indulge the flesh; rather, serve one another humbly in love." – Galatians 5:13 (NIV)

Encouragement: My journey is not solely a personal endeavor; it serves as a powerful testimony that has the potential to inspire those around me to pursue their own paths of liberation. When I embrace my freedom and live authentically, I become a beacon of hope, demonstrating that it is indeed possible to break free from the chains that bind us. Each step I take towards my own freedom reflects a commitment not just to myself, but to the larger community, encouraging others to explore the depths of their own potential and stand tall in their truths. By living boldly and with purpose, I create a ripple effect that empowers others, showing them that they too can embrace their God-given right to be free.

Moreover, as I choose to walk in freedom, I remember the call to serve one another humbly in love, as outlined in Galatians 5:13. This passage reminds me that true freedom is not simply about personal indulgence; it is about using my experience and insights to uplift and encourage those around me. In doing so, I cultivate an environment where others feel safe to express their own struggles and victories. My life, illuminated by love and humility, can inspire others to recognize their worth and to take courageous steps toward their own freedom. By shining my light, I invite others into a collaborative journey of growth, healing, and liberation, where together we can celebrate the beauty of our shared humanity.

Week 28

Embracing My Uniqueness

JULY 8

DAY 190

I AM FEARFULLY AND WONDERFULLY MADE

Affirmation: I am beautifully created by God, and I celebrate my uniqueness.

Scripture: "From him the whole body, joined and held together by every supporting ligament, grows and builds itself up in love, as each part does its work."– Ephesians 4:16 (NIV)

Encouragement: I am not a mistake; rather, I am a unique creation, thoughtfully designed with purpose in mind. Every detail about me, from the smallest characteristic to the grandest trait, reflects the intentionality of a loving Creator who knows me intimately. I choose to embrace the beauty of my individuality, recognizing that it adds richness and diversity to the tapestry of life. Each strength, flaw, and quirk contributes to the masterpiece that I am, and I celebrate this divine craftsmanship.

Moreover, just as Ephesians 4:16 reminds us, we are interconnected and essential parts of a larger body, and our unique contributions matter deeply. As I acknowledge my own worth and celebrate my uniqueness, I also encourage others to do the same. When we honor our individuality and celebrate the differences among us, we grow and flourish together in love. By fulfilling our distinct roles, we build each other up and create a supportive community where everyone can thrive in their authenticity. Let us rejoice in our differences and recognize that they are what make us beautifully and wonderfully made.

JULY 9

DAY 191

MY DIFFERENCES MAKE ME SPECIAL

Affirmation: What sets me apart is what makes me extraordinary.

Scripture: "Take delight in the Lord, and he will give you the desires of your heart."– Psalm 37:4 (NIV)

Encouragement: I will not shrink back or hide who I am, for I am beautifully and wonderfully made. Each unique trait I possess is a reflection of the intricate design of my Creator. My differences are not flaws; they are my strengths, gifts gifted to me to enrich my life and the lives of those around me. Embracing and celebrating these attributes allows me to contribute my distinct perspective and talents. I am compelled to walk confidently in my uniqueness, allowing my authentic self to shine brightly and inspire those I encounter.

As I delight in the Lord, I recognize that He takes joy in my individuality and encourages me to embrace it fully. The more I acknowledge my differences as divine strengths, the more I experience the fulfillment of my heart's desires. I am reminded that God's love and acceptance empower me to be unapologetically myself, and in this space of authenticity, I am able to bless others in ways only I can. By standing tall in my uniqueness, I not only honor the life I have been given but also invite others to celebrate their own differences, creating a beautiful tapestry of diverse and extraordinary lives.

JULY 10

DAY 192

I CELEBRATE MY INDIVIDUALITY

Affirmation: I choose to love every part of myself just as I am.

Scripture: "But by the grace of God I am what I am, and his grace to me was not without effect." – 1 Corinthians 15:10 (NIV)

Encouragement: I no longer seek to fit in—I choose to stand out! Embracing my individuality is a profound act of self-love, reflecting the unique path and experiences that have shaped who I am today. I recognize that every quirk, every challenge, and every success contributes to the beautiful tapestry of my life. By honoring my journey, I not only celebrate my own distinct qualities but also inspire others to recognize and cherish their own unique selves. This commitment to authenticity allows me to fully embrace the grace that God has bestowed upon me, empowering me to shine brightly as I am, unapologetically.

As I meditate on the words of 1 Corinthians 15:10, I am reminded that my uniqueness is a precious gift from God. His grace has intricately woven my identity, allowing me to blossom in my own way. I choose to acknowledge that I am wonderfully made, and I embrace the courage to express my true self. In doing so, I invite others to join me in a celebration of individuality, fostering a community where we uplift and support one another in our journeys. Together, we can create an environment where we all feel valued and accepted for who we truly are, reinforcing the beautiful truth that we are all masterpieces in our own right.

JULY 11

DAY 193

MY STORY IS A GIFT

Affirmation: My journey is unique, and it carries a powerful testimony.

Scripture: "They triumphed over him by the blood of the Lamb and by the word of their testimony." – Revelation 12:11 (NIV)

Encouragement: My story has incredible power, and it serves as a testament to the resilience and strength that I carry within me. Every moment of my journey, from the joyous peaks to the challenging valleys, has contributed to the person I am today. I have learned that my experiences—both the triumphs and the trials—are not just for me; they are meant to be shared. By embracing the uniqueness of my path, I honor the lessons learned and the growth achieved. My truth is not just a narrative; it is a beacon of hope that can resonate with others, encouraging them to see the beauty in their own journeys as well.

As I reflect on Revelation 12:11, I am reminded that my testimony is a powerful weapon. By sharing my story, I align myself with the truth that has the ability to transform lives. I will not shy away from the experiences that have shaped me; instead, I will present them with boldness and authenticity. This journey is not just mine; it is a gift that I can offer to the world, illuminating the paths of others who may be struggling or searching for guidance. In doing so, I stand firm in faith, knowing that my narrative carries the potential to inspire and uplift those around me.

JULY 12

DAY 194

I REFUSE TO COMPARE MYSELF TO OTHERS

Affirmation: I release comparison and embrace contentment in who I am.

Scripture: " Better the poor whose walk is blameless than a fool whose lips are perverse.." – Proverbs 19:1 (NIV)

Encouragement: I am not in competition with anyone else; my value comes from being the unique individual that God designed me to be. In a world that often encourages comparison, I choose to release that mindset and embrace contentment in who I am. Each of us has our own distinct journey, with divinely ordained paths tailored specifically for us. As I focus on my own walk, I can appreciate the beauty and growth that comes from my experiences, recognizing that I have been crafted for my own purpose, with strengths and gifts that are entirely mine.

By committing to this perspective, I can walk confidently in my own lane, nurturing my gifts and talents without the distractions of what others are doing. Just as Proverbs 19:1 reminds us, it is far better to lead a life of integrity and authenticity than to chase after superficial comparisons. My journey is uniquely mine, and I will honor it by staying focused on God's calling in my life. Let us celebrate our individuality and the extraordinary plans God has for each of us, finding joy in the journey rather than rivalry in comparison.

JULY 13

DAY 195

I SHINE MY LIGHT BRIGHTLY

Affirmation: I will not dim my light to make others comfortable.

Scripture: "To him who is able to keep you from stumbling and to present you before his glorious presence without fault and with great joy."– Jude 1:24 (NIV)

Encouragement: I was created to shine, a radiant reflection of my individuality and potential. Each one of us possesses a unique light that adds color and diversity to the world. It is tantamount to our growth and fulfillment that we refuse to hide who we are or minimize our gifts. When I embrace my true self, I not only honor my existence, but I also set a powerful example for those around me. By shining brightly, I encourage others to unlock their potential and embrace their own individuality, reminding them that their light is just as important as mine.

Shining my light involves stepping into my authentic self with confidence, knowing that I have been wonderfully made. I will not allow the fear of discomfort in others to dim my brilliance because I understand there is great strength in authenticity. Just as the scripture from Jude reminds us of God's ability to keep us steadfast and present us joyfully, I, too, can stand firm in my identity, unafraid to illuminate the path for myself and others. By shining my light, I contribute to a world where everyone feels empowered to live out their truth, fostering a community that celebrates uniqueness and shares in the joy of authentic living.

JULY 14

DAY 196

GOD LOVES ME JUST AS I AM

Affirmation: I am fully loved, accepted, and cherished by God.

Scripture: "See what great love the Father has lavished on us, that we should be called children of God!" – 1 John 3:1 (NIV)

Encouragement: There is profound freedom in recognizing that I do not need to alter my being to earn love or acceptance. God's love for me is not based on my performance, appearance, or any external metrics of worth. Instead, it is an unwavering and unconditional love that fully embraces me as I am. This realization allows me to release any burdens of trying to conform to others' expectations or societal standards. I am reminded that my identity as a beloved child of God is inherent, not something I must achieve or prove.

As I hold onto this truth, I can move through life with a renewed sense of self and purpose, knowing that I am cherished just as I am. The great love lavished upon me by the Father fills my heart with joy, empowering me to embrace my uniqueness and authenticity with confidence. In this space of acceptance, I can not only celebrate my individuality but also extend that same love to others, inviting everyone to feel the warmth of God's acceptance. By embracing who I truly am, I become a beacon of grace and love in the world, reflecting the very nature of God's heart toward all of His creation.

Week 29

My Voice Matters

JULY 15

DAY 197:

MY WORDS CARRY POWER

Affirmation: My voice has impact, and I use it with confidence.

Scripture: "The tongue has the power of life and death, and those who love it will eat its fruit." – Proverbs 18:21 (NIV)

Encouragement: I recognize the profound power of my words in shaping not just my own reality but also the lives of those around me. Every time I choose to speak, I am either sowing seeds of positivity and encouragement or allowing negativity to creep in. I understand that my voice has immense potential and with that comes the responsibility to use it wisely. By consciously deciding to speak life over myself and others, I can create an atmosphere filled with hope and inspiration. It's important for me to remember that my words can be a force for change, capable of uplifting spirits and igniting passion. Therefore, I embrace the power within my voice and commit to wielding it with intention and love.

As Proverbs 18:21 reminds us, the tongue holds the capability of both life and death, emphasizing the significance of how we communicate. When I speak words of affirmation, encouragement, and trust, I not only contribute to my own growth but also empower those around me to realize their potential. I become a catalyst for positivity, nurturing relationships and fostering an environment where everyone can thrive. Today, I choose to embrace the truth that my voice carries impact. By using it with confidence and conviction, I can inspire not only my journey but also the journeys of others, ultimately creating a ripple effect that spreads hope and encouragement far beyond just my immediate circle.

JULY 16

DAY 198

I SPEAK MY TRUTH BOLDLY

Affirmation: My truth deserves to be heard, and I share it fearlessly.

Scripture: "Keep me as the apple of your eye; hide me in the shadow of your wings." – Psalm 17:8 (NIV)

Encouragement: I will no longer be quiet or silence myself. My experiences, thoughts, and emotions are valid and deserve to be acknowledged. Each moment of my journey has shaped me, and it is through sharing my truth that I honor the lessons I've learned along the way. By embracing my authenticity, I not only empower myself but also create a space for others to do the same. I recognize that my voice has the power to inspire and uplift, and I will use it fearlessly to contribute to the world around me.

In this season of boldness, I draw strength from the promise found in Psalm 17:8. As I rest in the comfort of being the "apple of His eye," I am reminded that I am cherished and protected. Under the shadow of His wings, I gain the confidence to express my truth with courage and grace. I am compelled by love to share my story, and I trust that my honest reflections will resonate with others, creating connections that foster understanding and compassion. Each time I speak up, I affirm my worth and embrace the beauty of vulnerability, knowing that this journey is not just for me, but for all who seek authenticity and hope.

JULY 17

DAY 199

MY VOICE IS A GIFT

Affirmation: I use my voice as a tool to bring hope and encouragement.

Scripture: "Let your conversation be always full of grace, seasoned with salt, so that you may know how to answer everyone." – Colossians 4:6 (NIV)

Encouragement: My words have the incredible potential to heal, uplift, and inspire not only myself but also those who are fortunate enough to hear them. Each time I open my mouth to speak, I have the opportunity to create an atmosphere filled with hope and positivity. I choose to use my voice wisely, allowing it to resonate with kindness and compassion. By being intentional about the words I share, I can bring light into the lives of others, brightening their day even in the midst of challenges. As I engage in conversations, I remind myself that every word is a chance to either build up or tear down, and I aspire to be a force for encouragement and healing.

In a world where negativity can sometimes dominate, I recognize the power of uplifting speech to create a ripple effect of motivation and support. My voice is not merely a tool for communication; it's a vessel for transformation. When I speak with grace and intention, as emphasized in Colossians 4:6, I become a conduit for divine influence, responding to others with understanding and love. As I navigate my conversations, I commit to being mindful of the impact my words can have, striving to be a source of light and hope for everyone around me. This journey encourages me to cultivate a mindset that values grace, ensuring my speech reflects the profound love and encouragement that I wish to share with the world.

JULY 18

DAY 200

I ADVOCATE FOR MYSELF AND OTHERS

Affirmation: I stand up for what is right and use my voice to bring awareness.

Scripture: "Speak up for those who cannot speak for themselves, for the rights of all who are destitute." – Proverbs 31:8 (NIV)

Encouragement: I recognize that my voice holds immense power, capable of sparking significant change both in my own life and in the lives of those around me. It is essential to remember that silence in the face of injustice can perpetuate struggles not only for ourselves but for the vulnerable individuals who lack the means to defend themselves. By choosing to speak up, I embrace the responsibility that comes with my voice, allowing it to be a beacon of hope and awareness. Each time I advocate for myself or others, I contribute to creating a ripple effect that can transform despair into action, shining a light on those who invariably feel unseen and unheard.

Moreover, I commit to being a steadfast ally, intentionally using my words to uplift and empower those who may feel powerless. It is through this courageous act of advocacy that I honor the wisdom of

Proverbs 31:8, reminding myself that speaking up for the rights of the destitute is not merely a duty but a profound privilege. In doing so, I cultivate a sense of community and solidarity, encouraging others to join me in this vital pursuit of justice. Together, we can amplify our voices, fostering an environment where change is not just a possibility but a reality, and where every individual feels valued and heard.

JULY 19

DAY 201

MY VOICE REFLECTS MY STRENGTH

Affirmation: I am strong, and my voice carries authority and wisdom.

Scripture: "She speaks with wisdom, and faithful instruction is on her tongue." – Proverbs 31:26 (NIV)

Encouragement: My strength is truly reflected in my words, as they carry the power to uplift, inspire, and transform. When I speak, I do so with wisdom, kindness, and conviction, understanding that each word has the potential to impact those around me. I am reminded that my voice is not just an instrument of communication but a powerful tool that can influence the hearts and minds of others. In every conversation and interaction, I strive to share messages that embody truth and encouragement, resonating with the authority that comes from a place of inner strength.

As I embrace this truth, I recognize that my voice does not only convey information; it carries the warmth of compassion and the clarity of insight. I aim to be a source of faithful instruction, firmly grounded in the understanding that my words matter. Through attentive listening and thoughtful responses, I intend to nurture relationships and foster an environment where wisdom thrives. By embodying the strength of Proverbs 31:26, I commit to using my voice to reflect not just my own authority, but also the wisdom I have gathered along my journey. In doing so, I empower not only myself but also those who are fortunate enough to hear my voice.

JULY 20

DAY 202

I SHARE MY STORY WITH CONFIDENCE

Affirmation: My testimony is powerful, and I share it boldly.

Scripture: "They triumphed over him by the blood of the Lamb and by the word of their testimony." – Revelation 12:11 (NIV)

Encouragement: My journey holds immense power and purpose, intertwining both the struggles I have faced and the victories I have achieved. Each experience has uniquely shaped me and crafted a narrative that is worthy of sharing. When I openly share my story, I not only validate my own experiences but also create a space for others who may be walking a similar path to feel understood and empowered. By revealing my authentic self, I invite others to do the same, fostering a community built on shared truths and mutual support. Sharing my story becomes an act of courage and love, reminding everyone that we are not alone.

As I embrace my testimony, I speak it with confidence, recognizing that it is a powerful tool for transformation. My words carry the ability to inspire and uplift, as they resonate with those who may feel isolated in their struggles. In sharing the narrative of how I have triumphed over adversity, I not only reinforce my own resilience but also encourage others to find strength in their own stories. Each time I testify to the goodness and faithfulness that has accompanied me throughout my journey, I affirm the truth of Revelation 12:11, which tells us that we triumph through the blood of the Lamb and the word of our testimony. With every shared story, I contribute to a powerful legacy of hope and healing that can uplift the weary hearts around me.

JULY 21

DAY 203

GOD HAS GIVEN ME A VOICE FOR A REASON

Affirmation: My voice is a gift from God, and I use it with purpose.

Scripture: "The Sovereign Lord has given me a well-instructed tongue, to know the word that sustains the weary." – Isaiah 50:4 (NIV)

Encouragement: I am not here by accident—God has given me a voice for a reason that is far greater than I may fully understand. My voice is a powerful instrument for change and healing, and I refuse to squander it. Every word I speak holds the potential to uplift, inspire, and encourage those around me. Whether I am offering a kind word to a friend in need, sharing wisdom with colleagues, or simply expressing love to my family, I acknowledge that my voice matters. It is a divine gift, entrusted to me so that I can be a beacon of hope and a source of strength for others in their times of struggle.

As I reflect on the profound truth of Isaiah 50:4, I understand that the Sovereign Lord has equipped me with a well-instructed tongue. I recognize that I have been uniquely prepared to know the words that sustain the weary. This responsibility inspires me to choose my words wisely and to speak life into every situation. I commit to using my voice not only to express my own thoughts and feelings but also to serve the needs of others. In doing so, I take an active role in fulfilling God's purpose for my life, knowing that each word I share can bring comfort, courage, and encouragement to someone who may need it most.

Week 30

Loving Every Part Of Me

JULY 22

DAY 204

I LOVE MYSELF AS I AM

Affirmation: I embrace and love myself fully, just as I am.

Scripture: " Don't you know that you yourselves are God's temple and that God's Spirit dwells in your midst?" – 1 Corinthians 3:16 (NIV)

Encouragement: Self-love starts with me, and it is a fundamental aspect of our spiritual journey. I choose to embrace and accept myself wholly, recognizing that every part of my being is worthy of love and respect. This includes my strengths that make me unique, the challenges that shape my character, and the journey I am on that reflects my growth. We often underestimate our inherent worth and the beauty of being authentically ourselves. By affirming my self-love, I acknowledge that I am deserving of compassion, understanding, and acceptance, irrespective of my imperfections. This journey of loving myself fully allows me to cultivate a deeper sense of peace and fulfillment in my life.

In 1 Corinthians 3:16, we are reminded that we are God's temple, and His Spirit dwells within us. This profound truth reinforces the significance of honoring ourselves as vessels of divine love. By nurturing a loving relationship with ourselves, we create a sanctuary for the Spirit within us to thrive. When I recognize my worth, it empowers me to extend that same love to others, fostering a community of compassion and understanding. Embracing myself as I am not only enhances my own well-being but also enables me to shine brightly in the world around me. Therefore, I commit to loving myself fully, understanding that this love—which is rooted in my identity as a child of God—will radiate outward, positively affecting all those I encounter.

JULY 23

DAY 205

MY BODY IS A TEMPLE

Affirmation: I honor my body and treat it with love and care.

Scripture: "Do you not know that your bodies are temples of the Holy Spirit, who is in you, whom you have received from God? You are not your own." – 1 Corinthians 6:19 (NIV)

Encouragement: My body is a sacred vessel, meticulously crafted with purpose, and it is my responsibility to nurture it with unwavering kindness, intentional rest, and mindful care. Every part of me is not only valuable but is also deserving of deep love and respect. By honoring my body, I acknowledge the divine presence of the Holy Spirit within me, as described in 1 Corinthians 6:19. This realization compels me to treat myself with the same compassion and grace that I extend to others. I will choose to engage in activities that rejuvenate my spirit and fortify my physical health, recognizing that my well-being is intrinsically connected to my capacity to serve and love those around me.

Furthermore, understanding that I am not my own, but a cherished creation of God, inspires me to elevate my self-care practices. As I reflect on this truth, I choose to focus on what nourishes me holistically—spiritually, mentally, and physically. By doing so, I am not only honoring my body as a temple but also embracing the unique journey that accompanies my existence. I commit to cherishing my body as an integral part of my divine purpose, striving to create a lifestyle that embodies health, joy, and love. This commitment will ultimately empower me to live fully and authentically, modeling the love I wish to see in the world and glorifying the gift of life that I have been given.

JULY 24

DAY 206

I RELEASE SELF-DOUBT

Affirmation: I let go of negative self-talk and embrace confidence.

Scripture: "Let us throw off everything that hinders and the sin that so easily entangles. And let us run with perseverance the race marked out for us." – Hebrews 12:1 (NIV)

Encouragement: I no longer allow self-doubt to control me; instead, I actively choose to embrace a mindset rooted in confidence and self-acceptance. Each time a negative thought creeps in, I consciously replace it with a powerful declaration of my true worth. I affirm to myself that I am enough, just as I am, and I refuse to let any whispers of inadequacy dictate my actions or my perceptions. This intentional shift not only uplifts my spirit, but also empowers me to pursue my dreams with renewed vigor. As I shed the burdens of self-doubt, I open myself up to the possibilities that lie ahead and trust in my ability to navigate the challenges of life.

In embracing this journey of self-acceptance, I draw strength from the wisdom found in Hebrews 12:1. The scripture encourages me to shed those things that hinder my progress, including the sin of negative self-talk that so easily entangles me. Like a runner preparing for a race, I am reminded to lighten my load and focus on the path laid before me. With perseverance, I stride forward, empowered by my newfound confidence and guided by the knowledge that I am equipped with everything I need to succeed. Each step I take is a testament to my resilience, and I am grateful for the strength that flows through me as I continue my race with faith and determination.

JULY 25

DAY 207

I SEE MYSELF THROUGH GOD'S EYES

Affirmation: I am beautiful, valuable, and created in His image.

Scripture: " Many seek an audience with a ruler, but it is from the Lord that one gets justice." – Proverbs 29:26 (NIV)

Encouragement: When I look in the mirror, I see not just my physical appearance, but a beautiful reflection of God's handiwork. Each feature, each curve, and each imperfection tells a story of His design. I am divinely created, unique, and deeply loved by my Creator, who crafted me with intention and purpose. In this world that often encourages comparison, I am reminded to reject those negative thoughts and instead embrace my innate worth. I am not defined by the opinions of others, but rather by the truth that I am beautiful and valuable because I am made in His image.

Furthermore, it is essential to recognize that my value extends beyond mere appearances or societal standards. When I remind myself of the scripture in Proverbs 29:26, I understand that true justice and affirmation come from the Lord, not from the fleeting approval of the world. God sees my heart, my struggles, and my strengths, and He loves me unconditionally. As I navigate life, I can find comfort in knowing that my worth is anchored in His love, and that every day I reflect His beauty, purpose, and divine image to the world around me. Embracing this perspective allows me to walk in confidence and grace, knowing I am cherished just as I am.

JULY 26

DAY 208

MY SCARS TELL MY STORY

Affirmation: Every part of me carries strength and resilience.

Scripture: " The generous will themselves be blessed, for they share their food with the poor.." – Proverbs 22:9 (NIV)

Encouragement: My scars, whether visible or invisible, tell a powerful story of endurance and growth. They serve as reminders of the challenges I have faced and the strength I have summoned to overcome them. Each mark I carry embodies a moment of transformation, showcasing how I have risen above adversity. In embracing every part of my journey, I learn to appreciate the wisdom gained from struggle and hardship. These scars are not symbols of pain; rather, they are emblems of my resilience and courage that speak to the tenacity of the human spirit.

As I reflect on the journey of healing, I am reminded of the profound truth in Proverbs 22:9, which emphasizes the blessings that flow from generosity. Just as I have weathered trials, I find joy in giving back to others who may also be facing difficulties. By sharing my strength and experiences, I not only honor my scars but also extend a hand of compassion to those in need. In this way, my story intertwines with the stories of others, creating a tapestry of hope and resilience. Every part of me truly carries strength, and I am continually inspired to uplift those around me, embodying the generous spirit that the scripture calls us to embrace.

JULY 27

DAY 209

I SPEAK TO MYSELF WITH LOVE

Affirmation: My words to myself are filled with kindness and grace.

Scripture: "Gracious words are a honeycomb, sweet to the soul and healing to the bones." – Proverbs 16:24 (NIV)

Encouragement: I am intentional with my self-talk, recognizing the profound impact it has on my emotional and spiritual well-being. Each day, I strive to replace criticism with compassion, transforming any negative thoughts into affirmations of self-love and understanding. Instead of succumbing to doubt, I actively choose to cultivate faith in my abilities and worth. Embracing this approach allows me to build a foundation of positivity that nurtures my soul, reminding me that I am deserving of the same kindness and grace that I readily offer to others.

With every affirmation, I become more aware of the power of my words; they hold the potential to uplift not only my spirit but to foster resilience and healing within me. The wisdom of Proverbs 16:24 resonates deeply, illustrating that gracious words function as a nourishing balm for the soul. By speaking to myself with love and compassion, I create a honeycomb of sweet, healing words that flow from my heart, reinforcing my self-worth and bolstering my journey toward grace and acceptance. I am committed to this practice, knowing that my inner dialogue shapes my reality and leads me to a place of peace and fulfillment.

JULY 28

DAY 210

I AM WONDERFULLY MADE BY GOD

Affirmation: I celebrate my uniqueness and love every part of me.

Scripture: " Ears that hear and eyes that see -the Lord has made them both.." – Proverbs 20:12 (NIV)

Encouragement: I honor the way God made me, fully recognizing that every aspect of my being is a marvelous reflection of His intricate design. Each unique trait, whether it be my physical appearance, personality, or talents, contributes to the beautiful tapestry of who I am. By celebrating my individuality, I affirm that it is not the comparison to others that defines my worth, but rather the distinct qualities that set me apart. Embracing myself with unwavering love allows me to express gratitude for the gifts that God has bestowed upon me. I understand that in a world that often pushes conformity, my authenticity is a true testament to God's creative genius.

As I reflect on the wisdom of Proverbs 20:12, I am reminded that my ears and eyes are not mere senses but divine instruments crafted by God. Each time I listen with intention or observe the beauty around me, I am connecting with that divine workmanship. Let me move forward with confidence, knowing that my uniqueness is not just to be accepted, but celebrated. I choose to engage with the world fully, appreciating the intricacies of my being while also recognizing the beauty in others. In doing so, I contribute to a world that values diversity, inspires love, and fosters acceptance. I am wonderfully made, and I embrace this truth wholeheartedly.

Week 31

Trusting The Process

JULY 29

DAY 211

GOD'S PLAN FOR ME IS PERFECT

Affirmation: I trust that God's plan for my life is unfolding exactly as it should.

Scripture: "Then you will shine among them like stars in the sky as you hold firmly to the word of life."

– Philippians 2:15 (NIV)

Encouragement: Even when I don't fully grasp the twists and turns of life, I remain confident that God's plan for me is not only good, but it's also tailored uniquely for my journey. Each step I take is woven into a greater tapestry that reflects His love and wisdom. Even in moments of uncertainty or difficulty, I can rest assured that there is a divine purpose at work. I choose to walk in faith, knowing that every experience, both the joyous and the challenging, is leading me closer to the fulfillment of my true purpose. As I trust in this process, I find joy in the belief that every moment is an opportunity for growth and learning.

Moreover, I hold fast to the promise found in Philippians 2:15, which reminds me that I have the potential to shine brightly among those around me as I embrace the word of life. My faith not only uplifts me, but it can also serve as a beacon of hope to others who may feel lost or uncertain. By trusting in God's intricate plan, I can illuminate the path for myself and others, reflecting His light in a world that often feels dark. As I embrace my journey with unwavering trust, I become a testament to the perfect nature of God's design for my life, emanating the brilliance of His love and purpose for all to see.

JULY 30

DAY 212

I AM GROWING THROUGH EVERY CHALLENGE

Affirmation: Every challenge I face is an opportunity for growth and strength.

Scripture: "Consider it pure joy, my brothers and sisters, whenever you face trials of many kinds, because you know that the testing of your faith produces perseverance." – James 1:2-3 (NIV)

Encouragement: I welcome the concept of growth, recognizing that it is often birthed through the challenges I encounter. Each obstacle I face serves as a powerful opportunity for transformation, allowing me to cultivate strength, wisdom, and resilience. In moments of hardship, I remind myself that these experiences are not merely burdens to bear but rather stepping stones that lead me to a greater understanding of my potential. Every trial I experience adds depth to my character, shaping me into a more compassionate and determined individual. This journey through adversity not only fortifies my spirit but also enriches my perspective, helping me appreciate the beauty of perseverance.

As I navigate life's inevitable difficulties, I am encouraged to view them through the lens of joy, as highlighted in James 1:2-3. It is through these trials that my faith is tested and my perseverance is forged. I acknowledge that each challenge presents a unique opportunity to grow deeper in my faith and to develop a stronger resilience within myself. I am continually reminded that growth often comes during times of discomfort; it is the delicious irony of life that within the struggle lies the promise of transformation. By welcoming and embracing each challenge, I allow myself to evolve, emerging stronger and more capable with each passing day.

JULY 31

DAY 213

I SURRENDER TO GOD'S TIMING

Affirmation: I release control and trust that God's timing is perfect.

Scripture: "What does the Lord require of you? To act justly and to love mercy and to walk humbly with your God."– Micah 6:8 (NIV)

Encouragement: In our fast-paced world, it can be tempting to feel the pressure to hurry plans along or force outcomes to align with our desires. However, it is essential to recognize that we do not have to rush or exert control over every situation. God is fully aware of our circumstances and is actively orchestrating events in our lives according to His perfect timing. By releasing our need to control the clock, we can embrace the peace that comes from knowing that everything will unfold as it should. It's a comforting reminder that we are not solely responsible for the timing of our lives; instead, we can trust that God has a sovereign plan at work, guiding us through each moment with wisdom and grace.

As we reflect on Micah 6:8, we are reminded that what the Lord requires is not our frantic efforts, but our willingness to act justly, love mercy, and walk humbly with Him. It's through this humble walk that we learn to trust His timing. This means allowing ourselves to be in the present, fully aware that God's timing is not only perfect but also transformative. Surrendering to this divine timing enables us to grow and develop in ways that we may not foresee. So let us rest in the assurance that God is working behind the scenes, aligning every detail of our lives precisely when we need it, allowing us to flourish in His perfect plan.

AUGUST 1

DAY 214

I AM EQUIPPED FOR MY JOURNEY

Affirmation: Everything I need to succeed is already within me.

Scripture: "His divine power has given us everything we need for a godly life through our knowledge of him who called us by his own glory and goodness." – 2 Peter 1:3 (NIV)

Encouragement: God has intricately woven within me the strength, wisdom, and abilities necessary for my journey. Each challenge I face is an opportunity for growth, and I can approach them with assurance because I am not alone. The divine power that has been bestowed upon me acts as a wellspring of resources, waiting to be tapped into as I navigate through life's twists and turns. With every step I take, I remind myself of the truth in 2 Peter 1:3: I have been called to a life of purpose and abundance, empowered by His glory and goodness.

As I move forward in faith, I recognize that my potential is limitless, grounded in the understanding that everything I need to succeed lies within me. I am equipped not just to survive but to thrive in my journey. With every decision I make, I carry the assurance that God's empowerment is guiding me, illuminating my path, and preparing me for the extraordinary. Embracing this truth instills a deep sense of confidence and fortitude, reinforcing the belief that I am capable of achieving all that I am called to accomplish. Let us take heart, knowing that the very essence of our being is infused with everything necessary to live a life of godliness and fulfillment.

AUGUST 2

DAY 215

I EMBRACE THE UNKNOWN WITH FAITH

Affirmation: I trust in God's guidance, even when I cannot see the path ahead.

Scripture: " Answer me, Lord, out of the goodness of your love; in your great mercy turn to me.

17 Do not hide your face from your servant; answer me quickly, for I am in trouble.." – Psalm 69:16-17 (NKJV)

Encouragement: Embracing the unknown can often feel daunting, but it's important to remember that we don't need to have all the answers to find peace in our journey. Trusting in God's guidance allows us to surrender our worries and uncertainties to Him. Each step taken in faith can turn our apprehensions into opportunities for growth and transformation. When we lean into our relationship with God, we find reassurance that He walks alongside us, illuminating the path ahead even when the way forward seems unclear. By resting in His love and mercy, we can cultivate a sense of calm amid life's storms, knowing that we are not alone in our struggles.

Our faith has the power to overcome fear, allowing us to face the unknown with courage and hope. Just as the psalmist pleads for God's attention and guidance in times of trouble, we too can call upon Him in our moments of need. Remember that it's in these times of vulnerability that we can experience His profound grace. By trusting in God's goodness and letting go of the need to control every outcome, we open ourselves up to divine possibilities. As we step forward, let us affirm our reliance on His wisdom, embracing the journey before us, knowing that each day brings new mercies and the opportunity to deepen our connection with Him.

AUGUST 3

DAY 216

GOD'S PROMISES ARE TRUE FOR ME

Affirmation: I stand on God's promises, knowing He is faithful.

Scripture: "Let us hold unswervingly to the hope we profess, for he who promised is faithful." – Hebrews 10:23 (NIV)

Encouragement: As I reflect on the unwavering truth embedded in God's word, I am reminded that His promises are never empty or unfulfilled. Each declaration He has made over my life carries immense power and purpose, ensuring that I can move forward with full confidence. In moments of doubt or uncertainty, I can take solace in the fact that God's faithfulness is a cornerstone of my hope. By choosing to stand firmly on His promises, I engage in an act of faith that not only strengthens my spirit but also aligns my heart with His divine plan for my life.

Moreover, the assurance provided in Hebrews 10:23 serves as a potent reminder that my hope is anchored in a faithful God who does not waver or falter. Instead of succumbing to the pressures of doubt, I choose to hold unswervingly to the hope I profess, knowing that His timing is impeccable. Each step I take is a testament to my belief that His promises will manifest in my life, just as He has ordained. This steadfast hope fuels my journey, allowing me to embrace each day with the anticipation of witnessing His promises come to fruition, reinforcing my faith and nurturing my soul.

AUGUST 4

DAY 217

I TRUST THE JOURNEY GOD HAS ME ON

Affirmation: My life is unfolding exactly as it should, and I embrace each step with faith.

Scripture: " But the Israelites said to the Lord, "We have sinned. Do with us whatever you think best, but please rescue us now." – Judges 10:15 (NIV)

Encouragement: I am exactly where I need to be, and this realization fills me with a profound sense of peace. Each step I take, whether it be smooth or laden with challenges, is a vital part of the unique journey that God has crafted for me. Just as the Israelites recognized their shortcomings and turned to the Lord for help, I too can acknowledge my own struggles while remaining steadfast in my belief that God is guiding me. I trust that even in moments of difficulty, there is a purpose and a lesson that will ultimately propel me toward my destiny. Embracing this truth empowers me to navigate through life with resilience and faith, knowing that every experience is shaping me into the person I am meant to become.

As I reflect on the affirmation that my life is unfolding exactly as it should, I find strength in the understanding that faith is not just a feeling but a commitment to trust in God's timing and plan. Each day presents new opportunities and lessons, and by embracing each moment, I am allowing God to work within me. Just as the Israelites pleaded for rescue with a humble heart, I hold on to the belief that God is actively involved in my journey, providing guidance and support as I move forward. With this mindset, I continue to walk in confidence, reassured that God's divine blueprint for my life is unfolding perfectly, and I am exactly where I need to be.

Week 32

Finding Strength In Vulnerability

AUGUST 5

DAY 218

VULNERABILITY IS A STRENGTH, NOT A WEAKNESS

Affirmation: I embrace my vulnerability as a sign of courage and strength.

Scripture: " This is what the Lord says—he who made you, who formed you in the womb, and who will help you: Do not be afraid, Jacob, my servant, Jeshurun, whom I have chose." – Isaiah 44:2 (NIV

Encouragement: I no longer see vulnerability as something to hide; instead, I embrace it as a powerful act of courage. True strength lies in the willingness to be open, to share our genuine selves with others, and to admit when we face challenges. When I allow myself to be vulnerable, I create a space for authenticity in my relationships and invite healing, love, and connection into my life. Rather than being a source of fear or shame, my vulnerability nurtures deeper bonds with those around me and helps foster a supportive community where we can all thrive together.

Furthermore, embracing vulnerability opens the door to personal growth and self-discovery. It encourages me to confront my fears and limitations, reminding me that it is okay to seek help and guidance when needed. As I reflect on the Scripture from Isaiah 44:2, I find reassurance in God's promise to support and guide me. Just as He formed me with purpose, I can trust that embracing my vulnerabilities aligns with His design, allowing me to walk my path with courage and authenticity. The embrace of vulnerability not only strengthens my spirit but also brings me closer to fulfilling the life I am called to lead.

AUGUST 6

DAY 219

IT'S OKAY TO ASK FOR HELP

Affirmation: I am not alone, and I welcome support from others.

Scripture: " The Lord has done it this very day; let us rejoice today and be glad." – Psalm 118:24 (NIV)

Encouragement: It's important to remember that we are not meant to navigate the complexities of life in isolation. God has gifted us with relationships and community for a reason; He knows that we need each other. Embracing the support of those around us and allowing ourselves to lean on others can be a transformative experience. It's a beautiful testament to our shared humanity and a recognition that we are all in this together, facing our own battles and triumphs. By inviting help into our lives, we open ourselves up to strength that exists in unity, and we embody the spirit of love and friendship that God intends for us.

As we reflect on Psalm 118:24, we are reminded to rejoice in the present moment and be glad for the blessings that surround us, including the support we receive from others. It's easy to forget just how impactful a listening ear or a kind word can be when we're overwhelmed by our struggles. However, when we acknowledge the help that is available to us, we find comfort and encouragement in the knowledge that we are truly never alone. As we invite others into our journeys, we not only lighten our own burdens but also enrich the lives of those around us. Together, let us celebrate the love and support from God and our fellow friends and family, for it is in these connections that we find hope and strength to overcome even the toughest of challenges.

AUGUST 7

DAY 220

MY STORY HAS PURPOSE

Affirmation: My experiences, even the difficult ones, serve a greater purpose.

Scripture: "Look at the birds of the air; they do not sow or reap or store away in barns, and yet your heavenly Father feeds them. Are you not much more valuable than they?" – Matthew 6:26 (NIV)

Encouragement: Every part of my journey has meaning, and I am learning to recognize the significance embedded in both triumphs and tribulations. My struggles, while often challenging, are not without purpose; they are shaping me into a stronger, more compassionate individual. Each experience adds depth to my character, allowing me to cultivate empathy and resilience. As I navigate through life's ups and downs, I hold onto the belief that these trials are not merely obstacles, but stepping stones that enrich my narrative and equip me to connect with others on a deeper level.

With this understanding, I trust that my story will not only bring inspiration to my own life but also serve as a beacon of hope for those around me. Just as the birds rely on God's provision without worrying about their needs, I too can lean into the assurance that I am cared for and valued. My experiences—no matter how difficult—will transform into a testament of strength and hope, uplifting others who may be walking similar paths. By embracing the notion that every challenge has a greater purpose, I can share my journey with authenticity and encourage others to see the beauty in their struggles, knowing they, too, have a significant role to play in the tapestry of life.

AUGUST 8

DAY 221

I GIVE MYSELF PERMISSION TO FEEL

Affirmation: I allow myself to feel all emotions without judgment.

Scripture: " For great is his love toward us, and the faithfulness of the Lord endures forever." – Psalm 117:2 (NIV)

Encouragement: Today, I embrace the beautiful truth that I do not need to suppress my emotions; in fact, I actively choose to honor them. Each feeling I experience, whether joy, sorrow, anger, or peace, plays a vital role in shaping my journey and reflecting my humanity. God's presence is with me in each of these moments, reminding me that it's okay to feel deeply. I trust that, in my vulnerability, I am not alone. His love surrounds me, nurturing my spirit and providing the comfort I need to navigate life's challenges. I give myself permission to explore these emotions, knowing that they are part of my growth and healing.

As I acknowledge the complexity of my emotions, I am reassured by the enduring faithfulness of the Lord, as expressed in Psalm 117:2. His love toward me is vast and unwavering, providing a steadfast foundation in times of emotional turmoil. I can take solace in the fact that God does not abandon me when I feel overwhelmed or lost; instead, He is ever-present, ready to strengthen and uplift me. By allowing myself to feel without judgment, I open the door to deeper healing and connection with both myself and my Creator. Today, let me fully engage with my emotions, confident that His faithfulness will carry me through every high and low.

AUGUST 9

DAY 222

GOD'S LOVE COVERS MY INSECURITIES

Affirmation: I release my insecurities and rest in God's unconditional love.

Scripture: "Praise be to the God and Father of our Lord Jesus Christ! In his great mercy he has given us new birth into a living hope through the resurrection of Jesus Christ from the dead." – 1 Peter 1:3 (NIV)

Encouragement: My worth is not rooted in fleeting standards of appearance or the pursuit of perfection; rather, it is anchored in the deep and abiding love that God has for me. In moments when self-doubt creeps in and insecurities seem overwhelming, I can choose to remember that I am infinitely valued in the eyes of my Creator. His love is a constant, unchanging force that surrounds me, offering refuge from my worries and fears. It is through this divine love that I can find solace, knowing that I am accepted as I am, imperfections and all.

As I reflect on the scripture from 1 Peter 1:3, I am reminded that God's mercy has granted me a new birth into a living hope, a hope that is reinforced through the resurrection of Jesus Christ. This powerful promise transforms my insecurities into opportunities for growth and healing. In His loving embrace, I can let go of the burdens I carry and find renewed strength to walk confidently in my identity as a beloved child of God. The freedom that comes from releasing my fears and resting in His love empowers me to rise above my doubts and fully embrace the life He has called me to live.

AUGUST 10

DAY 223

I AM SAFE TO BE MY AUTHENTIC SELF

Affirmation: I show up as my true self, knowing I am accepted and loved.

Scripture: "You created my inmost being; you knit me together in my mother's womb." – Psalm 139:13 (NIV)

Encouragement: God designed me with intentionality, intricately crafting every facet of my being. I am a unique reflection of His creativity, and this realization empowers me to embrace my true self. No longer do I feel the need to conceal my authentic identity; instead, I celebrate the person God has called me to be. In a world that often pressures us to conform or fit into predefined molds, I find solace in the truth that I am wonderfully made. With each step I take towards authenticity, I grow stronger in my confidence and joy, knowing that I am fully accepted and loved just as I am.

As I live out this affirmation, I cultivate a deeper appreciation for my own uniqueness and remind myself that my worth does not depend on external validation. The assurance found in Psalm 139:13 resonates in my heart, affirming that I am fearfully and wonderfully made. This divine truth encourages me to be bold in expressing who I am, allowing my gifts and talents to shine brightly. With God's love as my foundation, I can be a source of inspiration to others who may feel the same struggle, encouraging them to step into their authenticity and embrace the beauty of their individuality. Together, we can create a supportive community where acceptance reigns, and we all thrive in being our true selves.

AUGUST 11

DAY 224

MY OPEN HEART LEADS TO HEALING

Affirmation: When I open my heart, I allow healing and love to flow in.

Scripture: " Your beginnings will seem humble, so prosperous will your future be." – Job 8:7 (NIV)

Encouragement: Healing begins when I allow myself to be open and honest with my feelings and experiences. It is in this vulnerable state that I can truly release the fear that often holds me captive, making room for the warmth of love to flow in. By embracing love, whether it is self-love, love from others, or divine love, I create a nurturing environment for my spirit and heart to heal. I trust wholeheartedly that God is at work, guiding and restoring me in every aspect of my life, even when it may not feel apparent at first. The process of healing requires patience and faith, both of which are cultivated in an open heart.

As I reflect on the scripture from Job 8:7, I am reminded that humble beginnings can lead to extraordinary futures. Just as the seed must break open to sprout and grow, I too must undergo a transformation that starts with my willingness to open my heart. I am encouraged to remember that the journey of healing, though it may seem small in its initial stages, holds the promise of abundant growth and prosperity ahead. In this journey, every act of bravery, every step of honesty, amplifies my capacity to receive and radiate love, ultimately leading me to a place of wholeness and restoration.

Week 33

Resting In God's Promises

AUGUST 12

DAY 225

GOD'S PROMISES NEVER FAIL

Affirmation: I trust that every promise God has spoken over my life will come to pass.

Scripture: "Not one of all the Lord's good promises to Israel failed; every one was fulfilled." – Joshua 21:45 (NIV)

Encouragement: God's word is truly unshakable and stands as a fortress in our lives. When we look at the Scriptures, we see a consistent track record of God's faithfulness to His people. Each promise He has spoken is like a seed planted in fertile soil, waiting for the right conditions to blossom. Our lives may feel turbulent at times, but the truth remains that God's promises are not contingent on our circumstances or feelings. Instead, they are rooted in His unwavering character and deep love for us. Trusting that every promise He has spoken over our lives will come to pass brings us a profound sense of peace, motivating us to hold steadfast through trials and uncertainties.

In the book of Joshua, we are reminded that "not one of all the Lord's good promises to Israel failed; every one was fulfilled" (Joshua 21:45 NIV). This verse resonates deeply, illuminating the certainty that God's faithfulness doesn't waver. It serves as a powerful reminder that His timing is divine and perfect. While we may not always see the immediate results of His promises, we can rest comfortably knowing that they will manifest at the right time and in the right way. Let this assurance stir within you a spirit of hope and expectation, enabling you to embrace each day with faith, as you walk forward with confidence in God's unfailing commitment to you.

AUGUST 13

DAY 226

I AM COVERED BY GOD'S GRACE

Affirmation: God's grace is more than enough for me in every situation.

Scripture: " See, I have engraved you on the palms of my hands; your walls are ever before me." – Isaiah 49:16 (NIV)

Encouragement: No matter the challenges or circumstances I encounter, I can find comfort and assurance in the boundless grace of God. His grace is not just a fleeting emotion; it is a profound source of strength and support that envelops me like a protective shield. When I feel overwhelmed, I am reminded that His grace is more than sufficient to meet all my needs. It empowers me to rise above the difficulties and trials in my life, helping me to persevere with resilience and courage. In every moment, whether filled with struggles or victories, I can trust that God's grace sustains me, allowing me to navigate through life with confidence and peace.

Furthermore, the assurance that I am engraved on the palms of God's hands serves as a powerful reminder of His unwavering love and attention toward me. This profound imagery highlights the intimate relationship I have with my Creator, illustrating that He is always aware of my circumstances and struggles. His grace not only strengthens me but also reassures me that I am never alone; my walls and challenges are always before Him. With this divine support, I am empowered to push through adversity and celebrate triumphs, knowing that God's grace will lead me through every season of life.

AUGUST 14

DAY 227

GOD IS MY PROVIDER

Affirmation: I lack nothing because God provides all my needs.

Scripture: "And my God will meet all your needs according to the riches of his glory in Christ Jesus." – Philippians 4:19 (NIV)

Encouragement: I do not have to live in fear or worry, for God's provision is abundant and unchanging. Each day, I am reminded that my needs—emotionally, physically, and spiritually—are met by a loving God who knows me intimately. His willingness to provide isn't just an abstract idea; it's a reality grounded in His promises. I can navigate life's uncertainties with the assurance that God sees my circumstances and is actively working on my behalf. There's a profound peace that comes from knowing that, regardless of what challenges I may face, I lack nothing because my needs are fully encompassed in His divine plans.

As I embrace this truth, I can rest in the understanding that God will always supply what I need in His perfect timing. His timing may not always align with my expectations, but I trust that His riches—rooted in Christ Jesus—are far greater than anything I could imagine. Each moment of waiting or uncertainty can deepen my faith and reliance on Him. So, I choose to release my fears and anxieties, knowing that my

Provider is faithful and abundant. I will look forward with hope, confident that every need will be met as I continue to trust in His goodness and grace.

AUGUST 15

DAY 228

GOD'S PEACE GUARDS MY HEART

Affirmation: I rest in the peace of God, knowing He is in control.

Scripture: " You simple people, use good judgment. You foolish people, show some understanding." – Proverbs 8:5 (NLT)

Encouragement: In the midst of uncertainty, I anchor myself in God's peace, allowing it to wash over me like a gentle wave. Life can present us with unpredictable challenges, but in these moments, I am reminded that I am not alone. His divine presence serves as an unwavering foundation in my life, calming my soul and reassuring me of His unfailing love and faithfulness. It is through this peace that I find the strength to persevere and the clarity to navigate the complexities of each day. Knowing that God is in control allows me to release anxieties and trust in His perfect plan, instilling a sense of hope that transcends my circumstances.

Moreover, embracing God's peace empowers me to approach decisions and situations with good judgment and understanding, as underscored in Proverbs 8:5. When I center my thoughts on His promises, I gain a perspective that enables me to respond rather than react. In every trial I face, I am committed to seeking His wisdom and guidance. By surrendering my worries and embracing His peace, I cultivate a heart that is open to His leading, allowing me to experience the fullness of life He intends for me. Through this divine connection, I can remain steadfast, trusting that His sovereign hand will guide me through all of life's uncertainties.

AUGUST 16

DAY 229

I TRUST IN GOD'S PERFECT TIMING

Affirmation: God's timing is always perfect, and I wait patiently for His plans to unfold.

Scripture: "The Lord is good, a refuge in times of trouble. He cares for those who trust in him." – Nahum 1:7 (NIV)

Encouragement: Although I may not always grasp the reasons behind God's timing, I find solace in the belief that His plans are intricately designed for my benefit. Life often presents challenges and uncertainties that can lead to feelings of impatience and confusion. However, I choose to trust in His divine wisdom and allow myself to be grounded in faith. When I focus on God's goodness and the truth that He is a refuge in times of trouble, I realize that every moment is a part of a larger tapestry crafted by His loving hand. In those moments of waiting, I remind myself that anxiety has no place in my heart when I rest in God's promises.

As I navigate through life's ups and downs, I take comfort in knowing that God sincerely cares for me, and His timing is always aligned with what is best for my journey. By choosing patience over worry, I can embrace each day with a hopeful spirit and an open heart. Trusting in

His plans allows me to find peace amid uncertainty, cultivating a deeper relationship with Him. I hold onto the assurance that as I wait, I am not idly standing by, but growing in strength and resilience, ready to receive His blessings when the time is right. In this season of preparation, I reaffirm my trust in God, knowing that He is working all things together for my ultimate good.

AUGUST 17

DAY 230

GOD IS FAITHFUL TO HIS WORD

Affirmation: I hold on to God's faithfulness, knowing He will never leave me.

Scripture: " Ah, Sovereign Lord, you have made the heavens and the earth by your great power and outstretched arm. Nothing is too hard for you." – Jeremiah 32:17 (NIV)

Encouragement: God is not a man that He should lie, and this truth offers us profound comfort and assurance in our daily lives. Each promise He has spoken over us is not only true but also anchored in His unwavering faithfulness. As we navigate through life's challenges and uncertainties, we can find strength in the knowledge that God's words are dependable and His commitments are eternal. When we hold on to His promises, we are reminded that He is always present, guiding us and walking alongside us, no matter the circumstances we face. In every moment, we can choose to lean into His faithfulness and trust that He will fulfill what He has ordained in our lives.

Furthermore, the scripture from Jeremiah 32:17 serves as a powerful reminder of God's omnipotence and sovereignty. "Ah, Sovereign Lord, you have made the heavens and the earth by your great power and outstretched arm. Nothing is too hard for you." This declaration not only highlights the magnitude of God's power but also reassures us that no situation in our lives is beyond His ability to transform. When we feel overwhelmed or burdened, we can take solace in knowing that the Creator of the universe is intimately involved in our lives and capable of orchestrating miracles. As we embrace this truth, let us nurture a spirit of hope and confidence, understanding that God's faithfulness is the bedrock upon which we can build our lives. He will never leave us, and with Him, we can face any trial that comes our way.

AUGUST 18

DAY 231

I REST IN GOD'S LOVE

Affirmation: God's love surrounds me, and I find rest in His embrace.

Scripture: "Come to me, all you who are weary and burdened, and I will give you rest." – Matthew 11:28 (NIV)

Encouragement: I do not have to carry my burdens alone. In times of weariness and anxiety, God gently beckons me to come to Him, offering me a safe haven where I can lay down my stress and concerns. His love envelops me like a warm embrace, reminding me that I am never forgotten or abandoned. By resting in Him, I acknowledge that His strength is sufficient for my weaknesses. I can release my burdens into His capable hands, knowing that He is eager to lighten my load. This invitation is not merely a suggestion; it is a profound promise that I can find solace in His presence.

As I draw closer to God, I discover the true meaning of rest, which is found in surrendering my struggles to His care. The assurance of His love serves as a shield against the pressures of the world. When I choose to rest in Him, I experience a renewal of spirit and clarity of mind. God's embrace reassures me that I can trust Him with my uncertainties, and in His arms, I regain my strength. It is in this sacred space of rest that I find the peace to navigate life's challenges, knowing that I am cherished and upheld by a love that is unchanging and ever-present.

Week 34

The Beauty Of Surrender

AUGUST 19

DAY 232

SURRENDERING TO GOD'S WILL

Affirmation: I release control and trust God's perfect plan for my life.

Scripture: "Commit your way to the Lord; trust in him and he will do this." – Psalm 37:5 (NIV)

Encouragement: True peace is a profound gift that emerges when we choose to stop striving and instead embrace the art of surrendering. In a world that often pressures us to take control and dictate the outcomes of our lives, there is an extraordinary freedom found in letting go and trusting God. It is in this quiet submission that we can truly experience the assurance that comes from knowing that God's will is always greater than our own aspirations. As we turn our hearts toward Him, we allow His perfect plan to unfold in our lives, leading us down paths we may have never imagined.

When we commit our ways to the Lord, as emphasized in Psalm 37:5, we are reminded that our trust in Him empowers us to step back and release the burdens of uncertainty and anxiety. This act of faith transforms the way we navigate our daily challenges. Rather than becoming overwhelmed by the complexities of life, we become grounded in His unwavering promise to guide us. Embracing God's perfect plan means we can rest assured that every step we take is part of a greater purpose, far beyond what we can perceive. In surrendering, we not only find peace but discover the boundless possibilities that await when we allow Him to lead our hearts and our paths.

AUGUST 20

DAY 233

LETTING GO OF FEAR

Affirmation: I release fear and embrace faith in all areas of my life.

Scripture: "He will cover you with his feathers, and under his wings you will find refuge; his faithfulness will be your shield and rampart." – Psalm 91:4 (NIV)

Encouragement: Fear can often feel like a heavy burden, threatening to weigh us down and cloud our vision. However, when we put our trust in God's promises, we realize that fear cannot coexist with faith. By consciously choosing to embrace courage, we allow ourselves to be enveloped in the protective embrace of God's unwavering presence. Just like a mother bird covering her young with her feathers, God provides us with the safety and comfort we need to face life's challenges. This divine protection becomes our stronghold, reminding us that we are never alone in our struggles.

As we navigate the complexities of life, we must continually remind ourselves of the faithfulness of God, which serves as both a shield and rampart against overwhelming fear. When we focus our hearts and minds on His loving care, we open ourselves up to the transformative power of faith. Each time fear tries to creep in, we can firmly reaffirm our commitment to trust in God's ever-present love and support. Let us hold fast to the assurance that with every step we take in faith, we are covered and protected by His wings, and in that knowledge, we find the courage to move forward. Together, let us release fear and embrace a life filled with faith, trusting that our Heavenly Father is guiding us through every storm.

AUGUST 21

DAY 234

GOD'S STRENGTH SUSTAINS ME

Affirmation: I surrender my weakness and receive God's strength.

Scripture: "The Lord will surely comfort Zion and will look with compassion on all her ruins; he will make her deserts like Eden, her wastelands like the garden of the Lord. Joy and gladness will be found in her, thanksgiving and the sound of singing.'" – Isaiah 51:3 (NIV)

Encouragement: I don't have to rely on my own strength, and I can find profound comfort in that truth. Life often presents us with challenges that can feel overwhelming, leading us to believe that we must bear them alone. However, when I surrender my struggles to God, I open myself up to His boundless strength and grace. Just as the Lord promises to comfort Zion and transform her wastelands into a place of joy and beauty, He can also work in the ruins of my life to restore hope and purpose. It's in these moments of surrender that I experience the transformative power of His love, reminding me that I am never alone in my battles.

Through the act of surrendering, I can embrace the assurance that God is with me, ready to support and uplift me in my weaknesses. His ability to bring joy and gladness into the most desolate parts of my life holds incredible power. I can take heart knowing that He sees my struggles with compassion and seeks to replace my despair with a garden of hope. As I open my heart to His healing, I can expect to find thanksgiving and the sound of singing in my spirit once more. No matter how barren my circumstances may appear, I trust that God's strength will sustain me, leading me toward a flourishing future filled with His joy.

AUGUST 22

DAY 235

RELEASING THE NEED FOR APPROVAL

Affirmation: I live for God's approval, not the approval of others.

Scripture: "Am I now trying to win the approval of human beings, or of God? Or am I trying to please people? If I were still trying to please people, I would not be a servant of Christ." – Galatians 1:10 (NIV)

Encouragement: In a world that often prioritizes validation from others, it can feel increasingly burdensome to seek approval from those around us. However, as individuals rooted in faith, we can release ourselves from this heavy obligation. By understanding that our identity and worth are anchored in God's love, we can embrace the liberation that comes from knowing our value isn't dictated by the fluctuating opinions of others. When we focus our hearts and minds on pleasing God instead of seeking the favor of people, we find a profound sense of peace and purpose.

God's love for each of us is unwavering and constant, providing a solid foundation upon which we can build our self-esteem and confidence. As we reflect on Galatians 1:10, we are reminded that our true calling is to serve God rather than seek the approval of others. This perspective allows us to live authentically and boldly, free from the constraints of societal expectations. When we shift our focus from the opinions of others and center ourselves in our relationship with God, we gain the strength to pursue our divine purpose with passion and courage. Let this truth resonate within you: you are inherently valuable in God's eyes, and His approval is what truly matters.

AUGUST 23

DAY 236

SURRENDERING MY WORRIES

Affirmation: I cast my cares on God, knowing He will take care of me.

Scripture: " I will give you a new heart and put a new spirit in you; I will remove from you your heart of stone and give you a heart of flesh." – Ezekiel 36:26 (NIV)

Encouragement: Worrying serves no constructive purpose in our lives; it only weighs us down and distracts us from experiencing the peace and joy that God intends for us. By intentionally choosing to surrender our concerns and anxieties to Him, we open ourselves to a deeper sense of tranquility and assurance. God invites us to cast our cares upon Him, for He is fully capable of handling our burdens and providing the guidance we need. In doing so, we free ourselves from the shackles of worry and embrace the peace that comes from trusting in His divine plan.

The promise found in Ezekiel 36:26 reminds us that God desires to transform our hearts, replacing our hardened worries and fears with a renewed spirit filled with hope and faith. He gently invites us to trust Him with every facet of our lives, assuring us that we are never alone in our struggles. As we lean into this promise, we can experience profound liberation and restoration, knowing that God is faithful in His care for us. Commit your worries to Him, and allow His love to restore your spirit, bringing a clarity that equips you to navigate the challenges ahead with grace and confidence.

AUGUST 24

DAY 237

TRUSTING GOD'S PROCESS

Affirmation: I embrace the journey, knowing God is leading me.

Scripture: "You have searched me, Lord, and you know me." – Psalm 139:1 (NIV)

Encouragement: As I navigate the twists and turns of my life's journey, I find solace in the knowledge that God is intimately aware of my every thought and emotion. Psalm 139:1 reminds me that I am seen and known by the Creator, who walks alongside me through every trial and triumph. In moments when uncertainty clouds my path and I struggle to understand the purpose behind my experiences, I am reassured that God is laying out a plan far beyond my comprehension. I choose to embrace this journey with an open heart, letting go of my need for control and trusting that God's wisdom will illuminate my steps.

Additionally, there is deep comfort in recognizing that the process of growth and transformation often requires patience and perseverance.

Trusting God's timing means understanding that every season has its purpose, designed to enrich my character and deepen my faith. By surrendering to His guiding hand, I open myself to the lessons and blessings hidden within each moment. Through the ebbs and flows of life, I can take heart in the assurance that I am not alone; God walks with me, illuminating my path and fostering a spirit of resilience within me. With each step I take, I not only gain greater clarity but also cultivate trust that ultimately, I am being led exactly where I need to be

AUGUST 25

DAY 238

FREEDOM IN SURRENDER

Affirmation: In surrendering to God, I find true freedom.

Scripture: "Then you will know the truth, and the truth will set you free." – John 8:32 (NIV)

Encouragement: Surrendering to God is a transformative journey that opens the door to profound freedom and liberation. It's essential to understand that surrender is not a sign of weakness or defeat; rather, it is an act of strength and courage. When we relinquish control and place our complete trust in God, we allow His peace to envelop us, dispelling the anxieties and burdens we often carry. By choosing to surrender, we experience an uplift in our spirits, and we uncover the joy that comes from embracing a life led by faith. Today, let us remind ourselves that in giving over our worries and challenges to the Lord, we are not losing anything; instead, we are gaining the opportunity to walk in faith and experience the beauty of His grace.

As highlighted in John 8:32, "Then you will know the truth, and the truth will set you free," we are invited to discover the liberating power of divine truth. This truth reassures us that when we let go and trust in God's plan for our lives, we are stepping into an abundant life filled with joy and purpose. Every moment we choose to surrender is an affirmation of our faith in His promises, leading us to a deeper understanding of His love and presence. So today, I consciously release everything into His capable hands, embracing the incredible peace that follows. In this act of faith, I am inviting His transformative power into my life, setting my heart free to pursue the abundant blessings He has in store for me.

Week 35

Claiming My Joy

AUGUST 26

DAY 239

JOY IS MY BIRTHRIGHT

Affirmation: I am worthy of joy and embrace it fully.

Scripture: " May the favor of the Lord our God rest on us; establish the work of our hands for us—yes, establish the work of our hands." – Psalm 90:17 (NIV)

Encouragement: Joy is not something that needs to be earned; it is inherently mine to claim and enjoy. Embracing joy means recognizing that it is a birthright bestowed upon me by God, one that is rooted in His love and grace. As I navigate the various seasons of life, I can tap into this divine joy as a source of strength, comfort, and resilience. It is a powerful reminder that, regardless of the challenges I may face, happiness and positivity are available to me. Each moment is an opportunity to experience this profound joy, allowing it to fill my heart and uplift my spirit.

Moreover, Psalm 90:17 emphasizes the importance of God's favor resting upon us, a reassurance that we are supported in our endeavors. When I acknowledge that my work and efforts are established by God, I can trust that my pursuit of joy is not just beneficial but also divinely orchestrated. This understanding empowers me to fully embrace joy, knowing that it is both a gift and a calling. By leaning into this truth, I cultivate a life rich in gratitude and positivity, where joy flows freely and illuminates even the darkest days. In doing so, I align myself with the abundant life God desires for me, allowing His joy to shine brightly through every circumstance.

AUGUST 27

DAY 240

MY JOY COMES FROM WITHIN

Affirmation: My joy is not dependent on circumstances; it comes from God.

Scripture: " I will instruct you and teach you in the way you should go; I will counsel you with my eye upon you.." – Psalm 32:8 (ESV)

Encouragement: External circumstances can often shift unexpectedly, leading us to seek joy in places that ultimately disappoint. However, true joy transcends these temporary experiences and is instead anchored in the unchanging presence of God. When we understand that our joy is a gift from Him, we can learn to navigate life's ups and downs with a sense of steadiness and peace. This inner joy does not waver with the tides of circumstance; instead, it remains a constant source of strength through every challenge and change. Our innermost joy is a reflection of our relationship with God, reminding us that we are never alone, and that He is there to guide us.

As Psalm 32:8 beautifully reassures us, God is not only aware of our journey but is actively involved in teaching us the path we should take. When we focus on His counsel and embrace His wisdom, we can cultivate a deeper understanding of our joy's true source. God's instruction is a gentle reminder that our joy isn't contingent on the external factors we often look to for happiness. Instead, it flourishes within us, rooted in our spirit and nurtured through our faith. Let us lean into this divine relationship, trusting that as we orient ourselves toward God, the joy we receive will be unwavering and will empower us through every season of life, anchoring us firmly in His love and guidance.

AUGUST 28

DAY 241

CHOOSING TO REJOICE

Affirmation: I choose to rejoice in all things, knowing God is working for my good.

Scripture: " Sitting down, Jesus called the Twelve and said, "Anyone who wants to be first must be the very last, and the servant of all."– Mark 9:35 (NIV)

Encouragement: In life's challenging moments, I reaffirm my ability to choose joy and embrace the power of gratitude. Even when circumstances may seem overwhelming or disheartening, I remind myself that joy is a deliberate choice, an act of will that allows me to rise above adversity. Each time I lift my voice in praise, I invite a sense of peace and hope into my heart, recognizing that God is always working behind the scenes for my good. This perspective not only transforms my outlook but also deepens my faith, fueling my spirit with the understanding that I am not alone in my struggles.

Moreover, as I reflect on the words of Jesus, I find profound wisdom in the call to humility and service. When He teaches us about prioritizing others over ourselves, it becomes clear that true joy stems from selflessness and generosity. By serving those around me, I cultivate a sense of fulfillment that transcends my personal challenges. In doing so, I not only honor God but also experience the uplifting power of community, as we support each other in faith and love. With each act of service, I strengthen my connection to others and to God, fortifying my soul with a joy that is rooted in purpose and compassion.

AUGUST 29

DAY 242

RELEASING WHAT STEALS MY JOY

Affirmation: I let go of anything that does not bring me joy and peace.

Scripture: " "In my distress I called to the Lord, and he answered me. From deep in the realm of the dead I called for help, and you listened to my cry.." – Jonah 2:2 (NIV)

Encouragement: Life is often filled with challenges that can easily burden our hearts and minds, making it difficult to experience true joy. However, I choose to stand firm against the pressures of stress, fear, and negativity that seek to overshadow my spirit. By actively letting go of anything that does not uplift or nurture my well-being, I open myself to the vibrant energy of joy and peace that the Lord so graciously offers. Just as Jonah cried out in his time of distress and received attention from the Lord, I am reminded that I too can call upon Him in my moments of need. His listening ear and compassionate heart assure me that I am never alone, even when navigating through life's tumultuous waters.

In embracing God's peace, I find strength and encouragement to release any burdens that chain me to worry or despair. The act of letting go is not just a release, but also a conscious decision to fill my life with that which brings me delight and tranquility. By focusing on joy, I align my heart with God's promises, choosing to dwell in His presence rather than in the noise of the world. I affirm today that I will walk in faith, knowing that as I surrender my fears and anxieties, I am enveloped in divine peace that transcends understanding. Each step I take in this process brings me closer to a life overflowing with joy, gratitude, and an unwavering trust in the Lord's goodness.

AUGUST 30

DAY 243

OVERFLOWING WITH GRATITUDE

Affirmation: Gratitude fills my heart, and my joy overflows.

Scripture: " Do not make friends with a hot-tempered person, do not associate with one easily angered,

or you may learn their ways and get yourself ensnared." – Proverbs 22:24-25 (NIV)

Encouragement: Gratitude has the extraordinary ability to transform my perspective, shifting my focus from the areas of my life that may feel deficient to the abundant blessings that surround me each day. By intentionally counting my blessings, I am reminded of the small and significant gifts that fill my life—whether it's the warmth of a smile from a friend, the beauty of nature, or the simple joy of a good meal. This practice not only nourishes my spirit but also cultivates a deep sense of contentment within me. The more I nurture an attitude of gratitude, the more my joy multiplies, overwhelming my heart and creating a ripple effect in my interactions with others.

Moreover, as I embrace gratitude, I become increasingly aware of the power of my associations. The wisdom found in Proverbs reminds me to be mindful of the company I keep, as negativity can easily influence my outlook. Surrounding myself with individuals who embody gratitude and positivity encourages me to foster these same qualities within myself. When I choose to engage with those who reflect kindness and joy, I reinforce my commitment to a grateful heart. In turn, this not only enriches my own life but also contributes positively to the lives of those around me. By focusing on the abundance I have, I create a space of encouragement and light that can uplift others, fostering a community steeped in gratitude together.

AUGUST 31

DAY 244

GOD FILLS ME WITH EVERLASTING JOY

Affirmation: God's joy is my constant source of strength and renewal.

Scripture: "Those who sow with tears will reap with songs of joy." – Psalm 126:5 (NIV)

Encouragement: Even my struggles are leading to something greater, revealing a divine plan that surpasses my understanding. In times of hardship and sorrow, I find comfort in the knowledge that God is at work behind the scenes, transforming my pain into a fertile ground for joy to blossom. Just as seeds must be sown in tears before they yield a harvest, I trust in God's perfect timing and His unshakeable promises. He will not let my struggles go to waste; rather, they are an essential part of the journey toward the abundant joy He has in store for me.

As I navigate through life's challenges, I remind myself that God's joy is my constant source of strength and renewal. His promise that I will ultimately reap songs of joy provides hope in my moments of despair. I choose to focus on the good that arises from my trials, knowing that each tear I shed today is watering the seeds of happiness that will bloom in the future. So, I hold tight to my faith, embracing the process of transformation, confident that joy is not just a fleeting feeling but a powerful gift from God that sustains me through every season of life.

SEPTEMBER 1

DAY 245

LIVING A JOYFUL LIFE

Affirmation: I radiate joy in all that I do, reflecting God's love to the world.

Scripture: "May the God of hope fill you with all joy and peace as you trust in him, so that you may overflow with hope by the power of the Holy Spirit." – Romans 15:13 (NIV)

Encouragement: Joy is a light within me that shines outward, touching the lives of those around me. It is not just an emotion; it is a profound expression of faith and gratitude that reflects my relationship with God. Each day, as I cultivate and embrace this God-given joy, I become a source of inspiration for others, encouraging them to tap into their own wellspring of joy. In these moments, I not only uplift myself but also create an atmosphere of positivity and hope, reminding others that joy is accessible and transformative, even amid life's challenges.

As I continue on this journey, I am reminded of the powerful promise found in Romans 15:13. This scripture reassures me that the God of hope longs to fill me with joy and peace, especially as I place my trust in Him. I recognize that my overflow of joy is not merely for my benefit; it is a divine gift meant to be shared with the world. With the support of the Holy Spirit, my joy becomes contagious, fostering a spirit of encouragement that can ripple through my community. By radiating joy in all that I do, I reflect God's unconditional love and grace, inviting others to experience the profound blessings that come from trusting in Him.

Week 36

Stepping Into My Best Self

SEPTEMBER 2

DAY 246

I AM BECOMING WHO I AM MEANT TO BE

Affirmation: Each day, I am growing into my best self with confidence and grace.

Scripture: "For the Lord gives wisdom; from his mouth come knowledge and understanding.

He holds success in store for the upright, he is a shield to those whose walk is blameless." – Proverbs 2:6-7 (NIV)

Encouragement: God has placed a purpose within me, and I am walking boldly in it. Every challenge I overcome strengthens me, and every lesson I learn shapes me into the person I am meant to be. It is crucial to remember that this journey is not always linear; there may be setbacks, but each twist and turn only serves to create a more resilient version of myself. Embracing the journey, with its peaks and valleys, is essential in realizing the beauty of becoming. God's grace envelopes us during the tough times, reminding us that we are never alone in this transformation.

Additionally, as I continue to evolve, I can find comfort in knowing that my growth is not solely for my benefit but can positively impact those around me. The wisdom I gain and the experiences I endure pave the way for me to uplift and encourage others who may be walking similar paths. With each step I take toward my true self, I am casting a light that can shine brightly into the lives of others. My journey serves as a testament to God's faithfulness, revealing that the process of becoming is a beautiful collaboration between His will and my willingness to follow His lead.

SEPTEMBER 3

DAY 247

MY GROWTH IS A PROCESS, NOT A DESTINATION

Affirmation: I give myself grace as I evolve into the best version of me.

Scripture: "Neither height nor depth, nor anything else in all creation, will be able to separate us from the love of God."– Romans 8:39 (NIV)

Encouragement: Transformation takes time, and I honor my journey. Each step I take brings me closer to the fullness of who I am in Christ. As I navigate this path of growth, I remind myself that setbacks are not failures but crucial parts of the learning process. Every challenge I encounter only deepens my understanding and strengthens my resolve. It's important to celebrate progress, no matter how small, because each moment of perseverance adds to the beautiful tapestry of my life in faith.

I also hold onto the truth that I am never alone in this journey. God's unwavering love envelops me, providing the comfort and strength I need to keep moving forward. As I experience different seasons, I will lean into His embrace and trust that He is continually shaping me into His image. By recognizing and embracing the process, I find peace in knowing that my evolution is a testament to His faithfulness and grace.

In this sacred journey, I am encouraged to walk with confidence, anticipating the beautiful transformations that lie ahead.

SEPTEMBER 4

DAY 248

I AM FEARFULLY AND WONDERFULLY MADE

Affirmation: I embrace the masterpiece God created me to be.

Scripture: "She is more precious than rubies; nothing you desire can compare with her." – Proverbs 3:15 (NIV)

Encouragement: I am not defined by my past, my struggles, or my appearance. I am defined by God's love and purpose for me. Each day, I am reminded that my worth transcends the challenges I face. God, in His infinite wisdom, has crafted me with unique gifts and attributes that serve a divine purpose. It's essential to see myself through His eyes, recognizing that I am a beloved creation, intricately designed to shine brightly in a world that often seeks to dim my light.

Moreover, embracing my identity as a masterpiece allows me to extend grace to myself. Just as I am beautifully made, I will cultivate the same appreciation for others, seeing them as God does. In moments of self-doubt or insecurity, I will remember that I am on a journey of growth and discovery, where every experience, whether good or challenging, contributes to the tapestry of my life. I am encouraged to celebrate my uniqueness, trusting that in God's plan, I am valued beyond measure, and my contributions to the world are significant and needed.

SEPTEMBER 5

DAY 249

I WALK IN PURPOSE AND CONFIDENCE

Affirmation: I am stepping boldly into my calling, trusting God's plan for my life.

Scripture: " Then our sons in their youth will be like well-nurtured plants, and our daughters will be like pillars carved to adorn a palace." – Psalm 144:12 (NIV)

Encouragement: My life has meaning, and my experiences shape the way I uplift others. I walk confidently, knowing I am called for something greater. Every challenge I face, every triumph I celebrate, adds depth to my story and equips me to inspire those around me. As I embrace my journey, I realize that my purpose is intricately woven into the lives of others, and my influence can ignite hope and motivation in their hearts.

When I step out with faith, I reflect the assurance that comes from knowing I am not alone in this journey. God walks beside me, nudging me forward and lighting the path ahead. This awareness fuels my courage and strengthens my resolve to fulfill my calling. As I cultivate confidence, I encourage others to recognize their own gifts, reminding them that they too have a unique purpose to fulfill. Together, we can create a legacy of support and empowerment, blossoming into the potential that God has lovingly crafted within each of us.

SEPTEMBER 6

DAY 250

I RELEASE ALL DOUBT AND STEP INTO GREATNESS

Affirmation: I let go of fear and trust God's divine timing in my life.

Scripture: "If you return to the Lord, then your fellow Israelites and your children will be shown compassion by their captors and will return to this land, for the Lord your God is gracious and compassionate. He will not turn his face from you if you return to him." – 2 Chronicles 30:9 (NIV)

Encouragement: I refuse to allow fear or self-doubt to hold me back. God has already paved the way for my greatness. When I feel the weight of uncertainty pressing down on me, I remind myself of the countless times throughout history where individuals stepped out in faith, despite their doubts. They chose to trust in God's guidance and timing, leading them to incredible outcomes that they could never have orchestrated on their own. This serves as a powerful reminder that my journey is unique, and though challenges may arise, I am equipped with the strength and courage to overcome them.

As I embrace this truth, I become more aware of the opportunities that lie ahead. Each moment is a chance to grow into the person God intended me to be, and every step forward is a testament to my resilience. I recognize that greatness is not defined by external achievements, but by the unwavering faith I cultivate in my heart. With each decision I make to release doubt and negativity, I am opening the door to a brighter tomorrow. I am not walking this path alone; God walks beside me, guiding my steps and reminding me that I am capable of so much more than I can imagine. It is in this spirit of faith that I can truly step into my greatness and fulfill my purpose.

SEPTEMBER 7

DAY 251

MY CONFIDENCE COMES FROM GOD

Affirmation: I stand boldly in my truth, knowing that I am enough just as I am.

Scripture: "The Son is the radiance of God's glory and the exact representation of his being, sustaining all things by his powerful word." – Hebrews 1:3 (NIV)

Encouragement: True confidence does not come from external validation but from knowing that God created me with purpose. I walk in that assurance daily. When I fully embrace my identity in Christ, I recognize that I am a unique masterpiece, designed with care and intention. Each of my strengths and weaknesses plays a role in the grand tapestry of His plan for my life, reminding me that I am inherently valuable simply because I was made in His image.

In moments of doubt or insecurity, I remind myself of the promises in Scripture that affirm my worth and purpose. I can trust that God sees the potential within me, even when I fail to recognize it. This understanding frees me to pursue my passions and step into my calling without hesitation, knowing that my confidence is rooted not in comparison with others but in the unwavering truth of who I am in Him. I am empowered to face challenges with grace, understanding that

His strength is made perfect in my weakness, and I am more than enough as I walk this journey of faith.

SEPTEMBER 8

DAY 252

I AM LIVING AS MY BEST SELF TODAY

Affirmation: I am not waiting for tomorrow—I step into my best self right now.

Scripture: " My heart is steadfast, O God, my heart is steadfast; I will sing and give praise.." – Psalm 57:7 (NKJV)

Encouragement: I choose to live fully in this moment. My best self is not a future version of me—it is who I decide to be today. I walk in joy, confidence, and faith. Each day, I am presented with countless opportunities to embrace my strengths and acknowledge my worth. It is within my reach to cultivate an attitude of gratitude for the present and to appreciate the growth that has led me here. By focusing on how I can serve others and uplift those around me, I reinforce my commitment to living authentically and purposefully.

In embracing my best self, I also recognize the importance of self-compassion. It's natural to experience challenges and setbacks, but I refuse to allow these moments to define me. Instead, I see them as stepping stones on my journey. Each day brings a fresh start and the chance to learn and evolve. So, I stand firm in the knowledge that I am enough, just as I am. With a heart full of gratitude, I will continue to strive for my dreams, knowing that my best self is already within me, waiting to shine

Week 37

Speaking Truth Over Lies

SEPTEMBER 9

DAY 253

THE TRUTH OF WHO I AM

Affirmation: I reject every lie spoken over me and embrace the truth of who God says I am.

Scripture: "Let us then approach God's throne of grace with confidence, so that we may receive mercy and find grace to help us in our time of need." – Hebrews 4:16 (NIV)

Encouragement: The world may try to define me, but only God's truth matters. I choose to walk in His word and not in the opinions of others. As I immerse myself in the scriptures, I become increasingly aware of my identity in Christ, which is unshakeable and steadfast. The whispers of doubt and insecurity may come from various sources, but I have the power to reject them and stand firm in the assurance that I am fearfully and wonderfully made.

Additionally, it's vital to surround myself with reminders of God's promises and affirmations. Embracing a community that uplifts and encourages me in my journey helps reinforce the truth of my identity. Together, we can celebrate our uniqueness and point each other back to the life-giving word of God. Each day is an opportunity to refresh my mind with His truth and to declare boldly that I am a beloved child of the King, destined to walk in His purpose and grace.

SEPTEMBER 10

DAY 254

I AM NOT MY STRUGGLES

Affirmation: My challenges do not define me—God's promises do.

Scripture: "For we know, brothers and sisters loved by God, that he has chosen you."

– 1 Thessalonians 1:4 (NIV)

Encouragement: My struggles are not my identity. I am more than my circumstances, and God has a purpose for my life beyond what I can see today. Even when I feel overwhelmed, I can find strength in the knowledge that God is with me, guiding me through each trial. It is during these challenging moments that He often shapes and molds me, preparing me for the future He has in store. Understanding this allows me to shift my perspective; instead of seeing my difficulties as barriers, I can view them as opportunities for growth and deeper faith.

Furthermore, I can remind myself that every challenge I face is temporary and serves a greater purpose in the tapestry of my life. When I lean on God's promises, I find comfort in the fact that He has chosen me, despite my struggles. I can embrace the journey—knowing that it refines my character and brings me closer to the person God created me to be. Each day is a fresh start, filled with possibilities, and I can confront my difficulties with renewed hope, trusting that God's love and guidance will lead me through.

SEPTEMBER 11

DAY 255

I SPEAK LIFE OVER MYSELF

Affirmation: My words have power, and I choose to speak life, not doubt.

Scripture: "For to be sure, he was crucified in weakness, yet he lives by God's power. Likewise, we are weak in him, yet by God's power we will live with him in our dealing with you." – 2 Corinthians 13:4 (NIV)

Encouragement: I will not allow negativity to take root in my spirit. Instead, I speak blessings, truth, and faith over my life every day. Each time I declare positivity, I am sowing seeds of hope and resilience within my heart. These words have the power to shape my reality, creating an atmosphere where joy can flourish and fears can diminish. By consciously choosing to speak life, I position myself to embrace the abundance that God has promised, allowing His truth to guide my thoughts and actions.

Furthermore, as I proclaim life over myself, I am reminded that this practice not only transforms my own mindset but can also be a source of encouragement to those around me. My words can uplift and inspire others, creating a ripple effect of positivity in our communities. Whenever I face challenges, I will remember that speaking life is a choice that empowers not just me, but those who hear my voice. By embracing the truth of God's power in my life, I become a vessel of His love and strength, reflecting His light in a world that often feels heavy and daunting.

SEPTEMBER 12

DAY 256

I AM WHOLE AND COMPLETE IN CHRIST

Affirmation: I lack nothing because I am made whole in Him.

Scripture: "For in Christ all the fullness of the Deity lives in bodily form, and in Christ you have been brought to fullness." – Colossians 2:9-10 (NIV)

Encouragement: I am not missing anything. I am complete just as I am, created in God's image and filled with His love. This wholeness is not dependent on external circumstances or the approval of others; it is an intrinsic truth that is rooted in my identity in Christ. When I face moments of doubt or insecurity, I can remind myself that I am crafted perfectly for the purposes God has for my life. Each of my unique qualities has been intentionally designed, enabling me to fulfill my calling and contribute to His kingdom in significant ways.

In a world that often promotes the idea of lack, I am invited to embrace the truth that through Christ, I have every resource I need to thrive. My worth is not measured by achievements or possessions but by the extraordinary love God has poured into my life. As I walk in this truth, I gain the strength to confront challenges, to step out in faith, and to love others deeply, knowing that my completeness is rooted in Him. Today, I choose to celebrate the wholeness I have in Christ and live confidently as the beautiful reflection of His love that I am.

SEPTEMBER 13

DAY 257

I AM FEARLESS IN TRUTH

Affirmation: I will not let fear silence the truth within me.

Scripture: "Your hands made me and formed me; give me understanding to learn your commands."– Psalm 119:73 (NIV)

Encouragement: Fear has no place in my life. I am bold, I am strong, and I walk in the power of God's truth daily. I recognize that every challenge I face is an opportunity for growth, and with each step taken in faith, I am embodying the courage bestowed upon me by my Creator. When doubt tries to creep in, I will stand firm, knowing that the truth ignites my spirit and provides clarity in turbulent times. I commit to being a vessel of the truth, shining brightly in the shadows of fear.

Each encounter I have with the truth strengthens my resolve and reinforces my identity as a child of God. I remember that the truth is not only a guiding light for my journey but also a source of liberation from the chains of anxiety and uncertainty. As I embrace this fearless mindset, I also encourage others to discover their own strength and voices within. Together, we can create a community where honesty and transparency flourish, reminding one another that we are never alone in our pursuit of truth. With God's guidance, I will continue to rise above the whisper of fear, confident in the steadfast truth that shapes my life.

SEPTEMBER 14

DAY 258

GOD'S TRUTH IS MY FOUNDATION

Affirmation: I stand on the unshakable truth of God's word.

Scripture: "Heaven and earth will pass away, but my words will never pass away." – Matthew 24:35 (NIV)

Encouragement: The world may change, but God's truth remains the same. I build my confidence on His promises, knowing they will never fail. In moments of uncertainty, when the world feels chaotic, I can turn to His Word as my refuge and strength. It is a constant source of hope that reminds me I am not alone in my struggles; He is with me always, guiding and comforting me through life's storms.

No matter how daunting life's challenges may seem, I can draw upon the unchanging nature of God's truth to remind myself that I am grounded in something much bigger than my circumstances. Each promise He has made is a firm foundation upon which I can stand. As I meditate on His Word, I find renewed strength and encouragement, knowing that even when everything else seems to falter, His truth will be my anchor, keeping me steady and secure in His love.

SEPTEMBER 15

DAY 259

I AM WHO GOD SAYS I AM

Affirmation: My identity is rooted in God, not in the opinions of others.

Scripture: "But you are a chosen people, a royal priesthood, a holy nation, God's special possession, that you may declare the praises of him who called you out of darkness into his wonderful light." – 1 Peter 2:9 (NIV)

Encouragement: I do not need validation from anyone—I am already chosen, loved, and set apart by God. Today, I walk boldly in that truth. It can be easy to become entangled in the opinions and expectations of others, but we must remind ourselves that our worth is intrinsic, defined by our relationship with the Creator. Our identity as His beloved children cannot be altered by external circumstances or the fleeting judgments of those around us. Instead, let us anchor ourselves in the eternal truth that we are precious to Him.

As we go about our day, let's cultivate a mindset that reflects our royal identity. This means embracing our uniqueness and recognizing the gifts and talents God has placed within us. When doubt creeps in or when we feel inadequate, we can remind ourselves that we are designed with purpose. By walking confidently in our identity, we not only affirm who we are but also inspire those around us to embrace their own worth as God's chosen people. Let the knowledge of His love empower you to shine brightly wherever you go, declaring His praises through your very existence.

Week 38

I Am Whole as I Am

SEPTEMBER 16

DAY 260

I AM ENOUGH

Affirmation: I am enough just as I am, lacking nothing in God's eyes.

Scripture: "He has made everything beautiful in its time. He has also set eternity in the human heart; yet[a] no one can fathom what God has done from beginning to end. " – Ecclesiastes 3:11 (NIV)

Encouragement: God created me with intention and purpose. I don't need to strive for perfection because I am already enough. Each day is a gift, and within it lies the potential for growth and transformation. It's vital to remember that our worth is not determined by our achievements or the opinions of others but is rooted in God's love for us. When we embrace this truth, we can let go of the burdens of comparison and self-doubt, choosing instead to walk in the freedom and joy that come from knowing we are perfectly made.

As we navigate through life's challenges, let us remind ourselves that God's definition of "enough" transcends our limited understanding. It invites us to see our weaknesses as opportunities for His strength to shine through us. When insecurities arise, we can reaffirm our identity in Christ by meditating on Scripture and surrounding ourselves with community that uplifts and encourages us. In recognizing our inherent value, we become empowered to live authentically, allowing our true selves to flourish in the beauty that God has woven into our lives.

SEPTEMBER 17

DAY 261

MY WHOLENESS IS IN CHRIST

Affirmation: My identity is rooted in Christ, and in Him, I am whole.

Scripture: "Yet to all who did receive him, to those who believed in his name, he gave the right to become children of God."– John 1:12 (NIV)

Encouragement: No flaw, condition, or struggle can take away the completeness I have in Christ. I am whole and secure in Him. In moments when self-doubt creeps in, it's vital to remember that our worth isn't contingent upon our perceived imperfections or the standards set by the world. Instead, it is firmly established in the reality that we are loved and accepted by our Creator. He sees us in our entirety—flaws and all—and still calls us His children. Embracing this truth transforms how we view ourselves and our circumstances, reassuring us that we are deserving of love and grace.

Moreover, as we navigate the challenges of life, we can take comfort in knowing that Christ's grace is sufficient for every weakness we encounter. Each struggle can serve as an opportunity for growth, illuminating areas where we can learn to lean on His strength rather than our own. When we shift our focus from our imperfections to His unwavering love, we begin to experience the peace that comes from recognizing that our identity is not shaped by our shortcomings, but by God's incredible purpose and design for our lives. Let this truth resonate within you, guiding you toward a deeper understanding of your wholeness in Him.

SEPTEMBER 18

DAY 262

NOTHING IS MISSING FROM ME

Affirmation: I release the idea that I am lacking. I am full of purpose and love.

Scripture: " The lions may grow weak and hungry, but those who seek the Lord lack no good thing.." – Psalm 34:10 (NIV)

Encouragement: Society may try to tell me I need more to be complete, but God says I am already whole. I embrace His truth today. In this world, it's easy to fall into the trap of comparison, measuring our worth by the possessions we accumulate or the accolades we earn. Yet, when I shift my focus to my identity in Christ, I realize that my value lies not in external validation but in the love and grace I have received. Every day I can choose to walk in the assurance that I am filled with divine purpose, and that my life is enriched by God's presence within me.

As I continue to seek Him, I understand that completeness doesn't come from outside influences; it stems from my relationship with my Creator. I can release the burdens of inadequacy and self-doubt that the world imposes on me, knowing that I lack nothing. With God on my side, I am equipped to handle all that life presents. Today, I will celebrate the wholeness that He has instilled in me and focus on the blessings that overflow from this divine connection.

SEPTEMBER 19

DAY 263

I AM PERFECTLY DESIGNED BY GOD

Affirmation: God's design for me is perfect, and I embrace myself fully.

Scripture: "Yet you, Lord, are our Father. We are the clay, you are the potter; we are all the work of your hand." – Isaiah 64:8 (NIV)

Encouragement: I am handcrafted by the Almighty. Every detail of my being is intentional and beautiful in His sight. As I navigate through life, it's essential to remember that I was created with a unique purpose. Each trait and characteristic is a reflection of God's creative genius, crafted to fulfill His specific plan for me. When I feel inadequate or question my value, I can look to the truth that my existence is a testament to His love and intention.

Moreover, I can find comfort in knowing that every challenge I face has been woven into the tapestry of my life to help shape me into the person He designed me to be. Just as a potter molds clay with care and precision, God is continually refining my character and helping me grow. I can embrace my imperfections, knowing they are part of my journey. Each moment is an opportunity to celebrate not just who I am but also who I am becoming in Him. His hands shape me, guide me, and empower me to step boldly into my calling, just as He envisioned.

SEPTEMBER 20

DAY 264

I AM NOT DEFINED BY SOCIETY'S STANDARDS

Affirmation: My worth is not based on society's expectations, but on God's truth.

Scripture: "We were therefore buried with him through baptism into death in order that, just as Christ was raised from the dead through the glory of the Father, we too may live a new life." – Romans 6:4 (NIV)

Encouragement: I release the need for validation from the world. I stand firm in the truth that I am whole, worthy, and valuable just as I am. It can be challenging to resist the pull of societal standards and expectations. Everywhere we look, there are messages that try to dictate our worth based on our appearance, accomplishments, or status. However, by intentionally choosing to focus on God's love and acceptance, we can dismantle these false narratives and embrace the identity God has given us. Remember that He sees you as uniquely valuable, deserving of love and grace, not because of what you do, but simply because of who you are in Him.

Moreover, let us take solace in the fact that God's view of us is far greater and more profound than any superficial metric the world might impose. Each day presents a new opportunity to reaffirm our identity in Christ and to bask in the truth that we are fearfully and wonderfully made. When doubts arise or when we feel the temptation to compare ourselves to others, let us return to His Word, meditate on His promises, and remind ourselves that our lives are defined by His purpose. We are not alone in this journey; God walks alongside us, imparting His peace and assurance every step of the way.

SEPTEMBER 21

DAY 265

MY INNER BEAUTY SHINES BRIGHTLY

Affirmation: My inner beauty radiates far beyond what is seen on the surface.

Scripture: "Come now, let us settle the matter," says the Lord. "Though your sins are like scarlet,

they shall be as white as snow; though they are red as crimson, they shall be like wool.." – Isaiah 1:18 (NIV)

Encouragement: True beauty comes from within. I nurture my spirit, and it shines brighter than anything physical ever could. As I cultivate love, kindness, and compassion in my heart, I become a vessel of God's light in the world. Every time I choose to speak words of encouragement or offer a helping hand to someone in need, I not only reflect my inner beauty but also inspire others to recognize and embrace their own. My actions, rooted in love and authenticity, create ripples of beauty that extend far beyond myself.

Each day is an opportunity to engage in practices that enhance my inner beauty, such as prayer, meditation, and gratitude. By setting aside time to connect with myself and with God, I invite the divine presence to transform my heart and mind. When I fill my thoughts with positivity and forgiveness, I become more radiant, and my light becomes a beacon for those around me. This commitment to nurturing my inner self not only deepens my faith but also allows my true beauty to shine in a world that often emphasizes superficial appearances.

SEPTEMBER 22

DAY 266

I CELEBRATE MYSELF TODAY

Affirmation: I celebrate who I am in this moment, without condition or comparison.

Scripture: " Who keeps our soul among the living, And does not allow our feet to [a]be moved.

For You, O God, have tested us; You have refined us as silver is refined.." – Psalm 66:9-10 (NKJV)

Encouragement: Today, I choose joy. I celebrate myself, my journey, and the beautiful life God has given me. I am whole, I am loved, and I am enough. Each day is a new opportunity to recognize the incredible worth that resides within me. I release the burdens of self-doubt and the urge to measure my value against anyone else's accomplishments. Instead, I embrace my individuality, understanding that my path is distinct and intricately designed for my growth and fulfillment.

As I reflect on my experiences, both joyful and challenging, I acknowledge the lessons that have shaped my character and resilience. These moments of testing are not merely obstacles; they are stepping stones guiding me toward a deeper understanding of myself and my purpose. I choose to honor every part of my journey, knowing that God celebrates me with love and grace. Today, I am empowered to shine brightly, to love myself fiercely, and to recognize the divine potential within me, fully embracing the unique journey that is mine alone.

Week 39

No More Apologies

SEPTEMBER 23

DAY 267

I WILL NOT DIM MY LIGHT

Affirmation: I refuse to shrink myself for the comfort of others.

Scripture: "Neither do people light a lamp and put it under a bowl. Instead, they put it on its stand, and it gives light to everyone in the house." – Matthew 5:15 (NIV)

Encouragement: My light was meant to shine. I will not apologize for the brightness God has placed within me. Each time I embrace my uniqueness and allow my true self to illuminate the world, I honor the gifts and talents that the Creator has generously bestowed upon me. It's easy to feel pressure to conform or dim my brilliance for the sake of others' comfort, but I am reminded that my light is a beacon of hope and inspiration. When I shine brightly, I empower those around me to recognize their own light and encourage them to let it shine as well.

Moreover, I understand that there will be times when my light may attract attention, both positive and negative. However, as I stand firm in my identity and purpose, I choose to focus on the impact I can make. Every act of kindness, every passionate pursuit, and every bold step forward creates a ripple effect, encouraging others to be courageous in their own journeys. I embrace the fullness of who I am, knowing that my shining light is not just for me but serves to uplift and enrich the lives of everyone I encounter. In this way, I fulfill my calling to be a light in the darkness, bringing warmth, clarity, and hope to those searching for their own light.

SEPTEMBER 24

DAY 268

I AM WORTHY OF TAKING UP SPACE

Affirmation: I deserve to take up space in every room I enter.

Scripture: "Rejoice always." – 1 Thessalonians 5:16 (NIV)

Encouragement: I belong here. I am not an afterthought. I walk in confidence, knowing that I am fearfully and wonderfully made. It is essential to remind ourselves of our intrinsic worth and the unique gifts we bring to the world. Each time I step into a room, I carry my experiences, my perspective, and my heart, which all contribute to the beautiful tapestry of humanity. No one else can take up the space in my way, and that is something to celebrate. We are all woven from the same threads of love and purpose, and that strength is reinforced with every breath we take.

Moreover, as we embrace our rightful place, we encourage others to do the same. Our confidence can be a catalyst for those around us, prompting them to recognize their own worthiness and encouraging them to take their rightful space as well. Together, we create an environment where everyone feels empowered to shine bright and fully express themselves. Let us remember that when we stand proudly in our truth, we not only affirm our own worth but also invite others to flourish alongside us in the spaces we share.

SEPTEMBER 25

DAY 269

MY CONFIDENCE IS GOD-GIVEN

Affirmation: I will not apologize for the confidence I carry.

Scripture: "We have this hope as an anchor for the soul, firm and secure." – Hebrews 6:19 (NIV)

Encouragement: God placed confidence within me, and I will not discard it. I embrace it fully and walk boldly. This divine confidence is not rooted in arrogance but in the truth of who I am in Christ. Each day, I choose to recognize that I am a reflection of His love and grace. This understanding empowers me to face challenges with a steadfast heart, knowing that I am never alone in my journey. My confidence is fortified by His promises, guiding me through uncertainty and into purpose.

As I move forward, I remind myself that confidence can inspire those around me. When I stand firm in my beliefs and embrace my God-given abilities, I become a beacon of hope for others who may struggle with self-doubt. By showcasing the strength and assurance that come from my relationship with God, I can encourage others to find and nurture their own confidence. Together, we can uplift each other, reflecting the light of His love and creating a community grounded in faith and courage.

SEPTEMBER 26

DAY 270

I STAND IN MY TRUTH WITHOUT SHAME

Affirmation: I refuse to apologize for who I am and the journey I have walked.

Scripture: " Be very careful, then, how you live—not as unwise but as wise." – Ephesians 5:15 (NIV)

Encouragement: My past, my struggles, my victories—all of it makes me who I am. I stand in my truth without fear or regret. Embracing my journey allows me to acknowledge the lessons learned and the growth achieved through every challenge and triumph. Each experience, whether painful or joyous, contributes to the rich tapestry of my life, reminding me that I am not defined by my mistakes but rather by how I choose to rise above them.

When I stand confidently in my truth, I empower others to do the same. My authenticity can spark courage in those around me who may still be hiding parts of their own stories. By sharing my journey openly, I create a space for vulnerability and connection, inviting others to step into their own truth without shame. Together, we can celebrate our unique paths and the wisdom we have gained, reinforcing that we are beautifully made and worthy of love and acceptance exactly as we are.

SEPTEMBER 27

DAY 271

I AM DONE SEEKING APPROVAL

Affirmation: I do not need permission to be myself.

Scripture: " In everything set them an example by doing what is good. In your teaching show integrity, seriousness." – Titus 2:7 (NIV)

Encouragement: I no longer seek validation from others. God's approval is enough for me. Embracing this truth frees me from the shackles of comparison and the pressure to conform to the expectations of those around me. When I anchor my identity in Christ, I can confidently walk the path He has laid out for me without the burden of needing to please anyone else. This journey toward self-acceptance allows me to fully experience the joy of being uniquely created by God, instilling in me a deep sense of purpose and belonging that transcends human affirmation.

Furthermore, understanding that I am already beloved by God strengthens my resolve to live authentically. I am reminded that my worth is not contingent on external accolades or the opinions of others; rather, it is firmly rooted in His unconditional love. As I delve deeper into this realization, I find courage to express the gifts and talents He has bestowed upon me without hesitation. I surrender the need for approval, knowing that my true calling is to serve Him and reflect His light in the world. In doing so, I discover a profound sense of freedom that empowers me to be unapologetically myself.

SEPTEMBER 28

DAY 272:

I SPEAK MY TRUTH WITHOUT FEAR

Affirmation: I will no longer apologize for my voice, my opinions, or my perspective.

Scripture: " Do not trust in extortion or put vain hope in stolen goods; though your riches increase,

do not set your heart on them.." – Psalm 62:10 (NIV)

Encouragement: My voice matters. I will speak with clarity, grace, and conviction, knowing that my words hold power. Each time I express my truth, I contribute to a larger conversation and create an opportunity for others to share their perspectives as well. Speaking my truth not only empowers me but also encourages those around me to embrace their own voices. It's in this shared authenticity that we find connection and strength, breaking the chains of silence that often hold us back.

Moreover, I recognize that sharing my truth can be daunting, yet I am strengthened by the understanding that vulnerability is a courageous act. When I articulate my thoughts and feelings, I give permission for others to do the same. Embracing openness fosters a culture of acceptance and understanding, reminding us that our differences can coexist harmoniously. In moments of doubt, I will remember that every word I speak contributes to a greater journey of self-discovery and communal growth, and that the beauty of humanity lies in our diverse voices.

SEPTEMBER 29

DAY 273

I WILL NOT APOLOGIZE FOR BEING ME

Affirmation: I am unapologetically me, and that is enough.

Scripture: " For the Lord gives wisdom; from his mouth come knowledge and understanding. He holds success in store for the upright, he is a shield to those whose walk is blameless." – Proverbs 2:6-7 (NIV)

Encouragement: I embrace my identity fully. I am no longer apologizing for being exactly who God created me to be. Each of us is made uniquely, woven with intricate details that reflect God's creativity and purpose. Embracing my true self allows me to shine in the light of His love and grace. This journey of self-acceptance is not always easy, especially in a world that often pressures us to conform. Yet, when I stand in the truth of who I am, I give glory to the One who knows every part of me and loves me unconditionally.

Furthermore, recognizing my worth in God's eyes empowers me to celebrate others in their authenticity as well. Each person bears the image of our Creator and has a unique contribution to offer. By letting go of the fear of judgment and the need for validation, I can foster an environment of acceptance and encouragement around me. The more I embrace my individuality, the more I inspire others to do the same, creating a ripple effect of love that honors the diversity of God's masterpiece. Together, we can create a community where everyone feels free to express their true selves, knowing that we are all enough in Him.

Week 40

Embracing the Journey

SEPTEMBER 30

DAY 274

MY JOURNEY IS PURPOSEFUL

A**ffirmation:** Every step I take is leading me to my destiny.

Scripture: "Whoever is patient has great understanding, but one who is quick-tempered displays folly." – Proverbs 14:29 (NIV)

Encouragement: My journey may have twists and turns, but every step has a purpose. God is guiding me, and I trust the path He has set before me. In moments of uncertainty or frustration, I remind myself that the detours I face are often opportunities for growth and learning. Each challenge strengthens my resolve and equips me with the tools I need to navigate the future. This journey is about more than just reaching a destination; it's about becoming the person I am meant to be along the way.

As I embrace the uniqueness of my journey, I can find joy in the little victories and the lessons learned through trials. I am reminded that my faith is not just a guiding light; it also fuels my perseverance. The patience I cultivate now will serve me well as I move forward, allowing me to acknowledge each moment as an integral part of God's divine plan. With each step, I am drawing closer to my purpose, trusting that every experience is shaping me for the destiny that awaits.

OCTOBER 1

DAY 275

I AM LEARNING AND GROWING

Affirmation: Every experience is an opportunity for growth.

Scripture: "Be strong, and let us fight bravely for our people and the cities of our God. The Lord will do what is good in his sight." – 2 Samuel 10:12 (NIV)

Encouragement: Challenges are not roadblocks; they are stepping stones. I embrace each lesson as a way to grow stronger and wiser. Each experience, whether joyful or difficult, plays a vital role in shaping who I am becoming. The discomfort that often accompanies growth is temporary, but the strength and wisdom I gain from navigating these moments will last a lifetime. Every setback can prepare me for a comeback, and so I choose to view my challenges through the lens of opportunity instead of defeat.

Moreover, it's essential to remember that I'm not navigating this journey alone. As I face obstacles, I can lean on my faith and those who support me. In moments of doubt, reaching out to friends or trusted mentors can provide new perspectives and encouragement. Together, we can remind each other of our resilience and the light that shines through challenges. By fostering a mindset that sees growth in difficulties, I can not only uplift myself but also inspire those around me to embrace their own journeys with courage and hope.

OCTOBER 2

DAY 276

I TRUST GOD'S PLAN

Affirmation: Even when I don't understand, I trust in His divine timing.

Scripture: "May our Lord Jesus Christ himself and God our Father, who loved us and by his grace gave us eternal encouragement and good hope, encourage your hearts and strengthen you in every good deed and word." – 2 Thessalonians 2:16-17 (NIV)

Encouragement: I may not always see the bigger picture, but I trust that God's plan for me is filled with hope, prosperity, and purpose. In times of uncertainty or confusion, it's essential to remember that God's perspective is far greater than our own. He sees every twist and turn in our lives, expertly weaving them together according to a divine design that is ultimately for our good. When things feel chaotic or disjointed, we can lean into faith, reassured that there is a meaning behind every moment we encounter. His timing may not align with our expectations, but therein lies the beauty of trusting a God who knows us intimately.

Additionally, I can find comfort in the collective experiences of those who have walked similar paths. It's empowering to hear the testimonies of others who, in moments of distress, chose to trust God and saw His faithfulness manifest in extraordinary ways. When we share our struggles and triumphs, we strengthen each other, creating a community of support that mirrors God's love and encouragement. Therefore, I will embrace my present circumstances as opportunities to grow in faith, reminding myself that God's promises are unwavering and His plans for my life are perfectly crafted with love and intention.

OCTOBER 3

DAY 277

MY JOURNEY IS UNIQUELY MINE

Affirmation: I do not compare my path to others; I walk in my own purpose.

Scripture: " A person's wisdom yields patience; it is to one's glory to overlook an offense." – Proverbs 19:11 (NIV)

Encouragement: My story is mine alone. I release the need to compare and embrace my unique walk with confidence. It's essential to remember that every journey unfolds differently, shaped by personal experiences, lessons learned, and the distinctive dreams we've cultivated. In moments of doubt or insecurity, we can draw strength from the fact that our individual paths were intentionally designed. It's a reminder that each step we take holds significance and contributes to a greater tapestry that only we can weave.

Moreover, comparing ourselves to others can cloud our vision and diminish our joy. As we embrace our uniqueness, we must also celebrate the victories—big and small—that come our way. Each achievement, regardless of its size, is a testament to our resilience and the faith we have in ourselves and our purpose. Let us foster a spirit of gratitude for our own journeys, acknowledging the beauty and lessons within them. By doing so, we grow in wisdom, allowing our patience to flourish as we trust the process, nurture our growth, and honor our own timing.

OCTOBER 4

DAY 278

I AM EXACTLY WHERE I NEED TO BE

Affirmation: I am not behind; I am on time in God's plan.

Scripture: "The Lord is my helper, and I will not fear what man shall do unto me."– Hebrews 13:6 (NIV)

Encouragement: I resist the urge to rush. I am right where I need to be, and I trust God's timing in every aspect of my life. In moments when I feel the pressure to move ahead or when I compare my journey to others, I pause and remember that each path is uniquely designed by God. The steps I take today, even if they seem small or slow, are part of a greater purpose that is unfolding just as it should. It is in these moments of stillness that I am reminded that every delay, every setback, and every challenge is simply a stepping stone to divine alignment.

Moreover, I choose to embrace the lessons that come with each stage of my journey. Just as a seed must break before it sprouts, I too must undergo periods of growth and reflection. These experiences shape me, build my character, and prepare me for the wonderful things that God has in store. Instead of feeling anxious about what lies ahead, I will celebrate who I am becoming in the process. I trust that by being present in my current season, I am setting the foundation for a bright future filled with endless possibilities.

OCTOBER 5

DAY 279

I WALK IN FAITH, NOT FEAR

Affirmation: I move forward with faith, knowing God is with me.

Scripture: " One who has unreliable friends soon comes to ruin, but there is a friend who sticks closer than a brother." – Proverbs 18:24 (NIV)

Encouragement: Even when I cannot see the outcome, I choose faith over fear. God is directing my steps, and I trust Him completely. In every situation I face, I remember that my faith is a powerful tool that can guide me through uncertainty. It is in the moments of doubt that I need to cling to the promise that God is holding my hand throughout this journey. By leaning into Him, I am reminded that every step I take is supported by His infinite wisdom and love, which equips me to confront my fears head-on.

In addition to this, I recognize that my journey in faith is not meant to be walked alone. Surrounding myself with a community of fellow believers encourages me to stay anchored in hope. Together, we can lift each other up during difficult times and celebrate the victories we experience along the way. By sharing our stories and testimonies, we reinforce the truth that God is ever-present and working in our lives, inspiring us to keep moving forward in faith, no matter how daunting the path may seem.

OCTOBER 6

DAY 280

I CELEBRATE MY PROGRESS

Affirmation: I honor every step forward, no matter how small.

Scripture: " When he arrived and saw what the grace of God had done, he was glad and encouraged them all to remain true to the Lord with all their hearts." – Acts 11:23 (NLT)

Encouragement: Progress is progress, no matter the pace. I celebrate my journey and give myself grace, knowing that each step forward is a victory. Each moment of growth, no matter how insignificant it may seem, contributes to the beautiful tapestry of my life. The moments when I feel stuck or overwhelmed are merely pauses in the journey, and they remind me of the importance of perseverance. Just like a seed takes time to grow into a mighty tree, my development also requires patience and nurturing. I will honor the process and trust that each effort I make is building towards a greater purpose.

Moreover, it's essential to remember that progress isn't always linear. There will be ups and downs, twists and turns; yet, each experience will teach me something valuable. When faced with challenges, I can lean on the assurance that I am never alone in my struggles. God's grace surrounds me, guiding my steps and encouraging my heart as I strive to move forward. By choosing to focus on the progress I've made rather than the distance I still need to cover, I cultivate a spirit of gratitude and resilience, which will empower me to keep pressing on, celebrating every milestone along the way.

Week 41

Resilience is My Superpower

OCTOBER 7

DAY 281

I AM STRONGER THAN MY STRUGGLES

Affirmation: My challenges do not define me; my strength does.

Scripture: "Though the mountains be shaken and the hills be removed, yet my unfailing love for you will not be shaken nor my covenant of peace be removed, says the Lord, who has compassion on you."

– Isaiah 54:10 (NIV)

Encouragement: Every challenge I face is an opportunity to witness my own resilience. God's grace empowers me to rise above every obstacle. In moments of struggle, it is easy to feel overwhelmed and isolated, but I must remember that these trials are temporary and that I am not alone. God has equipped me with the strength to navigate through life's toughest moments. Each setback is a stepping stone leading me closer to the person I am meant to become, refining my character and deepening my faith along the way.

It's important to remind myself that my struggles are an integral part of my journey. They serve to remind me of my capabilities and to awaken the strength within me that I may not realize I possess. With each battle I face, I become stronger, more compassionate, and more deeply connected to God's love. As I lean into His unfailing support, I find peace amidst the chaos, knowing that every challenge is an invitation to grow and to embrace the powerful truths of my identity in Christ.

OCTOBER 8

DAY 282

I AM BUILT TO OVERCOME

Affirmation: I am equipped with everything I need to succeed.

Scripture: "He chose to give us birth through the word of truth, that we might be a kind of first fruits of all he created." – James 1:18 (NIV)

Encouragement: I am never without the tools to overcome. With God's strength within me, there is no battle too great, no challenge too big. Each day, I can draw from the well of His wisdom, love, and guidance that empowers me. When difficulties arise, I can remind myself that those who trust in Him will find renewed strength. This assurance equips me to face obstacles head-on, knowing that I am not facing them alone. I can lean into His promises, which serve as my shield and my sword, helping me to forge ahead with courage and confidence.

Moreover, it is essential to remember that overcoming is not just about victory in the moment but also about growth. Each challenge I face is an opportunity to cultivate resilience and deepen my faith. God uses these experiences to shape my character and prepare me for the purpose He has for my life. By embracing this journey, I become a living testament of His grace, showcasing not just how I have overcome but how His presence in my life continuously prevails. With every step, I become more equipped to face future trials, transforming adversity into a platform for His glory.

OCTOBER 9

DAY 283

I WILL NOT BREAK

Affirmation: I may bend, but I will not break.

Scripture: "Though I walk in the midst of trouble, you preserve my life." – Psalm 138:7 (NIV)

Encouragement: Life may test me, but I refuse to be broken. I am resilient, protected, and victorious through Christ. Each challenge I encounter serves as an opportunity for growth and learning, molding my character and deepening my faith. Even when I feel overwhelmed, I can take comfort in knowing that every difficulty I face is not the end of my journey but a stepping stone toward something greater. With each bend, I am becoming stronger, more flexible, and more equipped to handle whatever comes my way.

In moments of doubt, I will remember the countless times I have overcome obstacles by leaning on God's unfailing love and strength. He walks beside me in the midst of chaos, reminding me that I am never alone. Those moments of endurance build my perseverance and pave the way for a testimony of His goodness. I will hold tightly to the truth that I can stretch and sway, but I will remain steadfast, because with God, I am always anchored.

OCTOBER 10

DAY 284

MY SCARS TELL A STORY OF VICTORY

Affirmation: My past struggles are proof of my triumph.

Scripture: " They will wage war against the Lamb, but the Lamb will triumph over them because he is Lord of lords and King of kings—and with him will be his called, chosen and faithful followers." – Revelations 17:14 (NIV)

Encouragement: My scars remind me of how far I've come. They are not signs of weakness, but of my resilience and strength in God. Each scar carries a story—a journey through challenges, heartaches, and growth. It is through these trials that I have learned to trust in God's unwavering faithfulness. With every struggle, I have gained wisdom and understanding, and I have become more equipped to face the challenges that lie ahead. My scars are truly a testament to God's grace, showing how He has brought me through the storms and into the light.

As I look at my scars, I am encouraged to remember that they serve a greater purpose; they can help others who are facing similar struggles. My experiences are not just for me but can be a beacon of hope for someone else who might feel lost or defeated. Sharing my story can inspire others to see that they, too, can overcome their challenges. The journey may be difficult, but with faith and perseverance, we emerge stronger and more compassionate. Embracing my scars allows me to own my story and encourages me to uplift others who are still navigating their own paths of healing and victory.

OCTOBER 11

DAY 285

I RISE ABOVE FEAR

Affirmation: Fear has no place in my heart; I walk in faith.

Scripture: "Surely God is my salvation; I will trust and not be afraid. The Lord, the Lord himself, is my strength and my defense; he has become my salvation."– Isaiah 12:2 (NIV)

Encouragement: Fear is a liar. I choose faith over fear, trusting that God's power within me is greater than anything I face. In the moments when fear whispers in my ear, I remind myself of the countless times God has delivered me. Each victory strengthens my resolve and serves as a testament to His unwavering faithfulness. I can stand firm in the knowledge that I am not alone; God walks beside me through every challenge, guiding my steps and illuminating my path.

As I embrace this journey of faith, I find that each act of courage, however small, lays the groundwork for greater bravery. When I confront my fears with faith, I become a living testament to God's grace. This not only transforms my own experience but also serves as an encouragement to others who may be grappling with their own uncertainties. By sharing my journey and triumphs, I ignite hope in those around me, reminding them that through faith, we can rise above even the most daunting fears. Together, we can cultivate a community rooted in love, strength, and unwavering trust in God.

OCTOBER 12

DAY 286

MY RESILIENCE IS A GIFT

Affirmation: My ability to rise again is my superpower.

Scripture: "The righteous may fall seven times, but they rise again." – Proverbs 24:16 (NIV)

Encouragement: No matter how many times life knocks me down, I get back up. That is my power, my resilience, and my testimony. Each time I rise, I learn something new about myself and my strength. The very act of getting back up reinforces my belief that I am capable of overcoming any obstacle. In moments of struggle, it's essential to remember that each setback is not a dead end, but rather a stepping stone on my journey. I can choose to see challenges as opportunities for growth, shaping me into a stronger and wiser individual.

Moreover, my resilience is not just for my own benefit; it serves as an inspiration to others. When I share my journey of rising against the odds, I encourage those around me to confront their own challenges with courage. It creates a ripple effect, where my resilience empowers friends, family, and even strangers to harness their own strengths and persevere through adversity. Each time I rise again, I not only affirm my own capacity for resilience but also uplift the spirits of those walking their paths alongside me.

OCTOBER 13

DAY 287

I AM VICTORIOUS IN CHRIST

Affirmation: I walk in victory every day of my life.

Scripture: " In vain you rise early and stay up late, toiling for food to eat— for he grants sleep to those he loves." – Psalm 127:2 (NIV)

Encouragement: Victory is mine because God has already won the battle. I live each day knowing I am more than a conqueror through Him. As I go through life's challenges, I can remind myself that my identity is rooted in His strength and love. Each hurdle is an opportunity to experience and demonstrate the grace that empowers me to rise above any circumstance. God's promise to grant rest to those He loves reassures me that I don't have to carry my burdens alone; I can lay them at His feet and trust His perfect plan.

In this victory, I find peace in the midst of chaos and confidence in times of uncertainty. Even when I face difficulties, I celebrate the truth that I am not defined by my struggles but by the resilience that comes from being anchored in Christ. Knowing that He has gone before me, I can approach each day with renewed hope and a joyful spirit, ready to embrace whatever comes my way, because my victory is secured in Him. I can take heart, knowing that He is my guide and strength, and with Him, I can overcome all obstacles.

Week 42

Choosing to Shine

OCTOBER 14

DAY 288

MY LIGHT CANNOT BE DIMMED

Affirmation: I am a light in this world, and I will not hide.

Scripture: "The Lord will fight for you; you need only to be still." – Exodus 14:14 (NIV)

Encouragement: God placed a light within me that no circumstance can extinguish. I choose to let it shine boldly and unapologetically. In times of difficulty, when shadows seem to close in around me, I remind myself that my light is not dependent on my circumstances. Rather, it is a reflection of God's unwavering love and presence in my life. Each challenge I face offers me an opportunity to show others how the light of hope can shine through even the darkest times. By embracing this truth, I can encourage those around me to seek their own inner light and trust in the power of divine intervention.

Moreover, I must remember that my light can have a ripple effect, igniting flames of hope in those who witness my resilience. When I stand firm in my faith and radiate positivity, I invite others to do the same. Just as stars shine brightest against the night sky, my light becomes even more powerful in turbulent seasons. Today, I choose to be a beacon of encouragement, sharing my testimony, love, and kindness with everyone I encounter. In doing so, I not only honor the light within me but also inspire others to embrace the brilliance they carry within themselves.

OCTOBER 15

DAY 289

I RADIATE CONFIDENCE AND LOVE

Affirmation: My presence brings warmth and encouragement to others.

Scripture: "Though my father and mother forsake me, the Lord will receive me." – Psalm 27:10 (NIV)

Encouragement: My confidence isn't just for me—it inspires those around me. I shine with love, kindness, and authenticity. When I embrace my own worth, I create a ripple effect, encouraging others to recognize their own greatness. In moments of doubt or hardship, I can extend my warmth and support to those who might be struggling, reaffirming that they are valued and needed. It's a beautiful cycle of love and empowerment, where my positive energy uplifts others and, in turn, they inspire me to continue radiating confidence.

Furthermore, by embodying this spirit of encouragement, I foster an environment where everyone feels safe to share their vulnerabilities. It's through my genuine heart that I can help others see that they, too, are deserving of love and acceptance. Each act of light I share invites others to shine alongside me, forming a community rooted in support and mutual encouragement. Together, we can uplift each other, reminding everyone that they are never alone in their journey.

OCTOBER 16

DAY 290

I WAS CREATED TO SHINE

Affirmation: I step fully into the brilliance God designed for me.

Scripture: " Therefore put on the full armor of God, so that when the day of evil comes, you may be able to stand your ground, and after you have done everything, to stand. Stand firm then, with the belt of truth buckled around your waist, with the breastplate of righteousness in place." – Ephesians 6:13-14 (NIV)

Encouragement: God didn't create me to hide or shrink back. I embrace the beauty of being fully seen. Each day is a new opportunity to shine brightly in the world, reflecting the unique light that God has placed within me. I am reminded that my worth is not defined by the opinions of others or the challenges I face, but by the truth that I am a beloved creation of God. Embracing this truth allows me to stand confidently in my identity, knowing that I have something valuable to offer.

As I step into this brilliance, I understand that my light can also illuminate the paths of those around me. When I shine, I encourage others to do the same, creating a ripple effect of courage and empowerment within my community. It's not just about my journey but also about lifting up others, reminding them of their own worth and the light they carry. Together, we can form a constellation of hope and inspiration that points back to the Creator, enriching our lives and the lives of those we encounter.

OCTOBER 17

DAY 291

I AM WORTHY OF BEING SEEN

Affirmation: I refuse to shrink for the comfort of others.

Scripture: "And provide for those who grieve in Zion—to bestow on them a crown of beauty instead of ashes, the oil of joy instead of mourning, and a garment of praise instead of a spirit of despair."– Isaiah 61:3 (NIV)

Encouragement: I was not created to blend in. I take up space with confidence, knowing I am worthy of being seen and valued. Each time I choose to embrace my unique identity and shine my light, I am participating in the beautiful tapestry of life that God has woven. My presence has purpose, and I contribute to the world in ways that only I can. When I walk boldly in my truth, I not only honor myself but also inspire others to do the same. It's important to remember that my worth is not dependent on the approval of others; my significance comes from my Creator, who delights in the individuality He has crafted within me.

To nourish this sense of worthiness, I can reflect on the many gifts and talents I possess, allowing them to flourish and shine. I am encouraged to step outside the shadows of comparison and doubt, and instead, celebrate the unique potpourri of experiences that have shaped me. Each obstacle and triumph has further sculpted my character, creating a person deserving of recognition and love. As I continue to embrace my journey, I can trust that in being authentically me, I will attract connections and experiences that align with my true self, reaffirming the belief that I am indeed worthy of being seen.

OCTOBER 18

DAY 292

MY PRESENCE IS A GIFT

Affirmation: The world is better because I am in it.

Scripture: "God is within her, she will not fall; God will help her at break of day."– Psalm 46:5 (NIV)

Encouragement: My life has purpose, and my presence matters. I bless the world by simply being myself. Each day is an opportunity to radiate kindness, love, and joy just by showing up as my authentic self. The unique gifts and qualities that I possess contribute to the rich tapestry of life around me. When I embrace who I am, I uplift not only myself but also those who cross my path, reminding them that they, too, carry intrinsic value.

As I navigate life's challenges, I can take comfort in the assurance that I am never alone. God's presence is a constant source of strength and encouragement, guiding me through uncertainties and hardships. Knowing that I am a vessel for His love empowers me to face each day with confidence and grace. I am called to shine brightly not just for myself, but also to illuminate the way for others, reassuring them that they too are significant and cherished. In every moment, I can remind myself that my mere existence leaves an indelible mark on the world.

OCTOBER 19

DAY 293

I SHINE BRIGHTLY WITHOUT APOLOGY

Affirmation: I am confident in who God created me to be.

Scripture: "The Lord make his face shine on you and be gracious to you." – Numbers 6:25 (NIV)

Encouragement: There is no need to apologize for my brilliance. I walk in my purpose, knowing I am divinely created to shine. Embracing my unique gifts allows me to contribute to the world in a way that no one else can. Each talent and trait that God has bestowed upon me is an essential part of the beautiful tapestry of life, and when I fully express myself, I inspire others to do the same. Recognizing the divine intention behind my existence fuels my confidence, empowering me to take bold steps towards my goals and passions.

Moreover, in shining brightly, I invite others to join me in that light. My courage to step into the fullness of who I am can uplift those around me, encouraging them to reclaim their own brilliance as well. It is a powerful reminder that when I allow my light to radiate, it not only serves my journey but also impacts the lives of others. Together, we can create a world where authenticity and self-acceptance flourish, reminding each other that we are all deserving of a space to shine without fear or hesitation.

OCTOBER 20

DAY 294

I AM A REFLECTION OF GOD'S GLORY

Affirmation: My life is a testimony of God's goodness.

Scripture: " Hear my prayer, Lord; listen to my cry for mercy. When I am in distress, I call to you,

because you answer me.." – Psalm 86:6-7 (NIV)

Encouragement: When I shine, I reflect God's glory. My life is a testament to His goodness, and I embrace every opportunity to let His light shine through me. It is important to remember that reflecting His glory isn't about perfection; it's about allowing His love and grace to flow through us in our everyday lives. Each act of kindness, each moment of patience, and each gesture of compassion becomes a mirror for others to see the divine, reminding us that we don't need to have it all figured out to be a powerful witness to His majesty.

In moments of doubt or struggle, I hold on to the truth that even my imperfections can be used to showcase God's glory. He can transform my challenges into opportunities for growth, creating a story that inspires others. When I face adversity, I can choose to lean into my faith, trusting that He works all things for my good. By sharing my journey, authentically embracing both the highs and lows, I not only shine brighter as His reflection, but also offer hope and encouragement to those around me who may be facing their own battles.

Week 43

Fully and Completely Me

OCTOBER 21

DAY 29

I AM ENOUGH JUST AS I AM

Affirmation: I am whole, worthy, and complete just as I am.

Scripture: " All people will fear; they will proclaim the works of God and ponder what he has done." – Psalm 64:9 (NIV)

Encouragement: I don't need to change or conform to be valuable. God created me intentionally, and I am beautifully made in His image. Each imperfection I perceive in myself only becomes a canvas for God's grace and love to shine through. Just as a masterpiece is defined by unique brush strokes, my individuality is a testament to the creativity of the Creator. When I embrace who I am, I step into the fullness of my potential, knowing that I do not need to seek validation from others. My worth is inherent, anchored in the truth that I am fearfully and wonderfully made.

Additionally, it's important to remember that everyone is on their own journey of self-discovery. Just as I am learning to accept and celebrate who I am, others are doing the same. By embodying self-acceptance, I can extend compassion and kindness to those around me, creating a ripple effect of love and affirmation. Recognizing my own completeness allows me to uplift others, fostering a community where we can all thrive without fear of judgment. With each step I take in affirming my identity, I inspire others to do the same, building a network of strength grounded in the truth that we are all enough, just as we are.

OCTOBER 22

DAY 296

I CELEBRATE MY AUTHENTIC SELF

Affirmation: I honor and embrace my true self.

Scripture: "Put on the new self, created to be like God in true righteousness and holiness." – Ephesians 4:24 (NIV)

Encouragement: The more I walk in my authenticity, the more I shine. I am free to be fully and completely me without hesitation. Embracing my true self allows me to connect deeply with others, as authenticity fosters genuine relationships. When I present myself honestly, I invite those around me to do the same, creating an environment rich with trust and understanding. It's within this space that love and acceptance flourish, reminding me that vulnerability is a strength, not a weakness.

As I celebrate my uniqueness, I am reminded that my gifts and character traits are divinely designed. Each quirk and passion is a piece of the beautiful puzzle that reflects my Creator's handiwork. In a world that sometimes pressures us to conform, I invite the power of the Holy Spirit to guide me, assuring me that living authentically is a testament to faith. Celebrating my true self is a declaration of gratitude for the life I've been given and a commitment to honoring the person God intended me to be.

OCTOBER 23

DAY 297

MY IDENTITY IS IN CHRIST

Affirmation: My worth is defined by God, not the world.

Scripture: " Truly my soul finds rest in God; my salvation comes from him.– Psalm 62:1 (NIV)

Encouragement: The opinions of others do not define me. My identity is rooted in Christ, and that truth is unshakable. When I grasp the depth of God's love for me, I realize that I am cherished beyond measure. In a world that often shifts its standards of success and value, I can find solace in the unwavering nature of my Creator's gaze. He sees me for who I truly am—His beloved child, lovingly crafted and uniquely designed for a purpose.

As I walk through each day, I am encouraged to embrace my identity in Christ more fully. By continually seeking His presence, I can reject the labels that society may place upon me and instead dwell in the assurance of His acceptance. Every time the world tries to sway my perception of self-worth, I'll remind myself that my true identity is found not in accomplishments, popularity, or worldly validation but in the steadfast love and grace that God extends to me. This foundation empowers me to navigate life's challenges and rejoice in my unique journey, knowing that I am enough because I am His.

OCTOBER 24

DAY 298

I RELEASE THE NEED FOR APPROVAL

Affirmation: I am confident in who I am, without seeking validation.

Scripture: " When the righteous triumph, there is great elation; but when the wicked rise to power, people go into hiding." – Proverbs 28:12 (NIV)

Encouragement: I no longer measure myself by the approval of others. I am at peace knowing I am already accepted by God. This acceptance frees me to embrace my true self, allowing me to grow and evolve without the constraints of societal expectations. I understand that my worth is not determined by likes, accolades, or compliments. Instead, I find joy in my individuality and celebrate the unique gifts that I bring to the world. With every step I take in authenticity, I inspire others to do the same.

As I release the need for external validation, I cultivate a deeper connection with my inner self. Each day, I remind myself that I am enough, just as I am. I no longer seek permission or approval to be who I was created to be. I am learning to appreciate the journey of self-discovery, where I can actively choose to live in alignment with my values and beliefs. This newfound empowerment allows me to walk with confidence, knowing that my identity is firmly rooted in the love and acceptance that God offers me. In embracing this truth, I find strength and resilience, which empowers me to face the world with grace and courage.

OCTOBER 25

DAY 299

I WALK IN BOLD CONFIDENCE

Affirmation: I embrace my uniqueness with boldness and joy.

Scripture: "The Lord appeared to us in the past, saying: 'I have loved you with an everlasting love; I have drawn you with unfailing kindness.'" – Jeremiah 31:3 (NIV)

Encouragement: I refuse to shrink myself to make others comfortable. I stand tall, knowing I am fearfully and wonderfully made. Each day is an opportunity to celebrate the individual gifts and talents that contribute to my unique identity. By recognizing and honoring my own strengths, I inspire those around me to do the same. Just as a beautiful garden thrives on a diverse array of flowers, our differences enrich the world and weave a tapestry of extraordinary beauty.

In embracing my uniqueness, I create a ripple effect of empowerment. Courage and authenticity are contagious; when I allow myself to shine, I encourage others to step into their own light. I remember that God's love for me is unwavering and eternal. This love fuels my confidence, reminding me that I do not have to conform to societal expectations or opinions. Instead, I can boldly walk the path laid out for me, enriching my journey and allowing others to share in the joy of their own remarkable stories.

OCTOBER 26

DAY 300

I AM LOVED BEYOND MEASURE

Affirmation: God's love for me is infinite and unconditional.

Scripture: " And to know this love that surpasses knowledge—that you may be filled to the measure of all the fullness of God.." – Ephesians 3:19 (NIV)

Encouragement: No mistake, no flaw, no insecurity can separate me from God's love. I am cherished beyond measure. In moments of doubt or despair, it is essential to remember that His love is a constant in our lives, a beacon of hope that guides us through our darkest hours. God's love does not waver based on our circumstances or the weight of our past; instead, it surrounds us, reminding us of our inherent worth. It invites us to lean into grace, knowing that we are embraced just as we are.

Furthermore, when we truly grasp the depth of this love, it transforms our perspective—not only on ourselves but also on the world around us. Each person, too, is held in this same infinite love, which encourages us to extend compassion and kindness. Imagine the waves of change we can create if we allow ourselves to be vessels of that love! Let it flow through us as we navigate our relationships and challenges, reinforcing the truth that we are all deserving of love and acceptance, thus spreading the message of God's boundless grace.

OCTOBER 27

DAY 301

I FULLY ACCEPT MYSELF

Affirmation: I choose self-acceptance and self-love every day.

Scripture: " And because of my chains, most of the brothers and sisters have become confident in the Lord and dare all the more to proclaim the gospel without fear." – Philippians 1:14 (NIV)

Encouragement: I embrace myself with kindness and grace. I am fully and completely me, just as God intended. In every moment and in every circumstance, I am reminded that my worth is not defined by the opinions of others or my own self-doubt. Instead, I choose to celebrate my unique journey and recognize that my flaws make me human and my struggles make me resilient. Embracing all parts of myself allows me to grow and to flourish in God's light, knowing that His love is unconditional and covers me completely.

As I cultivate self-acceptance, I am empowered to face challenges with confidence and courage. I learn to appreciate the lessons that come from both triumphs and trials, understanding that each experience shapes who I am meant to be. When I accept myself fully, I open my heart to others, encouraging them to do the same. Together, we can create a circle of compassion, affirming one another's worth and sharing the love that God has poured into our lives. In this space of acceptance, we can boldly proclaim our faith and walk in confidence, free from the chains of insecurity.

Week 44

Transforming Pain into Purpose

OCTOBER 28

DAY 302

MY PAIN HAS A PURPOSE

Affirmation: My struggles are shaping me into someone stronger and wiser.

Scripture: "But seek first his kingdom and his righteousness, and all these things will be given to you as well." – Matthew 6:33 (NIV)

Encouragement: Every hardship I have faced has the potential to birth something beautiful. I trust that God is using my pain for a greater purpose. When I embrace the challenges in my life, I open myself up to the lessons they offer. Each moment of discomfort can serve as a stepping stone toward growth, propelling me to a deeper understanding of my own resilience. As I navigate the storms, I learn to rely more on God's strength than my own, developing a trust that transforms my view of suffering into an opportunity for divine alignment.

In times of pain, I am reminded that I am not alone in this journey. Others have faced similar trials and emerged with wisdom and insight. Sharing these experiences with my community can foster connections and provide support that illuminate the dark moments. I can take comfort in knowing that my struggles can resonate with others, encouraging them to find hope in their own adversities. As I grow stronger and wiser through my experiences, I play a part in a larger story of healing and redemption, becoming a source of encouragement for those around me.

OCTOBER 29

DAY 303:

I AM BEING REFINED

Affirmation: Every trial I face refines me into the person I am meant to be.

Scripture: " Better a dry crust with peace and quiet than a house full of feasting, with strife.." – Proverbs 17:1 (NIV)

Encouragement: Instead of resisting the difficulties, I embrace them as part of my growth. I am being refined, strengthened, and prepared for what's ahead. The challenges I encounter are not mere obstacles but rather opportunities to learn and develop resilience. Each trial shapes my character, helping me to discover inner strengths I may not have known I possessed. As I navigate through these experiences, I am reminded that the most remarkable transformations often arise from moments of struggle.

I am not alone in this journey of refinement. Each setback is an invitation for deeper reliance on the One who knows my path and purpose. In these times, I can seek comfort in knowing that God is at work within me, orchestrating circumstances for my good. This process may be uncomfortable, but it is also a sacred time of discovering grace and growth. I can rest assured that as I face trials with faith, I am being crafted into a more authentic version of myself. This truth nourishes my spirit and fuels my determination to persevere.

OCTOBER 30

DAY 30

MY STORY WILL INSPIRE OTHERS

Affirmation: My journey is a testimony that can uplift and encourage others.

Scripture: " In their hearts humans plan their course, but the Lord establishes their steps." – Proverbs 16:9 (NIV)

Encouragement: There is power in my testimony. By sharing my story, I offer hope and healing to those who need to hear it. Each time I reflect on my experiences, I realize that the struggles I have overcome can resonate with others who might feel lost or discouraged. My journey, filled with challenges and victories, serves as a beacon of light, showing that no matter how difficult things may seem, there is always a path toward growth. Embracing my unique narrative allows me to connect with individuals on a deeper level, reassuring them that they are not alone in their battles.

Moreover, as I share my story, I invite others into a space of vulnerability and authenticity. This openness not only fosters community but also encourages those around me to embrace their own journeys, no matter how messy they might be. Every experience contributes to a greater tapestry of resilience, and when we openly share these threads, we inspire courage in others to face their own trials. It is through our shared stories that we can cultivate hope, ignite faith, and ultimately create a network of support that uplifts one another. Together, our narratives weave a powerful message of perseverance and encouragement for all who encounter them.

OCTOBER 31

DAY 305

I RISE ABOVE MY CIRCUMSTANCES

Affirmation: I am not defined by my struggles; I am defined by how I overcome them.

Scripture: "Who is like the wise? Who knows the explanation of things? A person's wisdom brightens their face and changes its hard appearance." – Ecclesiastes 8:1 (NIV)

Encouragement: No matter what I face, I refuse to be defeated. I rise above my circumstances with faith and resilience. Each challenge is an opportunity for growth, and I choose to see them as stepping stones, not stumbling blocks. Even when the road ahead seems difficult, I hold onto the promise that every trial I encounter serves a purpose, refining my character and strengthening my spirit. With each victory, no matter how small, I am reminded that I have the power to shape my own narrative and emerge stronger than before.

As I navigate through the ups and downs of life, I keep my eyes fixed on hope. I remind myself that I am not alone in my journey; I have a community of support and a deep well of inner strength. When I feel overwhelmed, I take a moment to breathe, to pray, and to reflect on my past victories. This practice encourages me to acknowledge my progress and fuels my determination to keep moving forward, no matter the challenges that lie ahead. In doing so, I cultivate a sense of inner peace, knowing that I am equipped to rise, conquer, and thrive.

NOVEMBER 1

DAY 306

I TURN MY PAIN INTO STRENGTH

Affirmation: I use my challenges as stepping stones toward my purpose.

Scripture: "The Lord is good to those whose hope is in him, to the one who seeks him." – Lamentations 3:25 (NIV)

Encouragement: My pain does not weaken me; it strengthens me. I walk forward with the confidence that God's grace sustains me. Each challenge I encounter serves as a valuable lesson, shaping my character and deepening my resilience. It is through the trials that I discover the depths of my own strength, and in recognizing this truth, I learn to embrace my circumstances rather than resist them. With God's help, I can transform my struggles into motivations for growth, using each setback as a setup for a remarkable comeback.

In the moments when the weight of my pain feels unbearable, I remind myself that I am never alone. God walks alongside me, providing the comfort and support I need to persevere. I can lean on His promises and trust that every tear I shed waters the seeds of hope and purpose within me. No matter how challenging the journey gets, I can find solace in knowing that my pain has meaning and can bring forth new strength and vitality. I am a testament to His goodness, and I use my experiences to encourage others on their own journeys of transformation.

NOVEMBER 2

DAY 307

I CHOOSE PURPOSE OVER BITTERNESS

Affirmation: I let go of bitterness and embrace the lessons my pain has taught me.

Scripture: "Get rid of all bitterness, rage and anger, brawling and slander, along with every form of malice." – Ephesians 4:31 (NIV)

Encouragement: Holding on to resentment only weighs me down. I choose to turn my pain into purpose, letting go of what no longer serves me. By recognizing the lessons hidden within my struggles, I find the strength to transform my experiences into opportunities for growth. Every challenge can be a stepping stone toward greater understanding and compassion, both for myself and for others.

As I cultivate a heart of forgiveness, I open myself up to healing and renewal. I realize that bitterness only creates a barrier between me and the joy that life has to offer. Instead, by choosing to release my grudges, I empower myself to live fully in the present, where hope and purpose flourish. With each step away from bitterness, I reclaim my peace and invite a deeper sense of purpose into my life, allowing my journey to inspire those around me

NOVEMBER 3

DAY 308

MY HEALING WILL BLESS OTHERS

Affirmation: As I heal, I become a vessel of hope and encouragement for others.

Scripture: " I would find out what he would answer me, and consider what he would say to me." – Job 23:5 (NIV)

Encouragement: My healing is not just for me—it is meant to inspire and uplift others. My journey is a gift that will bring light to those who need it. In moments of struggle, it can be easy to retreat and feel isolated in our pain. However, sharing our healing journey with others can create bonds of support and understanding, showing that we are not alone. By being open about our experiences, we give permission for others to share their pain and begin their own healing. This kind of vulnerability allows us to create a community built on empathy and love, reminding everyone that valleys can lead to mountain tops.

Moreover, as I walk through the process of healing, I have the opportunity to reflect on the lessons learned and the strength gained. Each step I take brings me closer to the person I am meant to be, and that transformation can serve as a beacon for those who feel lost. By embracing my healing journey, I can demonstrate resilience and encourage others to trust their path, reminding them that every setback is an opportunity for growth. Through my story, I can be a testament to the power of hope, showing others that with faith and perseverance, healing is not only possible but can bring immeasurable blessings to our lives and the lives of those around us.

Week 45

The Strength Within Me

NOVEMBER 4

DAY 309

STRENGTH IS ALREADY WITHIN ME

Affirmation: I am strong, resilient, and equipped to handle whatever comes my way.

Scripture: "The Lord is my strength and my defense; he has become my salvation." – Exodus 15:2 (NIV)

Encouragement: I do not have to search for strength outside of myself. God has already placed it within me. I stand firm, knowing I am built to overcome. Each day presents its own challenges, but I can embrace each moment with confidence, knowing that the strength I need is already woven into the fabric of my being. This divine empowerment is my anchor, helping me to navigate life's difficulties without wavering. I remind myself that even when I feel weary or doubt my abilities, I can tap into this inner reservoir of strength and find the resilience to stand tall.

Moreover, in times of uncertainty, I can draw comfort from the knowledge that God walks alongside me. His presence reinforces the strength I carry, urging me to confront obstacles head-on, rather than retreating in fear. I am reminded that my struggles are not meant to diminish me; they are opportunities for growth and transformation. I choose to embrace each challenge, trusting that with God by my side, I have all the strength I need to persevere and thrive.

NOVEMBER 5

DAY 310

I AM EMPOWERED BY GOD'S STRENGTH

Affirmation: God strengthens me for every battle I face.

Scripture: "For you have been born again, not of perishable seed, but of imperishable, through the living and enduring word of God."– 1 Peter 1:23 (NIV)

Encouragement: When I feel weak, I remember that I am not fighting alone. God empowers me, and with Him, I am unstoppable. In times of struggle, it is vital to hold onto the truth that God's strength is made perfect in my weakness. Every challenge I encounter provides an opportunity for God to showcase His power in my life. As I lean into His strength, I can trust that I have the ability to overcome, not just for myself, but to inspire others as well. My battles serve a greater purpose, and I can be a beacon of hope for those around me.

I also remind myself of the incredible resources available to me through prayer and community. Connecting with fellow believers fortifies my spirit, as we encourage each other and share our burdens. Together, we can uplift one another, reinforcing our commitment to trust in God's promises. No matter what circumstance I find myself in, I am surrounded by a cloud of witnesses, and through the bonds of faith, I can draw strength from their journeys. With God's unwavering presence and the support of my fellow believers, I can face whatever comes my way with confidence and courage.

NOVEMBER 6

DAY 311

MY STRUGGLES MAKE ME STRONGER

Affirmation: Every challenge I face strengthens my faith and character.

Scripture: "Do not be afraid, you who are highly esteemed," he said. "Peace! Be strong now; be strong." – Daniel 10:19 (NIV)

Encouragement: I no longer see my struggles as obstacles but as opportunities for growth. I trust that through every hardship, I am being made stronger. Each trial I encounter has the potential to teach me invaluable lessons about resilience, patience, and perseverance. In these moments when I feel most challenged, I remind myself that discomfort is often the precursor to development. By pushing through adversity, I cultivate a deeper understanding of my own strength and faith.

Additionally, I look back at past struggles and recognize how they have shaped me into the person I am today. I am more equipped to handle future challenges because I have faced difficulties before and emerged on the other side, wiser and more confident. As I navigate through each situation, I hold onto the promise that I am not alone; my faith anchors me and gives me the courage to keep moving forward. Embracing this mindset, I can find peace amidst the storms and trust that every battle I face contributes to my growth in character and spirit.

NOVEMBER 7

DAY 312

I HAVE THE COURAGE TO KEEP GOING

Affirmation: I refuse to give up; I press forward with determination and faith.

Scripture: " Wait for the Lord; be strong and take heart and wait for the Lord.." – Psalm 27:14 (NIV)

Encouragement: There may be days when I feel like giving up, but I remind myself that I have already come so far. I keep going because I am worth the fight. Each challenge I face has the potential to strengthen me, and I can view these moments not as roadblocks but as stepping stones on my journey. Embracing perseverance allows me to uncover hidden reserves of strength and resilience within myself, proving that I have what it takes to push through adversity.

Moreover, I find comfort in remembering that I am not alone in this struggle. With faith in God's timing and guidance, I can rest assured that every delay and every struggle serves a greater purpose in my life. When I lean into my faith and trust the process, I transform my weariness into hope. I know that the path may not always be clear, but every step forward counts, and each effort I make is a testament to my courage and commitment to my dreams. I can hold on, for brighter days are ahead, and I will emerge stronger than before.

NOVEMBER 8

DAY 313

MY INNER STRENGTH IS UNBREAKABLE

Affirmation: Nothing can break me because my strength comes from within.

Scripture: "Above all else, guard your heart, for everything you do flows from it."– Proverbs 4:23 (NIV)

Encouragement: Life's challenges may shake me, but they will never break me. My strength is built on faith, perseverance, and self-love. In moments of doubt, I will remind myself of the resilience that lies within. Each trial I face is an opportunity for growth, and every setback is a stepping stone toward my greater purpose. I am not alone in my struggles; I carry the love and support of those who believe in me, and I draw from that collective strength when the weight feels heavy.

Furthermore, I recognize that my inner strength is unbreakable because it is rooted in my values and beliefs. I will choose to nourish my heart and mind with positive thoughts and empowering affirmations. I'll surround myself with uplifting influences and seek out moments of stillness where I can reconnect with my true self. This unwavering inner strength fortifies me against life's storms, enabling me to rise each time I fall and reminding me that I am capable of overcoming anything that comes my way.

NOVEMBER 9

DAY 314

I STAND FIRM IN MY IDENTITY

Affirmation: I know who I am, and I walk confidently in my truth.

Scripture: " Sin is not ended by multiplying words, but the prudent hold their tongues." – Proverbs 10:9 (NIV)

Encouragement: My identity is not defined by my circumstances. I am fearfully and wonderfully made, and nothing can take that truth away from me. In moments of doubt or insecurity, it's vital to remember that my worth is innate and unchangeable. Just as a masterpiece of art remains valuable regardless of external opinions, I am a unique creation intended for great purpose. Embracing this truth empowers me to stand firm in who I am, regardless of life's challenges or the opinions of others.

I must also surround myself with reminders of my worth—whether through scripture, uplifting music, or supportive friendships. By filling my mind and heart with truth, I can resist the lies that may try to shake my confidence. Encouragement comes from recognizing that I am not alone in this journey; countless others also seek to affirm their identity each day. Together, we can uplift one another, leaning on the strength we find in our shared belief that our true identity is rooted in love and purpose. As I confidently walk in my truth, I will inspire others to do the same, creating a ripple effect of empowerment and authenticity.

NOVEMBER 10

DAY 315

I AM VICTORIOUS

Affirmation: I walk in victory, knowing that God has already made a way for me.

Scripture: " You will eat the fruit of your labor; blessings and prosperity will be yours.." – Psalm 128:2 (NIV)

Encouragement: No matter what I face, I am already victorious. God has gone before me, and I trust that my strength and perseverance will lead me to my greatest triumphs. The challenges I encounter are not roadblocks but stepping stones guiding me toward a greater purpose. Each struggle is an opportunity to lean on God's everlasting grace and to remind myself that through His power, I can overcome anything. In the face of adversity, I choose to keep my eyes on the promised blessings that lie ahead.

In moments of doubt or uncertainty, I will hold onto the truth that victory is not just a distant goal, but a present reality through my relationship with God. As I navigate the ups and downs of life, I can find peace in knowing that every setback is a setup for a greater comeback. Each day brings me closer to the abundance that God has prepared for me, as long as I remain steadfast in my faith. With every step I take in obedience, I am demonstrating my trust in God's provision and timing, and I invite His blessings to pour into my life.

Week 46

I am More Than Enough

NOVEMBER 11

DAY 316

I AM CREATED WITH PURPOSE

Affirmation: I am enough just as I am.

Scripture: ""Like a gold ring in a pig's snout is a beautiful woman who shows no discretion." – Proverbs 11:22 (NIV)

Encouragement: I am not lacking anything. God created me with intention, and I am enough just as He made me. Each of us is infused with unique gifts and qualities that are designed for a specific purpose in this world. When we embrace our intrinsic value, we begin to see how our lives can reflect His brilliance and love. No matter the challenges we face or the doubts that creep in, we must hold fast to the truth that we are God's masterpieces—crafted deliberately for His plan.

As we navigate the complexities of life, it's essential to focus on our strengths rather than our perceived weaknesses. Remember that it is often our vulnerabilities that lead us to connect deeply with others and fulfill our purpose. By leaning into our true selves, we shine brightly in a world that desperately needs light. Whenever you feel inadequate, take a moment to remind yourself of God's promise: you are more than enough, uniquely equipped to step into the calling He has placed before you. Trust in His design, and let your authenticity inspire those around you.

NOVEMBER 12

DAY 317

MY WORTH IS NOT MEASURED BY OTHERS

Affirmation: My value is determined by God, not the opinions of others.

Scripture: " For the Lord takes delight in his people; he crowns the humble with victory." – Psalm 149:4 (NIV)

Encouragement: I release the need for outside validation. My worth is rooted in God's love, and that is more than enough. In moments when I feel the weight of comparison or the sting of judgment from others, I remind myself that I am a unique creation, crafted intentionally by my Creator. Each of us possesses intrinsic value, not based on achievements or the approval of those around us, but grounded firmly in the love and purpose that God has for our lives. It's within that love that I find true strength and assurance.

Additionally, I choose to focus on the gifts and talents that God has instilled in me. Instead of seeking affirmation from others, I will cultivate a heart of gratitude for who I am and the journey I am on. This perspective allows me to celebrate my individuality and recognize that my path is different from anyone else's — and that's perfectly okay. It is in fully embracing my identity as God's beloved that I can live authentically and encourage others to do the same. I trust that my worth does not waver with the opinions of the world, for God sees me, values me, and calls me His own.

NOVEMBER 13

DAY 31

I AM WHOLE AND COMPLETE

Affirmation: I am not broken; I am whole in Christ.

Scripture: "I am the vine; you are the branches. If you remain in me and I in you, you will bear much fruit; apart from me you can do nothing."– John 15:5 (NIV)

Encouragement: I refuse to believe the lie that I am incomplete. I am whole, loved, and fully accepted just as I am. It can be easy to let the world's perceptions and our own self-doubts cloud the truth of who we are in Christ. But God sees us not through the lens of our shortcomings or failures; He sees our potential and the beauty of His creation in us. Each day, as we choose to abide in Him, we can find freedom and strength in His presence, allowing His love to fill the gaps we may feel exist within us.

As we embrace this truth and stand firm in our identity as complete beings in Christ, we can overcome any pressure to conform to fickle standards. Our worth is not determined by accomplishments or external validations but by the unconditional love and grace extended to us through Jesus. Remember, you are not alone in this journey. God walks with you, nurturing the branches of your life, encouraging growth, and reminding you that you are more than enough in His eyes. Trust in that promise, and let it empower you to live fully and authentically.

NOVEMBER 14

DAY 319

MY LIFE HAS MEANING AND VALUE

Affirmation: My existence matters, and I am making a difference.

Scripture: "Indeed, the very hairs of your head are all numbered. Don't be afraid; you are worth more than many sparrows." – Luke 12:7 (NIV)

Encouragement: I am not here by accident. My life has purpose, and I choose to walk in the confidence of my God-given value. Each encounter I have, each moment I share with others, holds the potential to create ripples of impact that extend far beyond what I can see. It is essential to remember that even the smallest act of kindness or understanding can change someone's day—or even their life. I am equipped with unique gifts and talents that are meant to reach out to others, and I can use them to fill the world with light and love.

When I embrace my worth, I not only uplift myself but also encourage those around me to realize their value. My existence contributes to a greater tapestry, woven with threads of significance and influence. By trusting in my purpose, I find strength to overcome self-doubt and fear. I remind myself that I have been intricately designed for a purpose, and my journey matters. Therefore, I choose to walk forward with courage, knowing that I am valued and that my contributions—however small they may seem—are vital to the fabric of the community around me.

NOVEMBER 15

DAY 320

I CHOOSE SELF-LOVE OVER SELF-DOUBT

Affirmation: I speak love and kindness over myself every day.

Scripture: " My dear brothers and sisters, take note of this: Everyone should be quick to listen, slow to speak and slow to become angry,." – James 1:19 (NIV)

Encouragement: I no longer allow self-doubt to take residence in my heart. I fill my mind with truth, love, and confidence in who I am. Embracing self-love means recognizing my worth and celebrating my unique attributes. Each morning, I remind myself of my strengths and the potential that lies within me. This practice helps to cultivate a mindset rooted in positivity, allowing me to greet each day with enthusiasm and resilience. Rather than focusing on my shortcomings or the opinions of others, I choose to nurture my spirit and uplift my heart with affirmations that resonate deeply within me.

Additionally, I surround myself with influences that encourage self-acceptance and growth. I seek out supportive communities, uplifting literature, and inspiring individuals who reflect the love I wish to embody. Stepping away from negative self-talk and affirming my value becomes a powerful act of self-compassion. As I lean into this journey of self-love, I learn to extend the same kindness and understanding to myself that I readily offer to others. Each moment spent in self-affirmation strengthens my belief in my capabilities and allows me to walk forward in confidence, eager to embrace the opportunities that lie ahead.

NOVEMBER 16

DAY 321

I AM DESIGNED TO THRIVE

Affirmation: I am created to live abundantly and joyfully.

Scripture: "For our light and momentary troubles are achieving for us an eternal glory that far outweighs them all." – 2 Corinthians 4:17 (NIV)

Encouragement: God did not create me to live in fear, doubt, or lack. I step fully into the abundant, joy-filled life He has for me. I embrace the truth that each day is a new opportunity to experience His goodness and grace. When challenges arise, I remind myself that these are simply stepping stones on my journey, not the destination. The struggles I encounter in this life are temporary, and they serve a purpose in shaping me into a stronger, more resilient person.

I also find strength in knowing that God has equipped me with everything I need to overcome life's obstacles. His promises provide a firm foundation upon which I can stand, knowing that I am never alone in my battles. I choose to focus on the blessings He has placed in my life, cultivating an attitude of gratitude that fuels my joy. By aligning my thoughts and actions with His abundant love, I flourish and soar beyond limitations, manifesting the vibrant life I was designed to lead.

NOVEMBER 17

DAY 322

I WALK BOLDLY IN MY TRUTH

Affirmation: I stand firm in my identity and refuse to shrink back.

Scripture: "Let us then approach God's throne of grace with confidence, so that we may receive mercy and find grace to help us in our time of need." – Hebrews 4:16 (NIV)

Encouragement: I will not diminish my light or hide who I am. I am fearfully and wonderfully made, and I walk confidently in that truth. Each day, I am reminded that my uniqueness is a gift to the world, and I will embrace every part of myself with love and gratitude. When I face challenges or negativity, I will remember that my identity is not defined by the opinions of others but by the grace and love bestowed upon me by my Creator.

As I continue my journey, I will seek to uplift and inspire those around me, sharing my story and my truth without fear. Courage is not the absence of fear but the determination to move forward despite it. By standing boldly in my authenticity, I create space for others to do the same. Together, we can build a community of strength and empowerment, celebrating our differences and encouraging one another to shine brightly in our own unique ways.

Week 47

Flourishing In Faith

NOVEMBER 18

DAY 323

ROOTED IN GOD'S LOVE

Affirmation: My faith keeps me grounded and strong.

Scripture: "So then, just as you received Christ Jesus as Lord, continue to live your lives in him, rooted and built up in him, strengthened in the faith as you were taught, and overflowing with thankfulness." – Colossians 2:6-7 (NIV)

Encouragement: When I stay rooted in God's love, I grow in strength, wisdom, and peace. I flourish because my foundation is firm in Him. This deep connection allows me to weather the storms of life with confidence, knowing that I am never alone. As I cultivate my relationship with God, I begin to see challenges not as obstacles, but as opportunities for growth and transformation. With each step of faith, I allow His love to nourish my spirit, fostering resilience within me that reflects His grace.

Moreover, being rooted in God's love instills a sense of purpose that transcends daily struggles. I understand that I am part of a much larger story, one that is woven together with threads of hope and promise. This perspective offers me the motivation to extend kindness and compassion to others, helping to create a ripple effect of love. When I share the strength I've gained from being grounded in Him, it not only enriches my life but also uplifts those around me, reinforcing the profound truth that together we can embody the love of Christ to a world that desperately needs it.

NOVEMBER 19

DAY 324

FAITH OVER FEAR

Affirmation: I trust God's plan even when I cannot see the way.

Scripture: " Now this is eternal life: that they know you, the only true God, and Jesus Christ, whom you have sent." – John 17:3 (NIV)

Encouragement: Even when uncertainty surrounds me, I choose faith over fear. I know that God is guiding me every step of the way. In moments when I feel overwhelmed by doubt, I remind myself of the countless times God has been faithful in the past. Each challenge I've faced has been met with grace, and I have emerged stronger and more resilient. It's in these moments of vulnerability that I often discover the depth of God's love and provision. By embracing my faith, I allow it to illuminate the path ahead, turning anxiety into assurance.

Moreover, choosing faith means actively looking for the blessings hidden within life's trials. When I lean into my relationship with God, I gain peace that surpasses understanding. I recognize that every setback is an opportunity for growth and that every fear can be transformed into a testament of His power. With His word as my anchor, I confidently step forward, embodying a spirit of hope and courage. As I journey through the unknown, I hold fast to the truth that I am never alone; God walks with me, and His plans for me are ultimately good.

NOVEMBER 20

DAY 325

I AM A REFLECTION OF GOD'S GRACE

Affirmation: God's grace is abundant in my life, and I walk in it daily.

Scripture: "I will be like the dew to Israel; he will blossom like a lily. Like a cedar of Lebanon he will send down his roots; his young shoots will grow. His splendor will be like an olive tree, his fragrance like a cedar of Lebanon." – Hosea 14:5-6 (NIV)

Encouragement: I am not defined by my past or my struggles. God's grace is sufficient, and I flourish in His love and mercy. In times when I feel overwhelmed or discouraged, I remind myself that grace is not just a one-time gift but a continuous flow of divine support that nurtures my spirit. Each day presents an opportunity to experience His grace anew, allowing me to grow stronger in my faith. With every struggle I face, I can choose to see it as a stepping stone toward a deeper understanding of God's purpose in my life, rather than as a barrier that holds me back.

Moreover, as I embrace my identity as a reflection of God's grace, I can also extend that same grace to others. By remembering that everyone carries their burdens and stories, I can cultivate a spirit of compassion and love in my relationships. This not only enriches my connections with those around me but also deepens the roots of my own faith. Each act of grace I share creates a ripple effect, spreading encouragement and hope in a world that so desperately needs it. I am reminded that I am a vessel of God's grace, and as I walk in it each day, I become a source of inspiration for others, guiding them back to the gentle embrace of God's love.

NOVEMBER 21

DAY 326

GOD'S TIMING IS PERFECT

Affirmation: I trust that everything is happening in divine timing.

Scripture: "Humble yourselves before the Lord, and he will lift you up."– James 4:10 (NIV)

Encouragement: I release the need to control and trust in God's perfect plan. I know that every season has a purpose in my journey. Embracing the truth that God's timing is perfect allows me to experience peace in waiting. When I feel overwhelmed by the uncertainties of life, I remind myself that God is always working in the background, orchestrating the events of my life with wisdom and love. By surrendering my own timeline, I open myself up to the possibilities He has in store for me.

In moments of doubt, I can look back on the times when things seemed impossible but eventually fell into place in ways I couldn't have imagined. This reflection builds my faith and encourages me to trust that what lies ahead is part of a larger plan crafted with my growth and fulfillment in mind. As I humble myself before the Lord, I cultivate a posture of expectancy and hope, knowing that when the time is right, He will lift me up and lead me to the blessings He has promised. Each step of patience and faith deepens my relationship with Him and prepares my heart for the wonderful things that are on the horizon.

NOVEMBER 22

DAY 327

MY FAITH MAKES ME STRONGER

Affirmation: I am strengthened through my faith in God.

Scripture: "When God created mankind, he made them in the likeness of God."– Judges 6:12 (NIV)

Encouragement: No matter what comes my way, I stand firm in my faith. God's strength empowers me to overcome and thrive. In moments of challenge and uncertainty, I can draw upon the deep well of faith that resides within me. Each trial I face is not just a test, but an opportunity to deepen my trust in God's plan. As I turn my heart toward Him, I am reminded that His grace is sufficient and His power is made perfect in my weakness. As I cling to this truth, I find the courage to keep moving forward.

Furthermore, it is essential to remember that my faith not only strengthens me but also connects me to a larger community of believers. By sharing my struggles and victories, I help to uplift others and remind them of God's enduring love and faithfulness. Together, we can face life's storms, assured that we are never alone. In unity, we find encouragement and inspiration, knowing that our collective faith serves as a powerful reminder that with God, all things are possible. As we walk this journey together, I am bolstered by the understanding that my strength in faith extends beyond myself and becomes part of a greater testament to God's goodness in our lives.

NOVEMBER 23

DAY 328

GOD IS WORKING IN MY LIFE

Affirmation: Even when I cannot see it, God is moving in my favor.

Scripture: "Jesus looked at them and said, 'With man this is impossible, but not with God; all things are possible with God.'" – Mark 10:27 (NIV)

Encouragement: I am never alone. God is always working behind the scenes, orchestrating blessings in my life. Even in moments when I feel isolated or uncertain, it is essential to remember that God's presence surrounds me like a comforting embrace. He sees every struggle, hears every prayer, and understands the desires of my heart. Each challenge I face is an opportunity for growth, and every setback is a setup for a breakthrough. My faith empowers me to trust that God is weaving His perfect plan, even when circumstances seem daunting.

Moreover, God's faithfulness reminds me that His promises are sure and steadfast. Just as He parted the waters for Moses and provided manna in the wilderness, He is continuously preparing a way for me, making paths where I see none. I can take courage knowing that each step I take draws me closer to the fulfillment of His purpose. When the road ahead appears unclear, I hold on to the assurance that God is at work, transforming my trials into triumphs. With every breath, I lean into His grace, embracing the journey, confident that He is guiding me toward a destiny filled with hope and purpose.

NOVEMBER 24

DAY 329

I FLOURISH BECAUSE I AM FAITHFUL

Affirmation: As I trust in God, I continue to grow and thrive.

Scripture: "Blessed is the one who trusts in the Lord, whose confidence is in him. They will be like a tree planted by the water that sends out its roots by the stream. It does not fear when heat comes; its leaves are always green. It has no worries in a year of drought and never fails to bear fruit." – Jeremiah 17:7-8 (NIV)

Encouragement: I flourish not because life is always easy, but because I trust in God. My faith keeps me growing, thriving, and bearing fruit in every season. In times of challenge or uncertainty, I draw strength from the deep roots of my trust. Like a tree nourished by a steady stream, I find sustenance and support in my relationship with God. This trust empowers me to rise above adversity, transforming trials into opportunities for growth and resilience.

Moreover, it is in these moments of difficulty that my faith truly shines. When I face storms or drought, I remind myself that God is my anchor, and His promises are unfailing. Each challenge I encounter is merely a backdrop for God's goodness to be displayed in my life. As I continue to lean on Him, I will not only withstand the test of time but also flourish boldly, becoming a beacon of hope and encouragement for others. Through my steadfast faith, I contribute to a legacy of trusting God's goodness, demonstrating that even in the hardest seasons, He is at work, bringing forth new life and abundance.

Week 48

Living My Truth

NOVEMBER 25

DAY 330

EMBRACING MY AUTHENTICITY

Affirmation: I honor and embrace who I truly am.

Scripture: " Because of the Lord's great love we are not consumed, for his compassions never fail. They are new every morning; great is your faithfulnessr ." – Lamentations 3:22-23 (NIV)

Encouragement: I no longer shrink myself to fit into spaces that were never meant for me. I am fearfully and wonderfully made, and I stand confidently in my truth. Embracing my authenticity means recognizing that my unique qualities and experiences are gifts to the world. Each time I shine in my true colors, I inspire others to do the same. It's a powerful reminder that authenticity is not just a personal journey; it is an invitation for others to embrace their own individuality. When I fully accept myself, I create a ripple effect of courage, encouraging those around me to shed their masks and reveal their true selves.

Moreover, embracing my authenticity opens the door to deeper connections with others. When I present my genuine self, I attract relationships that are built on honesty and mutual respect. I am free to share my perspective and celebrate the differences that make each of us unique. As I continue this journey of self-acceptance, I realize that my worth is not determined by external validation but by the love and compassion I extend to myself and others. In this space of authenticity, I can nurture meaningful connections that uplift and support, echoing the profound truth that we are all beautifully created and deserving of love just as we are.

NOVEMBER 26

DAY 331

MY TRUTH SETS ME FREE

Affirmation: I release all fear and embrace my truth with boldness.

Scripture: " Not giving up meeting together, as some are in the habit of doing, but encouraging one another—and all the more as you see the Day approaching." – Hebrews 10:25 (NIV)

Encouragement: When I walk in my truth, I experience freedom like never before. No longer bound by the expectations of others, I am free to be who God created me to be. This journey leads me to newfound confidence as I embrace my unique gifts and talents, recognizing them as tools for His purpose. In this space of authenticity, I find joy in creating connections with others who celebrate my true self, encouraging an environment where vulnerability and honesty can flourish.

As I continue to share my truth, I invite others to do the same, fostering a community rooted in understanding and support. The more we lean into our authentic selves, the more we uplift and inspire those around us. Together, we can create a ripple effect of encouragement, reminding each other that in our honesty lies strength, and in our collective stories, we discover the beautiful tapestry of God's grace. Embracing this truth enables me to walk confidently forward, knowing that I am surrounded by love and acceptance, both from God and from those who share in this journey with me.

NOVEMBER 27

DAY 332

I AM ENOUGH JUST AS I AM

Affirmation: I am complete and whole in my truth.

Scripture: "You are already clean because of the word I have spoken to you." – John 15:3 (NIV)

Encouragement: I am not defined by my past or my struggles. In God's eyes, I am already enough, already worthy, and already loved. Each day is a fresh opportunity to embrace my true identity, to recognize that my worth is intrinsic and cannot be diminished by external circumstances or the opinions of others. Regardless of the challenges I have faced or the mistakes I have made, I can take solace in knowing that I am seen as a masterpiece created uniquely by God. This truth empowers me to walk in confidence, free from the shackles of self-doubt and insecurity.

As I continue to affirm my worthiness, I must also remember that the journey towards self-acceptance is ongoing. It's important to cultivate grace for myself while growing in this understanding. Even in moments of struggle, I am invited to lean into God's love and begin each day anew, knowing that His grace covers my imperfections. When I feel insufficient, I can turn to His promises and reflect on my inherent value, reminding myself that I am fearfully and wonderfully made. In doing so, I reinforce my belief that I am enough, just as I am.

NOVEMBER 28

DAY 333

GOD CREATED ME WITH PURPOSE

Affirmation: My truth aligns with God's divine purpose for me.

Scripture: "Gold there is, and rubies in abundance, but lips that speak knowledge are a rare jewel."

– Proverbs 20:15 (NIV)

Encouragement: God designed me with intentionality. Every part of me—my story, my strengths, and even my struggles—plays a role in my greater purpose. Just as a skilled artist carefully chooses each color for their masterpiece, God has woven together the threads of my life in a way that reveals His divine plan. When I embrace who I am, with all my unique qualities and experiences, I become more equipped to fulfill the mission He has for me. Each moment of joy and each moment of hardship can serve to deepen my understanding of myself and strengthen my resolve to carry out His purpose.

Moreover, it's essential to remember that my journey is not meant to be navigated alone. In times of doubt or discouragement, I can lean on the community God has placed around me. Others can reflect the beauty of God's purpose back to me when I struggle to see it in myself. Together, we can remind one another of the incredible potential we hold within us, anchored by God's promise. As I continue to walk in faith and seek His guidance, I can trust that every step I take is aligned with the incredible journey He has laid out for me, reminding me that I am truly valuable and purposeful in His eyes.

NOVEMBER 29

DAY 334

WALKING BOLDLY IN MY TRUTH

Affirmation: I stand confidently in who I am.

Scripture: " Commit thy way unto the Lord; trust also in him; and he shall bring it to pass." – Psalm 37:5 (KJV)

Encouragement: I no longer allow fear to dictate my life. I stand in my truth, knowing that God is with me every step of the way. Each day, I make a conscious choice to embrace my identity and pursue my purpose with courage. The journey may present challenges, but I understand that these obstacles only serve to strengthen my resolve. I remain focused on the promise that God has great plans for me, plans filled with hope and a future. When uncertainties arise, I remind myself that I can lean into my faith and trust that He is guiding my every decision.

As I walk boldly in my truth, I recognize the power in authenticity and vulnerability. Sharing my journey and experiences with others creates a ripple effect, encouraging those around me to also embrace their own truths. Together, we can build a community rooted in support, empowerment, and love. I am reminded that, although the path may not always be easy, each step I take is filled with purpose, and God's presence lightens my load. I choose to celebrate each victory, no matter how small, and to remain steadfast in my commitment to walking confidently in the person He created me to be.

NOVEMBER 30

DAY 335

MY TRUTH IS A GIFT

Affirmation: My truth is powerful, and I share it with grace.

Scripture: " God blessed them and said to them, "Be fruitful and increase in number; fill the earth and subdue it. Rule over the fish in the sea and the birds in the sky and over every living creature that moves on the ground." – Genesis 1:28 (NIV)

Encouragement: My truth is not something to hide but something to share. My story has the power to inspire, uplift, and glorify God. Each time I embrace and articulate my truth, I am acknowledging the unique journey that God has crafted for me. This journey, with all its twists and turns, can serve as a beacon of hope for others who may be navigating their own challenges. By expressing my experiences and the lessons gleaned from them, I invite others to see the transformative nature of faith and resilience. It is through vulnerability and openness that I can connect with those around me, allowing them to find solace and encouragement in knowing that they are not alone in their struggles.

Moreover, sharing my truth strengthens not only my own faith but also the community that surrounds me. As I recount the ways God has worked in my life, I create a space for dialogue, understanding, and shared growth. When I speak of my victories, I celebrate God's goodness; when I share my trials, I highlight His faithfulness. By doing so, I contribute to a collective tapestry of testimonies that can empower others to step into their own truths and recognize the gifts God has placed within them. In this way, my truth becomes a channel for healing, grace, and inspiration, furthering God's kingdom on earth as we all strive to fulfill the purpose He has for us.

DECEMBER 1

DAY 336

I LIVE IN MY TRUTH WITHOUT FEAR

Affirmation: I walk in confidence, fully embracing my truth.

Scripture: "The Lord your God is with you, the Mighty Warrior who saves. He will take great delight in you; in his love he will no longer rebuke you, but will rejoice over you with singing."– Zephaniah 3:17 (NIV)

Encouragement: Fear no longer holds me captive. I walk in my truth with power, love, and self-control, knowing that I am exactly who God created me to be. Embracing our true selves allows us to shine brightly in a world that may often try to dim our light. When we acknowledge and celebrate our unique identities, we inspire others to do the same. Each moment spent in authentic expression becomes a testament to the strength that lies within us, reminding us that vulnerability is not weakness; it is a pathway to deeper connections and understanding.

In this journey of living out our truth, we can find comfort in knowing that we are never alone. God walks beside us, wrapping us in His love and reminding us of our worth. It is in His presence that we gather the courage to face the challenges of life, drawing strength from His promises. As we continue to embrace who we are—fearlessly and unapologetically—let us remember that our authenticity can serve as a beacon of hope for those around us, fueling a beautiful ripple effect in our communities.

Week 49

Walking In Abundance

DECEMBER 2

DAY 337

ABUNDANCE IS MY BIRTHRIGHT

A**ffirmation:** I am open to receiving God's abundance in every area of my life.

Scripture: "And as for you, brothers and sisters, never tire of doing what is good.." – 2 Thessalonians 3:13 (NIV)

Encouragement: God's abundance is not just about material wealth but about joy, love, peace, and purpose. I walk in the overflow of His blessings, knowing that I lack nothing. It's important to remember that abundance also manifests as the relationships we nurture and the experiences we cherish. Each moment spent in gratitude and appreciation opens the door to even greater blessings, allowing us to witness the beauty in the little things. As we grow in our connection with God, we create a life rich in fulfillment and happiness, trusting that He always provides for our needs.

Moreover, embracing God's abundance requires a heart willing to share and uplift others. As we reflect on our own blessings, we are called to be conduits of love and generosity to those around us. This cycle of giving and receiving fosters a community centered on support and kindness, enhancing the richness of our lives. Every act of compassion and generosity enriches not only the lives of others but also our own, reminding us of the endless flow of God's goodness. In doing so, we align ourselves with His heart and purpose, recognizing that true abundance stems from a life lived in service and love.

DECEMBER 3

DAY 338

I ATTRACT GOODNESS AND FAVOR

Affirmation: I am aligned with God's favor and blessings.

Scripture: "Fixing our eyes on Jesus, the pioneer and perfecter of faith. For the joy set before him he endured the cross, scorning its shame, and sat down at the right hand of the throne of God. Consider him who endured such opposition from sinners, so that you will not grow weary and lose heart." – Hebrews 12:2-3 (NIV)

Encouragement: I am a magnet for God's goodness. As I trust in Him, I see blessings unfold in ways I never imagined. Each day, I am reminded that God's favor is not just a distant concept, but a tangible reality that I can experience in my daily life. When I open my heart to His guidance, I attract opportunities and relationships that reflect His love and grace. Even during challenging times, I can find comfort in knowing that these experiences are shaping me and bringing me closer to my purpose. God's grace surrounds me, and I can choose to walk in the light of His blessings.

No matter the obstacles I face, I can find strength in the fact that God's goodness is always within reach. Every trial I encounter offers a chance to deepen my faith and resilience. As I lean on Him, I am reminded that His plans for me are far greater than I can imagine. With each step forward, I can release my doubts and fears, allowing His kindness to manifest in my life. By grounding myself in gratitude, I actively acknowledge the blessings that flow from my relationship with God, making me ever more receptive to the inherent goodness that He surrounds me with daily.

DECEMBER 4

DAY 339

MY MINDSET IS ONE OF ABUNDANCE

Affirmation: I think abundantly, I live abundantly, and I give abundantly.

Scripture: "Give, and it will be given to you. A good measure, pressed down, shaken together and running over, will be poured into your lap." – Luke 6:38 (NIV)

Encouragement: When I shift my mindset to abundance, I see the richness of life all around me. I give freely, love deeply, and receive fully. Embracing an abundant mindset opens my heart to the possibilities that exist in every moment. I begin to recognize that there is more than enough to go around, from love and kindness to resources and opportunities. This perspective not only transforms my own life but also encourages those around me to adopt the same outlook. By sharing my abundance, I create a ripple effect that impacts my community, fostering an environment where love and generosity flourish.

Furthermore, an abundance mindset empowers me to face challenges with grace and resilience. Instead of focusing on limitations, I learn to see obstacles as stepping stones towards growth and new possibilities. Each setback is an invitation to dig deeper and uncover hidden strengths. By maintaining a perspective rooted in abundance, I trust that I am supported by a universe that conspires in my favor. This faith encourages me to dream bigger, take risks, and embrace the fullness of life, knowing that as I give, I also create space to receive even more.

DECEMBER 5

DAY 340

GOD IS MY SOURCE

Affirmation: I trust in God as my provider and sustainer.

Scripture: "The Lord is my shepherd, I lack nothing." – Psalm 23:1 (NIV)

Encouragement: God is my source. I release fear and trust in His divine provision. He provides exactly what I need at the perfect time. In moments when I feel overwhelmed or uncertain, I remind myself that God is intimately aware of my circumstances. His wisdom surpasses my understanding, and His timing is always perfect. Even in the midst of challenges, I can lean into His promises, knowing that He is working all things for my good. By embracing this truth, I can navigate life's ups and downs with a sense of peace and assurance.

Moreover, it's important to recognize that God's provision is not just about physical needs but extends to emotional and spiritual nourishment as well. When I seek Him first, I find comfort, guidance, and strength that sustain me through trials. I can rest in the knowledge that He holds my future and guides my steps daily. As I continue to trust in His unfailing support, I open my heart to receive His abundant blessings, knowing that all my needs—seen and unseen—are met in His perfect will.

DECEMBER 6

DAY 341

I PROSPER IN EVERY AREA OF MY LIFE

Affirmation: My health, relationships, and spirit thrive in God's abundance.

Scripture: "Dear friend, I pray that you may enjoy good health and that all may go well with you, even as your soul is getting along well." – 3 John 1:2 (NIV)

Encouragement: Abundance is not just financial; it is wholeness in every area of my life. I walk in divine prosperity, health, and joy. It is essential to recognize that true richness comes from nurturing our physical, emotional, and spiritual well-being. By striving for balance in these areas, we open ourselves to the fullness of God's blessings. When we focus on cultivating healthy relationships, prioritizing self-care, and fostering a vibrant spiritual life, we automatically expand the realms of abundance in which we live. Each positive choice we make acts as a seed that contributes to a bountiful harvest.

In addition, embracing the idea that we are inherently deserving of God's goodness can transform our perspective. When we allow ourselves to believe in our worthiness, we create a space for God's grace to overflow into our lives. This mindset empowers us to engage with the world around us, fostering connections that uplift us and bring joy. Remember, the journey towards abundance is ongoing; every small step we take in nurturing ourselves and our relationships amplifies our capacity to thrive. When we align our thoughts and actions with the truth of our affirmation, we radiate positivity, attracting even more blessings.

DECEMBER 7

DAY 342

I WALK IN OVERFLOW

Affirmation: My cup overflows with blessings.

Scripture: "You anoint my head with oil; my cup overflows." – Psalm 23:5 (NIV)

Encouragement: My life is not meant to be lived in lack. God fills my cup to overflow so that I may bless others with His goodness. Each time I recognize His abundant provision in my life, I am reminded that I have more than enough—not just for myself, but also to share generously with those around me. This is a divine design, where blessings flow like a river from the source of all good things, empowering me to make a difference in the lives of others and extend His love beyond my immediate circle.

Moreover, by choosing to embrace the overflow in my life, I cultivate an atmosphere of gratitude and joy. I become a beacon of light to those who may feel overwhelmed or depleted. When I share from my abundance, it not only reflects the nature of God's generosity, but it also invites others to experience the same fullness that I know. In every challenge I face, I can dissolve feelings of scarcity by focusing on the countless ways God has filled my cup, thus reinforcing my ability to overflow with blessings, hope, and encouragement to those around me.

DECEMBER 8

DAY 343

I AM WORTHY OF GOD'S BEST

Affirmation: I accept and embrace God's best for me.

Scripture: "Now to him who is able to do immeasurably more than all we ask or imagine, according to his power that is at work within us." – Ephesians 3:20 (NIV)

Encouragement: God desires to do more in my life than I can ever imagine. I step into His abundance with gratitude and confidence, knowing that I am worthy of every good thing He has in store for me. It's important to remember that our worthiness does not stem from our achievements or failures, but from the very fact that we are created in His image. Each day, as we walk in faith, we open ourselves to the incredible possibilities that God has planned for our lives. Trusting in His goodness allows us to release any self-doubt and to fully embrace the blessings that come our way.

As we acknowledge God's best for us, we also cultivate a spirit of joy and positivity that can influence others around us. When we recognize our worthiness and live in alignment with God's promises, we inspire those we encounter to seek the same blessings in their own lives. Sharing our journey of faith and abundance encourages others to step into their own worthiness, creating a ripple effect of love and compassion. Remember, when we embody the truth that we are deserving of God's best, we become vessels of His grace, illuminating the path for others to follow.

Week 50

The Gift Of Self-Love

DECEMBER 9

DAY 344

LOVING MYSELF AS GOD LOVES ME

Affirmation: I am deeply loved by God, and I choose to love myself the same way.

Scripture: "Be strong and courageous, and do the work. Do not be afraid or discouraged, for the Lord God, my God, is with you." – 1 Chronicles 28:20 (NIV)

Encouragement: God's love for me is unwavering, and I honor Him by embracing that same love for myself. I release self-doubt and welcome self-acceptance. It's essential to remember that loving ourselves is not a sign of selfishness but rather an acknowledgment of the worth that God has placed within us. By embracing our identity as beloved children of the Most High, we can foster a sense of confidence that permeates every aspect of our lives. When we allow His love to transform how we view ourselves, we begin to shed the burdens of shame and inadequacy that have held us captive for far too long.

As we lean into this divine love, we should also remind ourselves that it is okay to seek growth and improvement without the weight of perfectionism. God does not expect us to be flawless; instead, He desires a heartfelt journey of becoming who He has created us to be. Every step we take in loving and accepting ourselves is a step toward fulfilling our God-given potential. Let us celebrate the progress we make, however small, as a testament to His grace at work within us. In this way, we can actively reflect the love we receive from God, making it a powerful force in our lives and the lives of those around us.

DECEMBER 10

DAY 345

I AM WORTHY OF LOVE AND CARE

Affirmation: I am deserving of love, care, and kindness, starting with myself.

Scripture: " For God so loved the world that he gave his one and only Son, that whoever believes in him shall not perish but have eternal life." – John 3:16 (NIV)

Encouragement: I recognize my worth. I treat myself with the same love and grace I extend to others, knowing that I am a masterpiece of God's creation. It is essential to remind ourselves that our value does not hinge on external validation or accomplishments. Each day, we are invited to embrace the truth that we are worthy simply because we exist and are loved by God. This love is not contingent on perfection or achievements; it is a reflection of our identity as beloved children of the Creator.

As we cultivate a mindset of self-love, we create a nurturing environment where our hearts can flourish. This means setting boundaries, prioritizing self-care, and allowing ourselves the grace to rest and recharge. When we acknowledge our inherent worth, we can better equip ourselves to spread love and kindness to those around us. Just as the love of God reigns in our lives, let us be vessels of that love, sharing it freely with ourselves and others. Remember, embracing our worthiness is not an act of selfishness but rather an essential step in fulfilling our potential and spreading positivity in the world.

DECEMBER 11

DAY 346

MY SELF-LOVE IS A REFLECTION OF GOD'S LOVE

Affirmation: When I love myself, I honor the love God has for me.

Scripture: "And over all these virtues put on love, which binds them all together in perfect unity." – Colossians 3:14 (NIV)

Encouragement: Loving myself does not mean pride or arrogance—it means seeing myself through God's eyes. I choose to nurture and care for the person He created me to be. Understanding my worth as a beloved child of God allows me to embrace my unique qualities and imperfections. When I prioritize self-love, I free myself from the chains of comparison and self-doubt, recognizing that my journey is divinely orchestrated. This inner compassion not only transforms the way I treat myself but also how I interact with others, leading to a more authentic expression of love.

Moreover, as I cultivate self-love, I become a channel through which God's love flows, impacting those around me. My acceptance of self enables me to extend grace and support to others in their struggles, mirroring the unconditional love that God has for each of us. In moments of doubt or negativity, I remind myself that loving myself is an act of worship, honoring the Creator who designed me with purpose and intention. By choosing to see myself through this divine lens, I affirm my inherent value and capacity to contribute to the world in a meaningful way.

DECEMBER 12

DAY 347

I SPEAK TO MYSELF WITH LOVE AND KINDNESS

Affirmation: My words to myself are full of love, encouragement, and grace.

Scripture: " Be kind and compassionate to one another, forgiving each other, just as in Christ God forgave you." – Ephesians 4:32 (NIV)

Encouragement: I silence the inner critic and replace negativity with words of affirmation and truth. I uplift myself with kindness, just as God uplifts me. Each day, I choose to speak to myself in a manner that reflects my worth and value as a beloved creation of God. By intentionally nurturing a compassionate inner dialogue, I create a positive atmosphere that fosters growth and resilience. This practice empowers me to embrace my flaws and celebrate my strengths, knowing that I am always deserving of grace.

Furthermore, as I cultivate this habit of self-kindness, I open the door to greater empathy for others. When I learn to speak lovingly to myself, I naturally extend that same grace and understanding to those around me. It transforms not just my relationship with myself, but my interactions with family, friends, and even strangers. In a world that can often feel harsh and critical, I become a beacon of positivity and encouragement. Let every word I speak over myself resonate with love and affirmation, as I mirror the compassion that God extends to me each day.

DECEMBER 13

DAY 348

I HONOR MY NEEDS AND BOUNDARIES

Affirmation: I listen to my heart, honor my needs, and protect my peace.

Scripture: " Why, you do not even know what will happen tomorrow. What is your life? You are a mist that appears for a little while and then vanishes.." – James 4:14 (NIV)

Encouragement: Self-love means recognizing my limits and setting healthy boundaries. I give myself permission to rest, heal, and say no when necessary. It's important to remember that honoring your needs is not a sign of weakness; rather, it is an act of strength. By prioritizing what feeds your soul and protects your well-being, you are creating a foundation for deeper peace and fulfillment in your life. When you stand firm in your boundaries, you not only nurture your own spirit but also teach others how to respect and honor you, fostering healthier relationships all around.

Taking the time to check in with yourself is crucial. Are you feeling drained, overwhelmed, or stretched too thin? These feelings are your heart's way of signaling that it may be time to step back and reassess your commitments. Listen closely, and respond with kindness to yourself. Remember, it is okay to pause and recharge. When you honor your own needs and limitations, you are better equipped to engage fully with the world around you, bringing your most authentic and vibrant self to every situation. Embrace this journey of self-discovery and use it as an opportunity to grow in love and understanding for yourself.

DECEMBER 14

DAY 349

I CHOOSE TO LOVE MYSELF FULLY TODAY

Affirmation: I embrace all of who I am with love and acceptance.

Scripture: "May the Lord direct your hearts into God's love and Christ's perseverance.." – 2 Thessalonians 3:5

(NIV)

Encouragement: God designed every part of me with intention and care. I choose to love every aspect of myself, knowing that I am a divine creation. In this journey of self-acceptance, it is essential to remember that we are not defined by our flaws or past mistakes but by the love that God has for us. Every imperfection tells a story, and each moment of challenge has shaped us into who we are today. Embracing this truth helps us to see ourselves through God's eyes, filled with compassion and grace. When we acknowledge our worth based on His love, we free ourselves from the shackles of self-doubt and begin to walk confidently in our identity.

Moreover, as we cultivate the practice of loving ourselves, we open the door for deeper relationships with others. Our ability to truly love and accept ourselves paves the way for us to extend that same grace to those around us. When we honor our divine creation, we inspire others to do the same, creating a ripple effect of love and acceptance in our communities. Let us practice kindness toward ourselves, allowing our self-love to reflect God's magnificent love for all of His creations. With each positive affirmation, we usher in a brighter perspective and embrace the fullness of life that God has designed for us.

DECEMBER 15

DAY 350

MY SELF-LOVE RADIATES TO OTHERS

Affirmation: As I love myself, I inspire others to do the same.

Scripture: "Those who look to him are radiant; their faces are never covered with shame." – Psalm 34:5 (NIV)

Encouragement: When I embrace self-love, I encourage those around me to do the same. I am a beacon of light, reflecting the love of God in my life and the lives of others. As I nurture my own spirit, I create an environment where others feel safe and empowered to explore their own worth. This ripple effect of love and acceptance can transform communities, inspiring deeper connections and fostering a spirit of compassion that extends far beyond myself.

Furthermore, it's essential to recognize that self-love is not a self-centered act; it is a divine calling to nourish the soul so that love can overflow and touch the hearts of others. Each act of kindness and grace we bestow upon ourselves sends a powerful message: that we are all deserving of love, and that it starts from within. So let us continue to celebrate our individuality and imperfections, allowing our authentic selves to shine through. As we love ourselves more, we invite others to bask in that glow, encouraging them to embrace their worthiness and radiate their own unique light into the world.

Week 51

Reflecting On My Growth

DECEMBER 16

DAY 351

RECOGNIZING HOW FAR I'VE COME

Affirmation: I honor my journey and the growth I have experienced.

Scripture: " Your people settled in it, and from your bounty, God, you provided for the poor.." – Psalm 68:10 (NIV)

Encouragement: Every step I have taken has shaped me into the strong, resilient person I am today. I acknowledge my progress and celebrate my victories. Each challenge I've faced has been a building block, teaching me valuable lessons about perseverance, patience, and courage. Rather than dwelling on past hardships, I choose to focus on the wisdom I have gained through these experiences. By embracing both the highs and lows of my journey, I can appreciate the fullness of life and recognize the beauty in my growth.

As I look back, I also see the many moments of grace and support that have guided me along the way. The people who have uplifted me, the lessons learned through trials, and the quiet moments of reflection have all contributed to my development. By honoring my journey, I not only acknowledge my struggles but also the strength that has come from them. This perspective allows me to move forward with hope and gratitude, reminding me that every experience, no matter how challenging, serves a purpose in shaping the person I am becoming..

DECEMBER 17

DAY 352

EMBRACING EVERY LESSON

Affirmation: Every experience has contributed to my growth and wisdom.

Scripture: "For everything that was written in the past was written to teach us, so that through the endurance taught in the Scriptures and the encouragement they provide we might have hope." – Romans 15:4 (NIV)

Encouragement: Even the challenges I have faced were opportunities to learn and grow. I choose to see every lesson as a stepping stone to a greater me. Each experience, whether joyful or painful, plays a crucial role in shaping my character and fortifying my spirit. When I reflect on my past, I recognize that what once felt like stumbling blocks were actually building blocks that have strengthened my foundation. Embracing this perspective allows me to move forward with resilience and hope, knowing that I am constantly evolving into the person I was meant to be.

Moreover, as I embrace these lessons, I am reminded that I am not alone in this journey. There is a divine purpose behind every encounter, every struggle, and every triumph that guides me on my path. In moments of doubt or discouragement, I can lean into the knowledge that these experiences are paved with intention. By trusting in the process and allowing myself to be transformed through my challenges, I cultivate a deeper sense of gratitude and a renewed commitment to growth. Ultimately, I am empowered to use the wisdom gained from my experiences to uplift others, fostering a community of support and encouragement.

DECEMBER 18

DAY 353

THANKFUL FOR MY TRANSFORMATION

Affirmation: I am grateful for the transformation taking place in my life.

Scripture: " After Job had prayed for his friends, the Lord restored his fortunes and gave him twice as much as he had before." – Job 42:10 (NIV)

Encouragement: Growth is a continuous journey, and I am thankful for each moment of transformation. My heart is full of gratitude for all that I have overcome. Every challenge I face has been a stepping stone towards becoming the person I am meant to be, and with each obstacle, I discover deeper strength and resilience within myself. This transformation is not only about personal growth but also about finding purpose in my experiences. By embracing the lessons learned along the way, I can appreciate the richness that comes from the journey itself.

As I navigate this path, I recognize the importance of surrounding myself with positivity and support. Encouragement from others, along with my own self-compassion, allows me to remain open to change and to trust the process. I am reminded that transformation often begins with a single step, and every choice I make leads me closer to the life I envision. No matter how difficult the road may seem, I am confident that the progress I make today sets the foundation for a brighter tomorrow. My transformation is a testament to my resilience, and I choose to celebrate each victory, no matter how small, along the way.

DECEMBER 19

DAY 354

MY STRENGTH IS EVIDENT

Affirmation: My strength is undeniable, and I walk boldly in it.

Scripture: "God is our refuge and strength, an ever-present help in trouble." – Psalm 46:1 (NIV)

Encouragement: I have faced adversity, yet I have not been defeated. I am stronger, wiser, and more confident in who I am. Each challenge I have encountered has only served to deepen my resolve and illuminate my path forward. It is through these trials that I have learned the value of perseverance and the importance of leaning on faith. As I reflect on my journey, I realize that my resilience is not merely a product of my own efforts but a testament to the support and guidance from a higher power. I am reminded that I do not walk this path alone; I am surrounded and uplifted by grace.

In moments when I feel the weight of the world pressing down on me, I draw strength from the knowledge that I am equipped to handle whatever comes my way. My experiences have forged a tenacity within me that radiates confidence and fosters a belief in my capabilities. I am empowered not just by my past victories but also by the unwavering faith that drives me. With each step I take, I embrace the promise that I am capable of overcoming any obstacle, for my strength is not just mine—it's a reflection of the divine support that sustains me. In this journey, I will continue to walk boldly, knowing that I am fortified by both my own resilience and the everlasting strength gifted to me.

DECEMBER 20

DAY 355

I SEE THE FRUIT OF MY FAITH

Affirmation: My faith has carried me, and I see its rewards in my life.

Scripture: " Fear of the Lord is the foundation of wisdom. Knowledge of the Holy One results in good judgment.." – Proverbs 9:10 (NLT)

Encouragement: Through faith, I have endured, and I now see the beautiful results of trusting God's plan for my life. My journey is unfolding just as it should. In moments of doubt or uncertainty, I can look back and recognize the seeds of belief that have been sown along the way. Each challenge I faced was not a stumbling block but rather a stepping stone, leading me closer to the fulfillment of God's promises. The strength I have gained transforms my perspective, enabling me to embrace future obstacles with confidence, knowing they are part of the greater tapestry of my faith.

Furthermore, I am reminded that my faith is not merely for my own benefit but also a source of encouragement for those around me. As I share my experiences and the fruit of my trust in God, I inspire others to embark on their own journeys of faith. I recognize that we are all interconnected, and by living out my gratitude and reliance on God, I contribute to a collective narrative of hope and resilience. My faith serves as a beacon, shining light on the path for others to see that no matter the circumstances, trusting in God's plan yields profound rewards—both in this life and beyond.

DECEMBER 21

DAY 356

I AM PROUD OF MYSELF

Affirmation: I celebrate my achievements and the person I have become.

Scripture: "If any of you lacks wisdom, you should ask God, who gives generously to all without finding fault, and it will be given to you." – James 1:5 (NIV)

Encouragement: I take a moment to appreciate how much I have grown. I am proud of myself for the courage, faith, and determination that have brought me here. Every challenge I faced was not just an obstacle but a stepping stone that shaped my resilience. It is crucial to recognize the battles I fought, both big and small, and to honor the strength that carried me through. Each setback taught me important lessons that have enriched my character, adding depth to my journey and enhancing my ability to celebrate my unique story.

I invite myself to reflect on the goals I set for myself and how far I have come in achieving them. No achievement is too small to acknowledge; even the smallest steps forward contribute significantly to my growth. As I celebrate, I also recognize the role faith has played in my journey. My belief in God's guidance has illuminated my path, reinforcing that I am never alone in my pursuits. This moment of self-praise is not mere vanity; it is a recognition of the divine spark within me that propels me toward my dreams and aspirations.

DECEMBER 22

DAY 357

I STEP FORWARD WITH CONFIDENCE

Affirmation: I walk into the next chapter of my life with boldness and confidence.

Scripture: " Then they would put their trust in God and would not forget his deeds but would keep his commands." – Psalm 78:7 (NIV)

Encouragement: My journey is not over; there is still more to discover, learn, and achieve. I move forward with confidence, knowing that God's plan for me is greater than I can imagine. Each step I take brings me closer to the fulfillment of my purpose, and I embrace the lessons life presents. With each new chapter, I remind myself that courage is a choice I can make daily. This choice allows God's light to shine through me, illuminating my path and the paths of those around me.

As I face new challenges and opportunities, I carry the assurance that God walks with me. I am reminded to lean into His promises, trusting that He equips me for whatever lies ahead. Each experience, even the difficult ones, enriches my journey, molding me into the person He has created me to be. So, I will step forward boldly, not held back by fear or uncertainty, but propelled by the unwavering faith that God has greater plans in store for my life.

Week 52

A Year Of Transformation

DECEMBER 23

DAY 358

I CELEBRATE MY JOURNEY

Affirmation: I honor the path I have walked and the person I have become.

Scripture: "The Lord has done great things for us, and we are filled with joy." – Psalm 126:3 (NIV)

Encouragement: This year has been filled with challenges, growth, and transformation. Today, I take a moment to celebrate every step I have taken. Each experience, whether joyous or difficult, has contributed to my journey, shaping my character and resilience. It's essential to acknowledge not only the peaks of happiness but also the valleys of struggle, as both have played a vital role in my development. Embracing the entirety of my journey allows me to appreciate how far I have come and the valuable lessons I have learned along the way.

As I reflect on the year, I can find strength in the realization that every step has been guided by a purpose. Each challenge has been an opportunity for me to grow stronger in my faith and to deepen my understanding of myself and those around me. Celebrating my journey means embracing every facet of my experience and recognizing that I am continually evolving. The joy I feel today is a testament to my resilience and commitment to becoming the best version of myself. God's hand has been with me every step of the way, and for that, I am truly grateful.

DECEMBER 24

DAY 359

GRATEFUL FOR MY STRENGTH

Affirmation: My strength has carried me through, and I am grateful.

Scripture: "The Lord said to him, 'Who gave human beings their mouths? Who makes them deaf or mute? Who gives them sight or makes them blind? Is it not I, the Lord?'" – Exodus 4:11 (NIV)

Encouragement: I recognize the resilience I have built over the past year. I am stronger, wiser, and more confident because of it. Each challenge I faced has been an opportunity for growth, molding me into a version of myself that I am proud to embrace. It's essential to take a moment to reflect on these experiences and celebrate how far I have come. Every trial, every setback, and every moment of doubt has only served to deepen my understanding of my own capabilities, reminding me that I am equipped to handle whatever life throws my way.

As I stand on the brink of a new year, I choose to carry this sense of empowerment with me into the future. The strength I possess is not just a momentary gift; it is a testament to my journey and a promise of what is to come. I will continue to seek opportunities that challenge me, knowing that each step forward builds my character and resilience. With faith in the Lord who gives me sight and understanding, I will approach each day with gratitude for my strength and hopeful anticipation for how it will serve me in the days to come.

DECEMBER 25

DAY 360

WALKING BOLDLY INTO MY FUTURE

Affirmation: I step into my future with faith and courage.

Scripture: "He saved us, not because of righteous things we had done, but because of his mercy. He saved us through the washing of rebirth and renewal by the Holy Spirit." – Titus 3:5 (NIV)

Encouragement: The journey does not end here; it is just the beginning. I embrace the road ahead with confidence and hope. As I step into the future, I remember that each new chapter is filled with possibilities waiting to be unlocked. The boldness I carry does not come from my own strength but from the unwavering support of the Holy Spirit who guides me daily. In this unfolding story, obstacles may arise, but I choose to view them as opportunities for growth and transformation. Each challenge I face equips me with the resilience to step into new ventures with renewed courage.

Moreover, I am reminded that I am not alone on this journey. The community of faith surrounds me, offering encouragement and wisdom as I navigate the path ahead. Together, we can uplift one another, sharing our experiences and testimonies of God's faithfulness. As I walk boldly into my future, I hold onto the promise that His mercy and grace go before me, creating a way even when the path seems unclear. With every step, I declare that my future is filled with hope, purpose, and the boundless love of my Creator.

DECEMBER 26

DAY 361

LETTING GO OF FEAR

Affirmation: Fear has no place in my life; I move forward with trust.

Scripture: " Praise be to the Lord God, the God of Israel, who alone does marvelous deeds.." – Psalm 72:18 (NIV)

Encouragement: I have learned to release fear and trust God's plan for my life. I walk forward in peace. As I surrender my worries to Him, I find a deep sense of calm that transcends all understanding. Each day brings new opportunities to practice this trust, reminding me that every challenge I face is a stepping stone toward growth and understanding. It is in these moments of vulnerability that I truly experience the strength of God's presence in my life.

When fear begins to creep in, I take a moment to pause and reflect on the countless times God has carried me through difficulties. I remind myself of His promises and the marvels He has already accomplished in my journey. Focusing on His unwavering love allows me to embrace the future with courage, knowing that even the uncertainties hold the potential for remarkable transformation. Each step I take in faith reassures me that I am never alone; God walks alongside me, guiding and uplifting my spirit.

DECEMBER 27

DAY 362

ROOTED IN LOVE AND PURPOSE

Affirmation: I am deeply loved and created for a purpose.

Scripture: "Blessed is she who has believed that the Lord would fulfill his promises to her!" – Luke 1:45 (NIV)

Encouragement: My life has meaning and purpose. Everything I have gone through has shaped me for something greater. Each experience, whether joyous or challenging, serves as a building block in the foundation of my story. God carefully weaves our past into His divine tapestry, using each thread to create a unique narrative that reflects His love and grace. It's essential to recognize that even in the moments when we feel exposed or vulnerable, we are being equipped for the journey ahead. Just as a seed must be buried in darkness to bloom into a beautiful flower, we too must sometimes endure hardship to fulfill our God-given potential.

As I embrace my journey, I am reminded that I am not alone; God is always with me, guiding my steps and illuminating my path. His plans for me are filled with hope, and I can confidently trust that He is working all things together for my good. When I become rooted in love and purpose, I find strength and resilience to overcome obstacles. God's promises are true and everlasting, and as I stand firm in my faith, I can expect to see the fulfillment of His divine will in my life. I am cherished and called, and that knowledge fuels my passion to pursue my unique purpose with joy and anticipation.

DECEMBER 28

DAY 363

I EMBRACE NEW BEGINNINGS

Affirmation: I welcome fresh opportunities and new growth.

Scripture: "See, I am doing a new thing! Now it springs up; do you not perceive it? I am making a way in the wilderness and streams in the wasteland." – Isaiah 43:19 (NIV)

Encouragement: With every ending comes a new beginning. I step forward with excitement and expectation for what's next. Embracing new beginnings allows us to shed the weight of past experiences and step into a season filled with potential. Consider the beauty of the seasons; just as winter gives way to the blooms of spring, we too have the opportunity to grow and thrive in new environments. Each fresh start is a chance to redefine our path and explore possibilities we may have overlooked before. Therefore, let us approach each transition with open hearts, ready to embrace the lessons and joys that await us.

Moreover, new beginnings often challenge us to step outside of our comfort zones, igniting a transformative journey where we can discover hidden strengths. It is within these moments of change that we learn to trust in our resilience and adaptability. As we confront the unknown, we also open ourselves to deeper connections with others and greater insights into our own journeys. Remember, God is always ready to guide and support us as we navigate these transitions. So let us cherish each fresh opportunity, believing wholeheartedly that the best is yet to come.

DECEMBER 29

DAY 364

A LIFE TRANSFORMED

Affirmation: I have been transformed, and I continue to evolve.

Scripture: "However, as it is written: 'What no eye has seen, what no ear has heard, and what no human mind has conceived'— the things God has prepared for those who love him." – 1 Corinthians 2:9 (NIV)

Encouragement: I am not the same person I was when this journey began. I embrace my transformation and continue to grow. Each step I take on this path reminds me of the vast potential that lies within me, waiting to be unveiled. The experiences that once seemed daunting now serve as building blocks for the person I am becoming. I recognize the power of my choice to evolve, and with that, I open my heart to the infinite possibilities that God has prepared for me.

As I reflect on my journey, I find strength in the knowledge that transformation is not a destination, but a continuous process. Every challenge I meet and every leap of faith I take allows me to shed old layers and nurture the seeds of my growth. In moments of doubt, I remind myself of the beauty that lies ahead—an unfolding tapestry woven by God's hands. With each new experience, I draw closer to the vision He has for my life, trusting that my journey is guided by love and purpose. Embracing this truth fuels my determination to keep evolving, no matter the hurdles I face along the way.

DECEMBER 30

DAY 365

THANK YOU, GOD, FOR THIS JOURNEY

Affirmation: I give thanks for every moment of growth and discovery.

Scripture: "Give thanks to the Lord, for he is good; his love endures forever." – Psalm 107:1 (NIV)

Encouragement: I reflect on this incredible year with a heart full of gratitude. Every experience has been a gift, and I am thankful for it all. As I look back, I recognize that even the challenges and trials have been opportunities for profound growth. Each obstacle I faced cultivated resilience, teaching me lessons that will accompany me into the future. The moments of joy were amplified by the tough times, reminding me of the goodness and faithfulness of God in every circumstance.

I am reminded that gratitude is not just an end-of-year exercise but a daily practice that shapes my perspective on life. By intentionally acknowledging the blessings surrounding me, I open my heart to deeper joy and connection with others. I celebrate the relationships strengthened, the wisdom gained, and the transformative moments that have shaped my journey. In doing so, I invite God's presence into each new day, allowing His love to guide and inspire me as I step into a fresh year filled with limitless possibilities

DECEMBER 31

DAY 366

A NEW CHAPTER BEGINS

Affirmation: I step into this new season with faith, hope, and love.

Scripture: " Do not withhold good from those to whom it is due, when it is in your power to act." – Proverbs 3:27 (NIV)

Encouragement: My journey does not end here—it continues in new and beautiful ways. I welcome what's ahead with open arms and a joyful heart. Each new chapter offers an opportunity for growth and transformation that we may not yet fully understand. As I embrace this fresh beginning, I remind myself that my past is merely the foundation upon which I will build my future. Every lesson learned, every challenge overcome, and every moment of triumph prepares me for the richness of experiences yet to come. As I let go of what was, I make room for hope, faith, and love to blossom in my life anew.

Moreover, I am not alone on this journey. The connections I foster with others will shape my path as well. Each person I encounter has a role to play, whether as a source of inspiration, encouragement, or support. I am reminded to reach out and invest in those relationships, as we each have unique gifts to share. By actively participating in this tapestry of community, I not only enhance my own journey but also become a vessel of goodness and light for others. Together, we can amplify the power of kindness and grace, creating a ripple effect that transforms not just our own lives but the world around us.

From My Desk

Dear Reader,

As you turn the final pages of 52 Week Daily Devotionals and Alopecia Affirmations, I want to take a moment to celebrate you. Every day that you have shown up for yourself, spoken life over your journey, and embraced the power within you is a victory. My sincerest prayers are these devotionals and affirmations are as a source of strength, renewal, and never-ending self-love.

Alopecia does not define you—your resilience, faith, and spirit do. You are beautifully and wonderfully made, and your presence in this world is purposeful. Regardless of your journey, I want you to know you are not alone. I am with you, and more importantly, God is ever present with you.

May you continue to grow in confidence, walk boldly in your truth, and shine your light unapologetically. Keep affirming, keep believing, and most of all, keep loving yourself—because you are worthy, just as you are.

With love and empowerment,

Stephanie Anderson, DPC, MPC, BSM
The Alopecia Advocate

THE END

www.ingramcontent.com/pod-product-compliance
Lightning Source LLC
Chambersburg PA
CBHW021210090426
42740CB00006B/173